For Jae —
with all good wishes —
Julia Wolf M_____

The Woman Who Lost Her Names

THE WOMAN WHO

*Compiled and Edited
by Julia Wolf Mazow*

Cambridge London
Hagerstown Mexico City
Philadelphia Sao Paolo
New York Sydney

LOST HER NAMES

Selected Writings of
American Jewish Women

HARPER & ROW, PUBLISHERS

San Francisco

1817

To Claire, Leo, Joshua and Jack—
kindred spirits, good friends, loyal supporters.

FIRST EDITION
Designed by Leigh McLellan

Library of Congress Cataloging in Publication Data

The Woman Who Lost Her Names.

    1. American literature—Jewish authors.
2. American literature—Women authors.
3. Jews in the United States—Literary collections.
4. Women, Jewish—Literary collections.
I. Mazow, Julia Wolf.
PS508.J4W65 1980   810'.8'09287   79-2986
ISBN 0-06-250566-1
ISBN 0-06-250567-X pbk

80 81 82 83 84 10 9 8 7 6 5 4 3 2 1

Contents

Foreword

Carole Klein

THIS COLLECTION OF writings by American Jewish women represents the work of a group of people who, though diverse, are linked to each other by a common heritage. No matter what they write about—the search for identity, the need to rebel, ambition versus sublimation—their perspective is touched by the fact that they are women who were born into the Jewish faith.

A good deal has been written about how being a woman affects one's creative expression. But when a woman is also Jewish, the shape and content of her expression are even more molded to particular experience. Who our grandparents are, how we are viewed by the dominating culture, what pressures we feel to assimilate into that culture, become part of our identity and follow us to the typewriter or writing table.

Reading this book one gets, finally, beyond the mythology that has defined the American Jewish woman. And it is high

Carole Klein is the author of *Aline,* the biography of stage designer Aline Bernstein. Born and brought up in New York City, Klein attended Goddard College, where she now teaches. Her other books are *The Single Parent Experience* and *The Myth of The Happy Child.*

time. As women of all religious persuasions demand new images of themselves, Jewish women too must refuse to accept the easy generalizations that have been made about their lives. We are not the stereotypic, self-indulged daughters or grasping wives or salacious seductresses; we are not the smothering, obscenely over-protective mothers who imprison sons into cages of guilt and heterosexual conflict. These are the distorted images of male writers.

In truth, as these stories prove, women are thinking, caring, sensitive people with a high degree of consciousness about themselves and their world. They struggle to make themselves and the world better, to live in that world with joy, pride, and integrity. These are wonderful stories, and as we read them, we experience the full range of human emotion, from giddy delight to tragic terror.

Perhaps just as important as learning through this anthology what Jewish women are writing about is learning that they are writing at all. As Ms. Mazow suggests, one would not realize this by looking at anthologies compiled by men. Masculine editors have successfully created a self-fulfilling prophecy: they have drawn a trivial portrait of the Jewish woman's experience and then not taken seriously the often-powerful renditions of her experience that have come from her pen.

It is not easy for any woman in this society to be a writer. The cultural demands and expectations of the female role run counter to the freedom to create. It seems especially difficult for the Jewish woman writer, however. A Jewish daughter grows up with strong pulls toward family and domestic life, and internalizes values that say she should put herself and her own needs after her family's. In such an atmosphere, going into "a room of one's own" to write is no easy matter. It is a constant and wearying challenge to find a comfortable, guilt-free balance between personal accomplishment and family life.

The more I reflect on it, the more I am convinced that Jewish-American artists who are also women have the most confusing socialization. Ambivalence trails them from childhood; they are encouraged every bit as much as sons to do well in school, and then, when they reach marriageable age, are pressured (however lovingly), to spend energies on less intellectual pursuits. It is only recently, with the spreading feminist consciousness, that Jewish women artists have been able to measure the effects of that ambivalence on their creative well-being. Young Jewish women today are attempting to fashion new, less dissonant images of themselves, as some of the more recent writings in this anthology illustrate.

These rich pages merit the attention of men as well as women, of people of all religious faiths and cultural backgrounds. For by seeing what Jewish women are really like, and what Jewish women writers are really saying, we all move deeper into the circle of understanding that makes every life fuller. Certainly these stories are enriched by thousands of years of Jewish experience; yet they are far more universal than parochial in content.

Out of her particular history comes a new, strong voice of the Jewish-American woman writer: an occasion for pride and excitement to anyone who reads, writes, or reflects on the evolving human condition.

Acknowledgments

I WISH TO thank those who participated in the nine months of planning for Houston's 1976 lecture series on the Jewish woman. Our discussions helped me formulate the ideas behind this book, presented first as a lecture entitled "The Jewish Mother and the Jewish-American Princess: Where Are the Stereotypes of Yesteryear?" Given in a different form before the American Studies Association of Texas, it laid the groundwork for the introduction to this anthology.

The women of *Lilith* magazine introduced me to the network of American Jewish women writing today. June Arnold, Jack Mazow, Rosemary S. Minard, Miriam Kass, and Yaal Silberberg read early versions of the manuscript. Denise Weinberg, Rena Reisman, Mary Ross Taylor, Effie Feld, Beverly Freedenthal, and Robbie Odom Moses provided many valuable suggestions, as well as their friendship.

Most of all, I want to express gratitude to the women who wrote the works this anthology contains. They had the courage to tell their part of the story. And they have enriched the experience of us all.

J. W. M.

Introduction

Julia Wolf Mazow

A NY DISCUSSION OF Jewish women in America must acknowl-
edge a history and a tradition which go back more than 5000
years. For generations, being a Jew has meant living as an
outsider on the periphery of the larger society, often as a scape-
goat. Therefore, Jews also understand the meaning of discrimi-
nation and persecution. It is not surprising, then, that many
Jews worked hard for the Civil Rights movement in this country.
And it seems appropriate, as others have noted, that so many
of the theoreticians and leaders of the recent women's movement should be Jewish women.[1]

Jewish tradition is rich in ambiguous attitudes and ambiva-
lent feelings towards women. On the one hand, the Talmud tells
us that a woman is "lightheaded" and that she is seductive to
men; on the other hand, the picture that emerges in Proverbs
31 is of great competence and energy. No matter how repres-
sive a given historical period may have been towards both Jews
and women, there have always been individuals who managed

---

[1]See, for example, Ann Wolfe's "The Jewish Woman," *Dialogue on Diversity*
(New York: Institute on Pluralism and Group Identity, 1976).

to overcome the restrictions of their times.[2]

Following the emigration of Jews to America from Western Europe in the 1840s, and from Eastern Europe in the 1880s and well into the 1900s, many changes occurred in the lives of women and men. The man who had been a respected scholar in the *shtetl*, for example, might have become a shoemaker without a place in the world, like Schmendrik in Anzia Yezierska's "My Own People." Of course, not all men in the *shtetl* were scholars, and not all were without work in this country. And it was just as common for women to work alongside their husbands in the marketplace here as it was for them to contribute to the family upkeep in Europe.

Having bought the middle-class American dream of success, many immigrant Jews became economically well-off. For some, success was accompanied by assimilation into the larger society. Scholarship ceased to be a cultural ideal for most Jews; achievement in business and the professions replaced it—for the men. But their mothers, wives, daughters, and sisters, whose worlds once included both home and workplace, were relegated to the sphere of home and family. One sign of the man's success was that the family did not need the wife's financial contribution. Previously, perpetuating Jewish tradition in the home had been one of her many duties; now, it became one of her few options.[3]

I began this project with a search for short fiction and autobiographical writings by American Jewish women from the 1930s to the present, because I wanted to find out who these women were and what had happened to them.[4] What were the concerns of the post-immigrant generations? What kinds of stories did they tell about themselves? Were they really the spoiled daughters of castrating mothers, as they were sometimes depicted in books written by American Jewish men?

[2]See Sondra Henry and Emily Taitz, *Written Out of History: A Hidden Legacy of Jewish Women Revealed Through Their Writings and Letters* (New York: Bloch Publishing Company, Inc., 1978).

[3]*The Jewish Woman in America* by Charlotte Baum, Paula Hyman, and Sonya Michel (New York: The Dial Press, 1976) contains a full discussion.

[4]For a thorough listing, see Aviva Cantor's annotated *Bibliography on the Jewish Woman* (Fresh Meadows, New York: Biblio Press, 1979).

My first discovery was the relative absence of Jewish women authors from well-known anthologies. Azriel Eisenberg's *The Golden Land: A Literary Portrait of American Jewry, 1654 to the Present*, contains excerpts from eighty-eight works, only eight of them by women. Irving Malin and Irwin Stark's 1964 *Breakthrough: A Treasury of Contemporary American Jewish Literature* contains thirty-one pieces, two of them by women, while Harold Ribalow's 1968 *Autobiographies of American Jews 1880–1920* includes selections by six women out of a total of twenty-five. *The Rise of American Jewish Literature*, edited by Charles Angoff and Meyer Levin (1970), lists twenty-two entries in its table of contents; none are by women. Theodore Gross's *The Literature of American Jews* (1973) includes the work of forty-one writers, six of them women. Of those six, only Grace Paley and Muriel Rukeyser published in this century. Finally, Irving Howe's anthology *Jewish American Stories* (1977) lists twenty-six works; four of them are by women.

What does this cursory survey mean? To some it may indicate that Jewish women are not writing. But the sampling also suggests that some male anthologizers are oblivious to the work of writers who are women.

When we look at some of the better-known female creations of American Jewish male writers we may find a clue. What can we say about these women, the Sophie Portnoys, the Marjorie Morningstars?

Generally, they are competent enablers. And they are also destroyers—a familiar stereotype on whose shoulders, we are sometimes told, the survival of the Jewish people rests.

But for the reader concerned with reality rather than appearance, the negative stereotype of the Jewish American Princess who grows up to be a Jewish mother is limiting, divisive, and simplistic. It tends to stress inevitability, to deny individual natures their due.

When we examine works that American Jewish women have written about themselves and their relationships, a different picture emerges. Even stereotypes appear in a different light. For when we encounter a mother, deeply concerned with the lives of her children and her home, we see much more: a woman who feels, one who is introspective. The stereotype ceases to be rigid. Because stereotypes, by definition, do not allow for individual differences, once they are filled in and humanized they no longer exist. Another pattern evolves when the woman tells her story from her own point of view.

Instead of the conventional negative stereotypic qualities, the women in this collection exhibit vast amounts of energy which take diverse shapes and occur in works as dissimilar as Andrea Dworkin's "First Love," Nancy Datan's "Making Jews," and Gertrude Friedberg's "Where Moth and Rust." For Datan, the process of "Making Jews" is a conscious, ongoing choice that requires the hard work of constant, rigorous self-examination. Dworkin writes of the intense drive to know and tell and do all that is possible, remembering always that, "There is no place on earth, no day or night, no hour or minute, when one is not a Jew or a woman." Friedberg's Mrs. Fortrey, on the other hand, uses her energy to forestall the disaster which would occur if she were to stop the obsessive performance of household tasks. Once she redirects her energy, she uncovers a new idea of what is possible for her.

In these pieces there is no single vision. In some there is no overtly Jewish content; in others, of course, there is. As Cheike says in "My Mother Was a Light Housekeeper," "Anarchy and variety are our beginning characteristics." There are no simplistic stereotypes. Rather, there are diverse women telling their stories.

The divisions of the book reflect the themes of the stories as they recur in the lives of many women, past and present. Section One, "Familiar Connections," deals with tradition, with families, and the need for roots. The families portrayed here range from Emma Goldman's to the newly created unit in "What Must I Say to You?" Rosen's story reveals an unexpected communion between the woman and her baby's nurse, one that is closer than other, more "familiar" relationships—for familiar also refers to the traditional aspects of our lives, those that we have become accustomed to. Sophie Sapinsky of Yezierska's "My Own People" comes to see just how strong her familiar connections are. The mother of five in Tillie Olsen's "I Stand Here Ironing" attempts to understand her experience with her first-born child, while the mother in Narell's "Papa's Tea" is a source of consternation to her small daughter, because she is *not* the stereotypic Jewish mother.

A sense of alienation and sometimes rebellion pervades the stories of "Seeking." Mrs. Fortrey of "Where Moth and Rust" ceases to perform her household duties, doing what she wants to do rather than what she should do. Some of the selections deal with personal loss. In *Riverfinger Women*, Inez, who has rejected many of her family's values, reveals her sadness that she has not yet found the voice to speak to her parents.

These pieces are about the need to re-establish a connection with the past. In "The Long-Distance Runner," Faith literally runs to her past and back to the present. Aviva Cantor's "The Phantom Child" shows a similar movement: as she weighs the question of abortion for herself, she explores her relationship with her mother and re-examines Judaism for its present meaning. And A of Andrea Dworkin's "First Love" writes a letter describing a hard-won self-knowledge, a synthesis of all that has happened to her.

The search for meaning is also an attempt to overcome aloneness, as it is for Sarah in "The Woman Who Lost Her Names." She marries, bears children, travels through America, and moves to Israel. But despite her gains, the loss of her names implies the loss of the power of naming, of language itself.

The selections listed under "Finding" tell of the acceptance that may evolve through time and understanding, as in Nancy Datan's "Making Jews." Sometimes it comes with recognition, as it does in "My Mother's Story" and "My Mother Was a Light Housekeeper," where it also signals a renewed relationship, based upon mutual knowledge of a shared past. Where conflicts once existed between husband and wife ("Anniversary"), young and old ("The Four Leaf Clover Story"), there is now some sense of affirmation. In this group of stories, to connect with the past becomes one way to find meaning in the present and hope for the future.

The two works that point toward "New Directions" are set in worlds different from those which most people encounter today. "X" is a fable of egalitarian child-rearing, far from the experience of all of us. The excerpt from *A Weave of Women* depicts a group of women in the Old City of Jerusalem striving to create their lives anew. The first is set in another time; the second, in another place.

For those with dreams of challenging the patriarchal bias of American culture, the inference is inescapable upon reading these two selections: Our dedication to change is not yet strong enough. We may have the imagination, but most of us lack the courage to risk and to make our visions reality.

Some selections could just as easily have been placed under another heading. For example, "The Fraychie Story" says as much about reconciliation, about finding, as it does about "familiar connections." And the life of Emma Goldman is certainly the life of a rebel. But the part of her autobiography reprinted here also shows the strength of her relationship with her family. The four divisions are thus suggestive rather than definitive.

This collection is only a beginning. It is not meant to be exhaustive, a task requiring many volumes. In the writings at hand, however, a picture of multiplicity emerges. The women portrayed are various; the thoughts and situations they have recorded are diverse. It is true that their Jewishness exists in greater or lesser degrees. It is also true that in some instances the language used to describe their experiences is somewhat rough-hewn.

But the American Jewish woman who is defining herself with language, as these writers are, is, in a sense, still at the beginning of a tradition. While she may once have lost the power of naming, she is about to regain it.

Meanwhile, those of us who wish can continue to search for each woman's story. We must learn what that story was and is. For some of us, the way to educate ourselves will be to write some fragment of it.

I
FAMILIAR
CONNECTIONS

My Own People

Anzia Yezierska

W ITH THE SUITCASE containing all her worldly possessions under her arm, Sophie Sapinsky elbowed her way through the noisy ghetto crowds. Pushcart peddlers and pullers-in shouted and gesticulated. Women with market-baskets pushed and shoved one another, eyes straining with the one thought— how to get the food a penny cheaper. With the same strained intentness, Sophie scanned each tenement, searching for a room cheap enough for her dwindling means.

In a dingy basement window a crooked sign, in straggling, penciled letters, caught Sophie's eye: "Room to let, a bargain, cheap."

The exuberant phrasing was quite in keeping with the extravagant dilapidation of the surroundings. "This is the very

In 1907, *Anzia Yezierska* and her family emigrated from Sukovoly, Russia, to New York. There she worked in a factory, in a Delancey Street sweatshop, and in a restaurant. A naturalized U.S. citizen, *Yezierska* began writing stories of ghetto life in 1918. *The Open Cage: An Anzia Yezierska Collection*, edited by Alice K. Harris, was published in 1979 by Persea Books. "My Own People" is reprinted from *Hungry Hearts* by permission of copyright owner, Louise Levitas Henriksen.

place," thought Sophie. "There could n't be nothing cheaper in all New York."

At the foot of the basement steps she knocked.

"Come in!" a voice answered.

As she opened the door she saw an old man bending over a pot of potatoes on a shoemaker's bench. A group of children in all degrees of rags surrounded him, greedily snatching at the potatoes he handed out.

Sophie paused for an instant, but her absorption in her own problem was too great to halt the question: "Is there a room to let?"

"Hanneh Breineh, in the back, has a room." The old man was so preoccupied filling the hungry hands that he did not even look up.

Sophie groped her way to the rear hall. A gaunt-faced woman answered her inquiry with loquacious enthusiasm. "A grand room for the money. I'll let it down to you only for three dollars a month. In the whole block is no bigger bargain. I should live so."

As she talked, the woman led her through the dark hall into an airshaft room. A narrow window looked out into the bottom of a chimney-like pit, where lay the accumulated refuse from a score of crowded kitchens.

"Oi weh!" gasped Sophie, throwing open the sash. "No air and no light. Outside shines the sun and here it's so dark."

"It ain't so dark. It's only a little shady. Let me only turn up the gas for you and you'll quick see everything like with sunshine."

The claw-fingered flame revealed a rusty, iron cot, an inverted potato barrel that served for a table, and two soapboxes for chairs.

Sophie felt of the cot. It sagged and flopped under her touch. "The bed has only three feet!" she exclaimed in dismay.

"You can't have Rockefeller's palace for three dollars a month," defended Hanneh Breineh, as she shoved one of the boxes under the legless corner of the cot. "If the bed ain't so steady, so you got good neighbors. Upstairs lives Shprintzeh Gittle, the herring-woman. You can buy by her the biggest bargains in fish, a few days older.... What she got left over from the Sabbath, she sells to the neighbors cheap.... In the front lives Shmendrik, the shoemaker. I'll tell you the truth, he ain't no real shoemaker. He never yet made a pair of whole shoes in his life. He's a learner from the old country—a tzadik, a saint; but every time he sees in the street a child with torn feet, he calls them in and patches them up. His own eating, the last bite from his mouth, he divides up with them."

"Three dollars," deliberated Sophie, scarcely hearing Hanneh Breineh's chatter. "I will never find anything cheaper. It has a door to lock and I can shut this woman out. . . . I'll take it," she said, handing her the money.

Hanneh Breineh kissed the greasy bills gloatingly. "I'll treat you like a mother! You'll have it good by me like in your own home."

"Thanks—but I got no time to shmoos. I got to be alone to get my work done."

The rebuff could not penetrate Hanneh Breineh's joy over the sudden possession of three dollars.

"Long years on you! May we be to good luck to one another!" was Hanneh Breineh's blessing as she closed the door.

Alone in her room—*her* room, securely hers—yet with the flash of triumph, a stab of bitterness. All that was hers—so wretched and so ugly! Had her eager spirit, eager to give and give, no claim to a bit of beauty—a shred of comfort?

Perhaps her family was right in condemning her rashness. Was it worth while to give up the peace of home, the security of a regular job—suffer hunger, loneliness, and want—for what? For something she knew in her heart was beyond her reach. Would her writing ever amount to enough to vindicate the uprooting of her past? Would she ever become articulate enough to express beautifully what she saw and felt? What had she, after all, but a stifling, sweatshop experience, a meager, night-school education, and this wild, blind hunger to release the dumbness that choked her?

Sophie spread her papers on the cot beside her. Resting her elbows on the potato barrel, she clutched her pencil with tense fingers. In the notebook before her were a hundred beginnings, essays, abstractions, outbursts of chaotic moods. She glanced through the titles: "Believe in Yourself," "The Quest of the Ideal."

Meaningless tracings on the paper, her words seemed to her

now—a restless spirit pawing at the air. The intensity of experience, the surge of emotion that had been hers when she wrote—
where were they? The words had failed to catch the lifebeat—
had failed to register the passion she had poured into them.

Perhaps she was not a writer, after all. Had the years and years
of night-study been in vain? Choked with discouragement, the
cry broke from her, "O—God—God help me! I feel—I see, but
it all dies in me—dumb!"

Tedious days passed into weeks. Again Sophie sat staring
into her notebook. "There's nothing here that's alive. Not a
word yet says what's in me ...

"But it *is* in me!" With clenched fist she smote her bosom. "It
must be in me! I believe in it! I got to get it out—even if it tears
my flesh in pieces—even if it kills me! ...

"But these words—these flat, dead words ...

"Whether I can write or can't write—I can't stop writing. I
can't rest. I can't breathe. There's no peace, no running away
for me on earth except in the struggle to give out what's in me.
The beat from my heart—the blood from my veins—must flow
out into my words."

She returned to her unfinished essay, "Believe in Yourself."
Her mind groping—clutching at the misty incoherence that
clouded her thoughts—she wrote on.

"These sentences are yet only wood—lead; but I can't help
it—I'll push on—on—I'll not eat—I'll not sleep—I'll not move
from this spot till I get it to say on the paper what I got in my
heart!"

Slowly the dead words seemed to begin to breathe. Her eyes
brightened. Her cheeks flushed. Her very pencil trembled with
the eager onrush of words.

Then a sharp rap sounded on her door. With a gesture of
irritation Sophie put down her pencil and looked into the burning, sunken eyes of her neighbor, Hanneh Breineh.

"I got yourself a glass of tea, good friend. It ain't much I got
to give away, but it's warm even if it's nothing."

Sophie scowled. "You must n't bother yourself with me. I'm
so busy—thanks."

"Don't thank me yet so quick. I got no sugar." Hanneh Breineh edged herself into the room confidingly. "At home, in
Poland, I not only had sugar for tea—but even jelly—a jelly that
would lift you up to heaven. I thought in America everything
would be so plenty, I could drink the tea out from my sugarbowl. But ach! Not in Poland did my children starve like in
America!"

Hanneh Breineh, in a friendly manner, settled herself on the
sound end of the bed, and began her jeremiad.

"Yosef, my man, ain't no bread-giver. Already he got consumption the second year. One week he works and nine weeks
he lays sick."

In despair Sophie gathered her papers, wondering how to get
the woman out of her room. She glanced through the page she
had written, but Hanneh Breineh, unconscious of her indifference, went right on.

"How many times it is tearing the heart out from my body—
should I take Yosef's milk to give to the baby, or the baby's milk
to give to Yosef? If he was dead the pensions they give to
widows would help feed my children. Now I got only the charities to help me. A black year on them! They should only have
to feed their own children on what they give me."

Resolved not to listen to the intruder, Sophie debated within
herself: "Should I call my essay 'Believe in Yourself,' or would
n't it be stronger to say, 'Trust Yourself'? But if I say, 'Trust
Yourself,' would n't they think that I got the words from Emerson?"

Hanneh Breineh's voice went on, but it sounded to Sophie
like a faint buzzing from afar. "Gotteniu! How much did it cost
me my life to go and swear myself that my little Fannie—only
skin and bones—that she is already fourteen! How it chokes me
the tears every morning when I got to wake her and push her
out to the shop when her eyes are yet shutting themselves with
sleep!"

Sophie glanced at her wrist-watch as it ticked away the precious minutes. She must get rid of the woman! Had she not left
her own sister, sacrificed all comfort, all association, for solitude and its golden possibilities? For the first time in her life
she had the chance to be by herself and think. And now, the

8 Familiar Connections

thoughts which a moment ago had seemed like a flock of fluttering birds had come so close—and this woman with her sordid wailing had scattered them.

"I'm a savage, a beast, but I got to ask her to get out—this very minute," resolved Sophie. But before she could summon the courage to do what she wanted to do, there was a timid knock at the door, and the wizened little Fannie, her face streaked with tears, stumbled in.

"The inspector said it's a lie. I ain't yet fourteen," she whimpered.

Hanneh Breineh paled. "Woe is me! Sent back from the shop? God from the world—is there no end to my troubles? Why did n't you hide yourself when you saw the inspector come?"

"I was running to hide myself under the table, but she caught me and she said she'll take me to the Children's Society and arrest me and my mother for sending me to work too soon."

"Arrest me?" shrieked Hanneh Breineh, beating her breast. "Let them only come and arrest me! I'll show America who I am! Let them only begin themselves with me! . . . Black is for my eyes . . . the groceryman will not give us another bread till we pay him the bill!"

"The inspector said . . ." The child's brow puckered in an effort to recall the words.

"What did the inspector said? Gotteniu!" Hanneh Breineh wrung her hands in passionate entreaty. "Listen only once to my prayer! Send on the inspector only a quick death! I only wish her to have her own house with twenty-four rooms and each of the twenty-four rooms should be twenty-four beds and the chills and the fever should throw her from one bed to another!"

"Hanneh Breineh, still yourself a little," entreated Sophie.

"How can I still myself without Fannie's wages? Bitter is me! Why do I have to live so long?"

"The inspector said . . ."

"What did the inspector said? A thunder should strike the inspector! Ain't I as good a mother as other mothers? Would n't I better send my children to school? But who'll give us to eat? And who'll pay us the rent?"

Hanneh Breineh wiped her red-lidded eyes with the corner of her apron.

"The president from America should only come to my bitter heart. Let him go fighting himself with the pushcarts how to get the eating a penny cheaper. Let him try to feed his children on the money the charities give me and we'd see if he would n't better send his littlest ones to the shop better than to let them starve before his eyes. Woe is me! What for did I come to America? What's my life—nothing but one terrible, never-stopping fight with the grocer and the butcher and the landlord . . ."

Suddenly Sophie's resentment for her lost morning was forgotten. The crying waste of Hanneh Breineh's life lay open before her eyes like pictures in a book. She saw her own life in Hanneh Breineh's life. Her efforts to write were like Hanneh Breineh's efforts to feed her children. Behind her life and Hanneh Breineh's life she saw the massed ghosts of thousands upon thousands beating—beating out their hearts against rock barriers.

"The inspector said . . ." Fannie timidly attempted again to explain.

"The inspector!" shrieked Hanneh Breineh, as she seized hold of Fannie in a rage. "Hellfire should burn the inspector! Tell me again about the inspector and I'll choke the life out from you—"

Sophie sprang forward to protect the child from the mother. "She's only trying to tell you something."

"Why should she yet throw salt on my wounds? If there was enough bread in the house would I need an inspector to tell me to send her to school? If America is so interested in poor people's children, then why don't they give them to eat till they should go to work? What learning can come into a child's head when the stomach is empty?"

A clutter of feet down the creaking cellar steps, a scuffle of broken shoes and a chorus of shrill voices, as the younger children rushed in from school.

"Mamma—what's to eat?"

"It smells potatoes!"

"Pfui! The pot is empty! It smells over from Cohen's."

"Jake grabbed all the bread!"

"Mamma—he kicked the piece out from my hands!"

"Mamma—it's so empty in my stomach! Ain't there nothing?"

"Gluttons—wolves—thieves!" Hanneh Breineh shrieked. "I should only live to bury you all in one day!"

The children, regardless of Hanneh Breineh's invectives, swarmed around her like hungry bees, tearing at her apron, her skirt. Their voices rose in increased clamor, topped only by their mother's imprecations. "Gotteniu! Tear me away from these leeches on my neck! Send on them only a quick death! . . . Only a minute's peace before I die!"

"Hanneh Breineh—children! What's the matter?" Shmendrik stood at the door. The sweet quiet of the old man stilled the raucous voices as the coming of evening stills the noises of the day.

"There's no end to my troubles! Hear them hollering for bread, and the grocer stopped to give till the bill is paid. Woe is me! Fannie sent home by the inspector and not a crumb in the house!"

"I got something." The old man put his hands over the heads of the children in silent benediction. "All come in by me. I got sent me a box of cake."

"Cake!" The children cried, catching at the kind hands and snuggling about the shabby coat.

"Yes. Cake and nuts and raisins and even a bottle of wine."

The children leaped and danced around him in their wild burst of joy.

"Cake and wine—a box—to you? Have the charities gone crazy?" Hanneh Breineh's eyes sparkled with light and laughter.

"No—no," Shmendrik explained hastily. "Not from the charities—from a friend—for the holidays."

Shmendrik nodded invitingly to Sophie, who was standing in the door of her room. "The roomerkeh will also give a taste with us our party?"

"Sure will she!" Hanneh Breineh took Sophie by the arm. "Who'll say no in this black life to cake and wine?"

Young throats burst into shrill cries: "Cake and wine—wine and cake—raisins and nuts—nuts and raisins!" The words rose in a triumphant chorus. The children leaped and danced in time to their chant, almost carrying the old man bodily into his room in the wildness of their joy.

The contagion of this sudden hilarity erased from Sophie's mind the last thought of work and she found herself seated with the others on the cobbler's bench.

From under his cot the old man drew forth a wooden box. Lifting the cover he held up before wondering eyes a large frosted cake embedded in raisins and nuts.

Amid the shouts of glee Shmendrik now waved aloft a large bottle of grape-juice.

The children could contain themselves no longer and dashed forward.

"Shah—shah! Wait only!" He gently halted their onrush and waved them back to their seats.

"The glasses for the wine!" Hanneh Breineh rushed about hither and thither in happy confusion. From the sink, the shelf, the windowsill, she gathered cracked glasses, cups without handles—anything that would hold even a few drops of the yellow wine.

Sacrificial solemnity filled the basement as the children breathlessly watched Shmendrik cut the precious cake. Mouths —even eyes—watered with the intensity of their emotion.

With almost religious fervor Hanneh Breineh poured the grape-juice into the glasses held in the trembling hands of the children. So overwhelming was the occasion that none dared to taste till the ritual was completed. The suspense was agonizing as one and all waited for Shmendrik's signal.

"Hanneh Breineh—you drink from my Sabbath wine-glass!"

Hanneh Breineh clinked glasses with Schmendrik. "Long years on us all!" Then she turned to Sophie, clinked glasses once more. "May you yet marry yourself from our basement to a millionaire!" Then she lifted the glass to her lips.

The spell was broken. With a yell of triumph the children gobbled the cake in huge mouthfuls and sucked the golden liquid. All the traditions of wealth and joy that ever sparkled from the bubbles of champagne smiled at Hanneh Breineh from her glass of California grape-juice.

"Ach!" she sighed. "How good it is to forget your troubles,

and only those that's got troubles have the chance to forget them."

She sipped the grape-juice leisurely, thrilled into ecstasy with each lingering drop. "How it laughs yet in me, the life, the minute I turn my head from my worries!"

With growing wonder in her eyes, Sophie watched Hanneh Breineh. This ragged wreck of a woman—how passionately she clung to every atom of life! Hungrily, she burned through the depths of every experience. How she flared against wrongs— and how every tiny spark of pleasure blazed into joy!

Within a half-hour this woman had touched the whole range of human emotions, from bitterest agony to dancing joy. The terrible despair at the onrush of her starving children when she cried out, "O that I should only bury you all in one day!" And now the leaping light of the words: "How it laughs yet in me, the life, the minute I turn my head from my worries."

"Ach, if I could only write like Hanneh Breineh talks!" thought Sophie. "Her words dance with a thousand colors. Like a rainbow it flows from her lips." Sentences from her own essays marched before her, stiff and wooden. How clumsy, how unreal, were her most labored phrases compared to Hanneh Breineh's spontaneity. Fascinated, she listened to Hanneh Breineh, drinking her words as a thirst-perishing man drinks water. Every bubbling phrase filled her with a drunken rapture to create.

"Up till now I was only trying to write from my head. It wasn't real—it wasn't life. Hanneh Breineh is real. Hanneh Breineh is life."

"Ach! What do the rich people got but dried-up dollars? Pfui on them and their money!" Hanneh Breineh held up her glass to be refilled. "Let me only win a fortune on the lotteree and move myself in my own bought house. Let me only have my first hundred dollars in the bank and I'll lift up my head like a person and tell the charities to eat their own cornmeal. I'll get myself an automobile like the kind rich ladies and ride up to their houses on Fifth Avenue and feed them only once on the eating they like so good for me and my children."

With a smile of benediction Shmendrik refilled the glasses and cut for each of his guests another slice of cake. Then came the handful of nuts and raisins.

As the children were scurrying about for hammers and iron lasts with which to crack their nuts, the basement door creaked. Unannounced, a woman entered—the "friendly visitor" of the charities. Her look of awful amazement swept the group of merrymakers.

"Mr. Shmendrik!—Hanneh Breineh!" Indignation seethed in her voice. "What's this? A feast—a birthday?"

Gasps—bewildered glances—a struggle for utterance!

"I came to make my monthly visit—evidently I'm not needed."

Shmendrik faced the accusing eyes of the "friendly visitor." "Holiday eating . . ."

"Oh—I'm glad you're so prosperous."

Before any one had gained presence of mind enough to explain things, the door had clanked. The "friendly visitor" had vanished.

"Pfui!" Hanneh Breineh snatched up her glass and drained its contents. "What will she do now? Will we get no more dry bread from the charities because once we ate cake?"

"What for did she come?" asked Sophie.

"To see that we don't over-eat ourselves!" returned Hanneh Breineh. "She's a 'friendly visitor'! She learns us how to cook cornmeal. By pictures and lectures she shows us how the poor people should live without meat, without milk, without butter, and without eggs. Always it's on the end of my tongue to ask her, 'You learned us to do without so much, why can't you yet learn us how to eat without eating?' "

The children seized the last crumbs of cake that Shmendrik handed them and rushed for the street.

"What a killing look was on her face," said Sophie. "Could n't she be a little glad for your gladness?"

"Charity ladies—gladness?" The joy of the grape-wine still rippled in Hanneh Breineh's laughter. "For poor people is only cornmeal. Ten cents a day—to feed my children!"

Still in her rollicking mood Hanneh Breineh picked up the baby and tossed it like a Bacchante. "Could you be happy a lot with ten cents in your stomach? Ten cents—half a can of condensed milk—then fill yourself the rest with water! . . . Maybe yet feed you with all water and save the ten-cent pieces to buy you a carriage like the Fifth Avenue babies! . . ."

The soft sound of a limousine purred through the area grating and two well-fed figures in sealskin coats, led by the "friendly visitor," appeared at the door.

"Mr. Bernstein, you can see for yourself." The "friendly visitor" pointed to the table.

The merry group shrank back. It was as if a gust of icy wind had swept all the joy and laughter from the basement.

"You are charged with intent to deceive and obtain assistance by dishonest means," said Mr. Bernstein.

"Dishonest?" Shmendrik paled.

Sophie's throat strained with passionate protest, but no words came to her release.

"A friend—a friend"—stammered Shmendrik—"sent me the holiday eating."

The superintendent of the Social Betterment Society faced him accusingly. "You told us that you had no friends when you applied to us for assistance."

"My friend—he knew me in my better time." Shmendrik flushed painfully. "I was once a scholar—respected. I wanted by this one friend to hold myself like I was."

Mr. Bernstein had taken from the bookshelf a number of letters, glanced through them rapidly and handed them one by one to the deferential superintendent.

Shmendrik clutched at his heart in an agony of humiliation. Suddenly his bent body straightened. His eyes dilated. "My letters—my life—you dare?"

"Of course we dare!" The superintendent returned Shmendrik's livid gaze, made bold by the confidence that what he was doing was the only scientific method of administering philanthropy. "These dollars, so generously given, must go to those most worthy. . . . I find in these letters references to gifts of fruit and other luxuries you did not report at our office."

"He never kept nothing for himself!" Hanneh Breineh broke in defensively. "He gave it all for the children."

Ignoring the interruption Mr. Bernstein turned to the "friendly visitor." "I'm glad you brought my attention to this case. It's but one of the many impositions on our charity . . . Come . . ."

"Kossacks! Pogromschiks!" Sophie's rage broke at last.

"You call yourselves Americans? You dare call yourselves Jews? You bosses of the poor! This man Shmendrik, whose house you broke into, whom you made to shame like a beggar—he is the one Jew from whom the Jews can be proud! He gives all he is—all he has—as God gives. *He is* charity.

"But you—you are the greed—the shame of the Jews! *All-right-niks*—fat bellies in fur coats! What do you give from yourselves? You may eat and bust eating! Nothing you give till you've stuffed yourselves so full that your hearts are dead!"

The door closed in her face. Her wrath fell on indifferent backs as the visitors mounted the steps to the street.

Shmendrik groped blindly for the Bible. In a low, quavering voice, he began the chant of the oppressed—the wail of the downtrodden. "I am afraid, and a trembling taketh hold of my flesh. Wherefore do the wicked live, become old, yea, mighty in power?"

Hanneh Breineh and the children drew close around the old man. They were weeping—unconscious of their weeping—deep-buried memories roused by the music, the age-old music of the Hebrew race.

Through the grating Sophie saw the limousine pass. The chant flowed on: "Their houses are safe from fear; neither is the rod of God upon them."

Silently Sophie stole back to her room. She flung herself on the cot, pressed her fingers to her burning eyeballs. For a long time she lay rigid, clenched—listening to the drumming of her heart like the sea against rock barriers. Presently the barriers burst. Something in her began pouring itself out. She felt for her pencil—paper—and began to write. Whether she reached out to God or man she knew not, but she wrote on and on all through that night.

The gray light entering her grated window told her that beyond was dawn. Sophie looked up: "Ach! At last it writes itself in me!" she whispered triumphantly. "It's not me—it's their cries—my own people—crying in me! Hanneh Breineh, Shmendrik, they will not be stilled in me, till all America stops to listen."

from Living My Life

Emma Goldman

I HAD WORKED IN factories before, in St. Petersburg. In the winter of 1882, when Mother, my two little brothers, and I came from Konigsberg to join Father in the Russian capital, we found that he had lost his position. He had been manager of his cousin's drygoods store; but, shortly before our arrival, the business failed. The loss of his job was a tragedy to our family, as Father had not managed to save anything. The only bread-winner then was Helena. Mother was forced to turn to her brothers for a loan. The three hundred roubles they advanced were invested in a grocery store. The business yielded little at first, and it became necessary for me to find employment.

Knitted shawls were then much in vogue, and a neighbour told my mother where I might find work to do at home. By keeping at the task many hours a day, sometimes late into the night, I contrived to earn twelve roubles a month.

At the age of seventeen, *Emma Goldman* came to the U.S. from Russia. Married briefly, she worked in sweatshops and factories and was a leader in the radical-anarchist circles of her time, lecturing and writing on diverse topics. She was deported to Russia after World War I and was never allowed to return to America. She died in 1940. Chapter 2 of *Living My Life*, Vol. II, by Emma Goldman is reprinted with permission of Dover Publications.

The shawls I knitted for a livelihood were by no means masterpieces, but somehow they passed. I hated the work, and my eyes gave way under the strain of constant application. Father's cousin who had failed in the dry-goods business now owned a glove factory. He offered to teach me the trade and give me work.

The factory was far from our place. One had to get up at five in the morning to be at work at seven. The rooms were stuffy, unventilated, and dark. Oil lamps gave the light; the sun never penetrated the work-room.

There were six hundred of us, of all ages, working on costly and beautiful gloves day in, day out, for very small pay. But we were allowed sufficient time for our noon meal and twice a day for tea. We could talk and sing while at work; we were not driven or harassed. That was in St. Petersburg, in 1882.

Now I was in America, in the Flower City of the State of New York, in a model factory, as I was told. Certainly, Garson's clothing-works were a vast improvement on the glove factory on the Vassilevsky Ostrov. The rooms were large, bright, and airy. One had elbow space. There were none of those ill-smelling odours that used to nauseate me in our cousin's shop. Yet the work here was harder, and the day, with only half an hour for lunch, seemed endless. The iron discipline forbade free movement (one could not even go to the toilet without permission), and the constant surveillance of the foreman weighed like stone on my heart. The end of each day found me sapped, with just enough energy to drag myself to my sister's home and crawl into bed. This continued with deadly monotony week after week.

The amazing thing to me was that no one else in the factory seemed to be so affected as I, no one but my neighbour, frail little Tanya. She was delicate and pale, frequently complained of headaches, and often broke into tears when the task of handling heavy ulsters proved too much for her. One morning, as I looked up from my work, I discovered her all huddled in a heap. She had fallen in a faint. I called to the foreman to help me carry her to the dressing-room, but the deafening noise of the machines drowned my voice. Several girls near by heard me and began to shout. They ceased working and rushed over to

Tanya. The sudden stopping of the machines attracted the fore-man's attention and he came over to us. Without even asking the reason for the commotion, he shouted: "Back to your ma-chines! What do you mean stopping work now? Do you want to be fired? Get back at once!" When he spied the crumpled body of Tanya, he yelled: "What the hell is the matter with her?" "She has fainted," I replied, trying hard to control my voice. "Faint-ed, nothing," he sneered, "she's only shamming."

"You are a liar and a brute!" I cried, no longer able to keep back my indignation.

I bent over Tanya, loosened her waist, and squeezed the juice of an orange I had in my lunch basket into her half-opened mouth. Her face was white, a cold sweat on her forehead. She looked so ill that even the foreman realized she had not been shamming. He excused her for the day. "I will go with Tanya," I said; "you can deduct from my pay for the time." "You can go to hell, you wildcat!" he flung after me.

We went to a coffee place. I myself felt empty and faint, but all we had between us was seventy-five cents. We decided to spend forty on food, and use the rest for a street-car ride to the park. There, in the fresh air, amid the flowers and trees, we forgot our dreaded tasks. The day that had begun in trouble ended restfully and in peace.

The next morning the enervating routine started all over again, continuing for weeks and months, broken only by the new arrival in our family, a baby girl. The child became the one interest in my dull existence. Often, when the atmosphere in Garson's factory threatened to overcome me, the thought of the lovely mite at home revived my spirit. The evenings were no longer dreary and meaningless. But, while little Stella brought joy into our household, she added to the material anxiety of my sister and my brother-in-law.

Lena never by word or deed made me feel that the dollar and fifty cents I was giving her for my board (the car fare amounted to sixty cents a week, the remaining forty cents being my pin-money) did not cover my keep. But I had overheard my brother-in-law grumbling over the growing expense of the house. I felt he was right. I did not want my sister worried, she was nursing her child. I decided to apply for a rise. I knew it was no use talking to the foreman and therefore I asked to see Mr. Garson.

I was ushered into a luxurious office. American Beauties were on the table. Often I had admired them in the flower shops, and once, unable to withstand the temptation, I had gone in to ask the price. They were one dollar and a half apiece—more than half of my week's earnings. The lovely vase in Mr. Garson's office held a great many of them.

I was not asked to sit down. For a moment I forgot my mission. The beautiful room, the roses, the aroma of the bluish smoke from Mr. Garson's cigar, fascinated me. I was recalled to reality by my employer's question. "Well, what can I do for you?"

I had come to ask for a rise, I told him. The two dollars and a half I was getting did not pay my board, let alone anything else, such as an occasional book or a theatre ticket for twenty-five cents. Mr. Garson replied that for a factory girl I had rather extravagant tastes, that all his "hands" were well satisfied, that they seemed to be getting along all right—that I, too, would have to manage or find work elsewhere. "If I raise your wages, I'll have to raise the others' as well and I can't afford that," he said. I decided to leave Garson's employ.

A few days later I secured a job at Rubinstein's factory at four dollars a week. It was a small shop, not far from where I lived. The house stood in a garden, and only a dozen men and women were employed in the place. The Garson discipline and drive were missing.

Next to my machine worked an attractive young man whose name was Jacob Kershner. He lived near Lena's home, and we would often walk from work together. Before long he began calling for me in the morning. We used to converse in Russian, my English still being very halting. His Russian was like music to me; it was the first real Russian, outside of Helena's, that I had had an opportunity to hear in Rochester since my arrival.

Kershner had come to America in 1881 from Odessa, where he had finished the *Gymnasium*. Having no trade, he became an "operator" on cloaks. He used to spend most of his leisure, he told me, reading or going to dances. He had no friends, because he found his co-workers in Rochester interested only in money-making, their ideal being to start a shop of their own. He had heard of our arrival, Helena's and mine—had even seen me on the street several times—but he did not know how to get acquainted. Now he would no longer feel lonely, he said brightly; we could visit places together and he would lend me his books to read. My own loneliness no longer was so poignant.

I told my sisters of my new acquaintance, and Lena asked me to invite him the next Sunday. When Kershner came, she was favourably impressed; but Helena took a violent dislike to him from the first. She said nothing about it for a long time, but I could sense it.

One day Kershner invited me to a dance. It was my first since I came to America. The very anticipation was exciting, bringing back memories of my first ball in St. Petersburg.

I was fifteen then. Helena had been invited to the fashionable German Club by her employer, who gave her two tickets, so she could bring me with her. Some time previously my sister had presented me with a lovely blue velvet for my first long dress; but before it could be made up, our peasant servant walked off with the material. My grief over its loss made me quite ill for several days. If only I had a dress, I thought, Father might consent to my attending the ball. "I'll get you material for a dress," Helena consoled me, "but I'm afraid Father will refuse." "Then I will defy him!" I declared.

She bought another piece of blue stuff, not so beautiful as my velvet, but I no longer minded. I was too happy over the prospect of my first ball, of the bliss of dancing in public. Somehow Helena succeeded in getting Father's consent, but at the last moment he changed his mind. I had been guilty of some infraction during the day, and he categorically declared that I would have to stay home. Thereupon Helena said she also would not go. But I was determined to defy my father, no matter what the consequences.

With bated breath I waited for my parents to retire for the night. Then I dressed and woke Helena. I told her she must come with me or I would run away from home. "We can be back before Father wakes up," I urged. Dear Helena—she was always so timid! She had infinite capacity for suffering, for endurance, but she could not fight. On this occasion she was carried away by my desperate decision. She dressed and we quietly slipped out of the house.

At the German Club everything was bright and gay. We found

Helena's employer, whose name was Kadison, and some of his
young friends. I was asked for every dance, and I danced in
frantic excitement and abandon. It was getting late and many
people were already leaving when Kadison invited me for another dance. Helena insisted that I was too exhausted, but I
would not have it so. "I will dance!" I declared; "I will dance
myself to death!" My flesh felt hot, my heart beat violently as my
cavalier swung me round the ball-room, holding me tightly. To
dance to death—what more glorious end!

It was towards five in the morning when we arrived home.
Our people were still asleep. I awoke late in the day, pretending
a sick headache, and secretly I gloried in my triumph of having
outwitted our old man.

The memory of that experience still vivid in my mind, I accompanied Jacob Kershner to the party, full of anticipation. My
disappointment was bitter: there were no beautiful ball-room,
no lovely women, no dashing young men, no gaiety. The music
was shrill, the dancers clumsy. Jacob danced not badly, but he
lacked spirit and fire. "Four years at the machine have taken the
strength out of me," he said; "I get tired so easily."

I had known Jacob Kershner about four months when he
asked me to marry him. I admitted I liked him, but I did not want
to marry so young. We still knew so little of each other. He said
he'd wait as long as I pleased, but there was already a great deal
of talk about our being out together so much. "Why should we
not get engaged?" he pleaded. Finally I consented. Helena's
antagonism to Jacob had become almost an obsession; she
fairly hated him. But I was lonely—I needed companionship.
Ultimately I won over my sister. Her great love for me could
never refuse me anything or stand out against my wishes.

The late fall of 1886 brought the rest of our family to Rochester—Father, Mother, my brothers, Herman and Yegor. Conditions in St. Petersburg had become intolerable for the Jews, and
the grocery business did not yield enough for the ever-growing
bribery Father had to practice in order to be allowed to exist.
America became the only solution.

Together with Helena I had prepared a home for our parents,
and on their arrival we went to live with them. Our earnings
soon proved inadequate to meet the household expenses. Jacob

Kershner offered to board with us, which would be of some help, and before long he moved in.

The house was small, consisting of a living-room, a kitchen, and two bedrooms. One of them was used by my parents, the other by Helena, myself, and our little brother. Kershner and Herman slept in the living-room. The close proximity of Jacob and the lack of privacy kept me in constant irritation. I suffered from sleepless nights, waking dreams and great fatigue at work. Life was becoming unbearable, and Jacob stressed the need of a home of our own.

On nearer acquaintance I had grown to understand that we were too different. His interest in books, which had first attracted me to him, had waned. He had fallen into the ways of his shopmates, playing cards and attending dull dances. I, on the contrary, was filled with striving and aspirations. In spirit I was still in Russia, in my beloved St. Petersburg, living in the world of the books I had read, the operas I had heard, the circle of the students I had known. I hated Rochester even more than before. But Kershner was the only human being I had met since my arrival. He filled a void in my life, and I was strongly attracted to him. In February 1887 we were married in Rochester by a rabbi, according to Jewish rites, which were then considered sufficient by the law of the country.

My feverish excitement of that day, my suspense and ardent anticipation gave way at night to a feeling of utter bewilderment. Jacob lay trembling near me; he was impotent.

My first erotic sensations I remember had come to me when I was about six. My parents lived in Popelan then, where we children had no home in any real sense. Father kept an inn, which was constantly filled with peasants, drunk and quarrelling, and government officials. Mother was busy superintending the servants in our large, chaotic house. My sisters, Lena and Helena, fourteen and twelve, were burdened with work. I was left to myself most of the day. Among the stable help there was a young peasant, Petrushka, who served as shepherd, looking after our cows and sheep. Often he would take me with him to the meadows, and I would listen to the sweet tones of his flute. In the evening he would carry me back home on his shoulders, I sitting astride. He would play horse—run as fast as his legs could carry him, then suddenly throw me up in the air, catch me in his arms, and press me to him. It used to give me a peculiar sensation, fill me with exultation, followed by blissful release.

I became inseparable from Petrushka. I grew so fond of him that I began stealing cake and fruit from Mother's pantry for him. To be with Petrushka out in the fields, to listen to his music, to ride on his shoulders, became the obsession of my waking and sleeping hours. One day Father had an altercation with Petrushka, and the boy was sent away. The loss of him was one of the greatest tragedies of my child-life. For weeks afterwards I kept on dreaming of Petrushka, the meadows, the music, and reliving the joy and ecstasy of our play. One morning I felt myself torn out of sleep. Mother was bending over me, tightly holding my right hand. In an angry voice she cried: "If ever I find your hand again like that, I'll whip you, you naughty child!"

The approach of puberty gave me my first consciousness of the effect of men on me. I was eleven then. Early one summer day I woke up in great agony. My head, spine, and legs ached as if they were being pulled asunder. I called for Mother. She drew back my bedcovers, and suddenly I felt a stinging pain in my face. She had struck me. I let out a shriek, fastening on Mother terrified eyes. "This is necessary for a girl," she said, "when she becomes a woman, as a protection against disgrace." She tried to take me in her arms, but I pushed her back. I was writhing in pain and I was too outraged for her to touch me. "I am going to die," I howled, "I want the *Feldscher* (assistant doctor)." The *Feldscher* was sent for. He was a young man, a new-comer in our village. He examined me and gave me something to put me to sleep. Thenceforth my dreams were of the *Feldscher*.

When I was fifteen, I was employed in a corset factory in the Hermitage Arcade in St. Petersburg. After working hours, on leaving the shop together with the other girls, we would be waylaid by young Russian officers and civilians. Most of the girls had their sweethearts; only a Jewish girl chum of mine and I refused to be taken to the *konditorskaya* (pastry shop) or to the park.

Next to the Hermitage was a hotel we had to pass. One of the clerks, a handsome fellow of about twenty, singled me out for his attentions. At first I scorned him, but gradually he began to exert a fascination on me. His perseverance slowly undermined my pride and I accepted his courtship. We used to meet in some quiet spot or in an out-of-the-way pastry shop. I had to invent all sorts of stories to explain to my father why I returned late from work or stayed out after nine o'clock. One day he spied me in the Summer Garden in the company of other girls and some boy students. When I returned home, he threw me violently against the shelves in our grocery store, which sent the jars of Mother's wonderful *varenya* flying to the floor. He pounded me with his fists, shouting that he would not tolerate a loose daughter. The experience made my home more unbearable, the need of escape more compelling.

For several months my admirer and I met clandestinely. One day he asked me whether I should not like to go through the hotel to see the luxurious rooms. I had never been in a hotel before—the joy and gaiety I fancied behind the gorgeous windows used to fascinate me as I would pass the place on my way from work.

The boy led me through a side entrance, along a thickly carpeted corridor, into a large room. It was brightly illumined and beautifully furnished. A table near the sofa held flowers and a tea-tray. We sat down. The young man poured out a golden-coloured liquid and asked me to clink glasses to our friendship. I put the wine to my lips. Suddenly I found myself in his arms, my waist torn open—his passionate kisses covered my face, neck, and breasts. Not until after the violent contact of our bodies and the excruciating pain he caused me did I come to my senses. I screamed, savagely beating against the man's chest with my fists. Suddenly I heard Helena's voice in the hall. "She must be here—she must be here!" I became speechless. The man, too, was terrorized. His grip relaxed, and we listened in breathless silence. After what seemed to me hours, Helena's voice receded. The man got up. I rose mechanically, mechanically buttoned my waist and brushed back my hair.

Strange, I felt no shame—only a great shock at the discovery

that the contact between man and woman could be so brutal and
so painful. I walked out in a daze, bruised in every nerve.

When I reached home I found Helena fearfully wrought up.
She had been uneasy about me, aware of my meeting with the
boy. She had made it her business to find out where he worked,
and when I failed to return, she had gone to the hotel in search
of me. The shame I did not feel in the arms of the man now
overwhelmed me. I could not muster up courage to tell Helena
of my experience.

After that I always felt between two fires in the presence of
men. Their lure remained strong, but it was always mingled
with violent revulsion. I could not bear to have them touch me.

These pictures passed through my mind vividly as I lay alongside my husband on our wedding night. He had fallen fast
asleep.

The weeks went on. There was no change. I urged Jacob to
consult a doctor. At first he refused, pleading diffidence, but
finally he went. He was told it would take considerable time to
"build up his manhood." My own passion had subsided. The
material anxiety of making ends meet excluded everything else.
I had stopped work; it was considered disgraceful for a married
woman to go to the shop. Jacob was earning fifteen dollars a
week. He had developed a passion for cards, which swallowed
up a considerable part of our income. He grew jealous, suspect-
ing everyone. Life became insupportable. I was saved from
utter despair by my interest in the Haymarket events.

After the death of the Chicago anarchists I insisted on a
separation from Kershner. He fought long against it, but finally
consented to a divorce. It was given to us by the same rabbi who
had performed our marriage ceremony. Then I left for New
Haven, Connecticut, to work in a corset-factory.

During my efforts to free myself from Kershner the only one
who stood by me was my sister Helena. She had been strenu-
ously opposed to the marriage in the first place, but now she
offered not a single reproach. On the contrary, she gave me
help and comfort. She pleaded with my parents and with Lena

in behalf of my decision to get a divorce. As always, her devotion knew no bounds.

In New Haven I met a group of young Russians, students mainly, now working at various trades. Most of them were socialists and anarchists. They often organized meetings, generally inviting speakers from New York, one of whom was A. Solotaroff. Life was interesting and colourful, but gradually the strain of the work became too much for my depleted vitality. Finally I had to return to Rochester.

I went to Helena. She lived with her husband and child over their little printing shop, which also served as an office for their steamship agency. But both occupations did not bring in enough to keep them from dire poverty. Helena had married Jacob Hochstein, a man ten years her senior. He was a great Hebrew scholar, an authority on the English and Russian classics, and a very rare personality. His integrity and independent character made him a poor competitor in the sordid business life. When anyone brought him a printing order worth two dollars, Jacob Hochstein devoted as much time to it as if he were getting fifty. If a customer showed a tendency to bargain over prices, he would send him away. He could not bear the implication that he might overcharge. His income was insufficient for the needs of the family, and the one to worry and fret most about it was my poor Helena. She was pregnant with her second child and yet had to drudge from morning till night to make ends meet, with never a word of complaint. But, then, she had been that way all her life, suffering silently, always resigned.

Helena's marriage had not sprung from a passionate love. It was the union of two mature people who longed for comradeship, for a quiet life. Whatever there had been of passion in my sister had burned out when she was twenty-four. At the age of sixteen, while we were living in Popelan, she had fallen in love with a young Lithuanian, a beautiful soul. But he was a *goi* (gentile) and Helena knew that marriage between them was impossible. After a great struggle and many tears Helena broke off the affair with young Susha. Years later, while on our way to America, we stopped in Kovno, our native town. Helena had arranged for Susha to meet her there. She could not bear to go away so far without saying good-bye to him. They met and parted as good friends—the fire of their youth was in ashes.

On my return from New Haven Helena received me, as always, with tenderness and with the assurance that her home was also mine. It was good to be near my darling again, with little Stella and my young brother Yegor. But it did not take me long to discover the pinched condition in Helena's home. I went back to the shop.

Living in the Jewish district, it was impossible to avoid those one did not wish to see. I ran into Kershner almost immediately after my arrival. Day after day he would seek me out. He began to plead with me to go back to him—all would be different. One day he threatened suicide—actually pulled out a bottle of poison. Insistently he pressed me for a final answer.

I was not naive enough to think that a renewed life with Kershner would prove more satisfactory or lasting than at first. Besides, I had definitely decided to go to New York, to equip myself for the work I had vowed to take up after the death of my Chicago comrades. But Kershner's threat frightened me: I could not be responsible for his death. I remarried him. My parents rejoiced and so did Lena and her husband, but Helena was sick with grief.

Without Kershner's knowledge I took up a course in dressmaking, in order to have a trade that would free me from the shop. During three long months I wrestled with my husband to let me go my way. I tried to make him see the futility of living a patched life, but he remained obdurate. Late one night, after bitter recriminations, I left Jacob Kershner and my home, this time definitely.

I was immediately ostracized by the whole Jewish population of Rochester. I could not pass on the street without being held up to scorn. My parents forbade me their house, and again it was only Helena who stood by me. Out of her meager income she even paid my fare to New York.

So I left Rochester, where I had known so much pain, hard work, and loneliness, but the joy of my departure was marred by separation from Helena, from Stella, and the little brother I loved so well.

The break of the new day in the Minkin flat still found me awake. The door upon the old had now closed for ever. The new was calling, and I eagerly stretched out my hands towards it. I fell into a deep, peaceful sleep.

I was awakened by Anna Minkin's voice announcing the arrival of Alexander Berkman. It was late afternoon.

I Stand Here Ironing

Tillie Olsen

I STAND HERE IRONING, and what you asked me moves tormented back and forth with the iron.

"I wish you would manage the time to come in and talk with
me about your daughter. I'm sure you can help me understand
her. She's a youngster who needs help and whom I'm deeply
interested in helping."

"Who needs help." . . . Even if I came, what good would it do?
You think because I am her mother I have a key, or that in some
way you could use me as a key? She has lived for nineteen years.

Born in Omaha, Nebraska, educated in public libraries, and a San Franciscan
most of her life, *Tillie Olsen* has received fellowships and grants from the Ford
Foundation, the National Endowment for the Arts, the Radcliffe Institute, and
the Guggenheim Memorial Foundation. She is the recipient of the Literary
Award of the American Academy and National Institute of Arts and Letters and
of an honorary Doctor of Arts and Letters degree from the University of
Nebraska. Her published works include *Yonnondio, Silences,* and *Tell Me a Riddle,*
a collection of her stories. The title selection in the latter won first prize in the
1961 O. Henry Awards. Olsen's works have been anthologized more than 45
times in various publications, among them *The Best American Short Stories* 1957,
1961, 1971 and *Fifty Best American Stories, 1915–1965.* "I Stand Here Ironing" is
excerpted from *Tell Me a Riddle* by Tillie Olsen, copyright © 1956 by Tillie
Olsen, and reprinted by permission of Delacorte Press/Seymour Lawrence.

There is all that life that has happened outside of me, beyond me.

And when is there time to remember, to sift, to weigh, to estimate, to total? I will start and there will be an interruption and I will have to gather it all together again. Or I will become engulfed with all I did or did not do, with what should have been and what cannot be helped.

She was a beautiful baby. The first and only one of our five that was beautiful at birth. You do not guess how new and uneasy her tenancy in her now-loveliness. You did not know her all those years she was thought homely, or see her poring over her baby pictures, making me tell her over and over how beautiful she had been—and would be, I would tell her—and was now, to the seeing eye. But the seeing eyes were few or nonexistent. Including mine.

I nursed her. They feel that's important nowadays. I nursed all the children, but with her, with all the fierce rigidity of first motherhood, I did like the books then said. Though her cries battered me to trembling and my breasts ached with swollenness, I waited till the clock decreed.

Why do I put that first? I do not even know if it matters, or if it explains anything.

She was a beautiful baby. She blew shining bubbles of sound. She loved motion, loved light, loved color and music and textures. She would lie on the floor in her blue overalls patting the surface so hard in ecstasy her hands and feet would blur. She was a miracle to me, but when she was eight months old I had to leave her daytimes with the woman downstairs to whom she was no miracle at all, for I worked or looked for work and for Emily's father, who "could no longer endure" (he wrote in his good-bye note) "sharing want with us."

I was nineteen. It was the pre-relief, pre-WPA world of the depression. I would start running as soon as I got off the street-car, running up the stairs, the place smelling sour, and awake or asleep to startle awake, when she saw me she would break into a clogged weeping that could not be comforted, a weeping I can hear yet.

After a while I found a job hashing at night so I could be with her days, and it was better. But it came to where I had to bring her to his family and leave her.

It took a long time to raise the money for her fare back. Then she got chicken pox and I had to wait longer. When she finally came, I hardly knew her, walking quick and nervous like her father, looking like her father, thin, and dressed in a shoddy red that yellowed her skin and glared at the pockmarks. All the baby loveliness gone.

She was two. Old enough for nursery school they said, and I did not know then what I know now—the fatigue of the long day, and the lacerations of group life in the kinds of nurseries that are only parking places for children.

Except that it would have made no difference if I had known. It was the only place there was. It was the only way we could be together, the only way I could hold a job.

And even without knowing, I knew. I knew the teacher that was evil because all these years it has curdled into my memory, the little boy hunched in the corner, her rasp, "why aren't you outside, because Alvin hits you? that's no reason, go out, scaredy." I knew Emily hated it even if she did not clutch and implore "don't go Mommy" like the other children, mornings.

She always had a reason why we should stay home. Momma, you look sick. Momma, I feel sick. Momma, the teachers aren't there today, they're sick. Momma, we can't go, there was a fire there last night. Momma, it's a holiday today, no school, they told me.

But never a direct protest, never rebellion. I think of our others in their three-, four-year-oldness—the explosions, the tempers, the denunciations, the demands—and I feel suddenly ill. I put the iron down. What in me demanded that goodness in her? And what was the cost, the cost to her of such goodness?

The old man living in the back once said in his gentle way: "You should smile at Emily more when you look at her." What *was* in my face when I looked at her? I loved her. There were all the acts of love.

It was only with the others I remembered what he said, and it was the face of joy, and not of care or tightness or worry I turned to them—too late for Emily. She does not smile easily, let alone almost always as her brothers and sisters do. Her face is closed and sombre, but when she wants, how fluid. You must have seen it in her pantomimes, you spoke of her rare gift for comedy on the stage that rouses a laughter out of the audience so dear they applaud and applaud and do not want to let her go.

Where does it come from, that comedy? There was none of it in her when she came back to me that second time, after I had had to send her away again. She had a new daddy now to learn to love, and I think perhaps it was a better time.

Except when we left her alone nights, telling ourselves she was old enough.

"Can't you go some other time, Mommy, like tomorrow?" she would ask. "Will it be just a little while you'll be gone? Do you promise?"

The time we came back, the front door open, the clock on the floor in the hall. She rigid awake. "It wasn't just a little while. I didn't cry. Three times I called you, just three times, and then I ran downstairs to open the door so you could come faster. The clock talked loud. I threw it away, it scared me what it talked."

She said the clock talked loud again that night I went to the hospital to have Susan. She was delirious with the fever that comes before red measles, but she was fully conscious all the week I was gone and the week after we were home when she could not come near the new baby or me.

She did not get well. She stayed skeleton thin, not wanting to eat, and night after night she had nightmares. She would call for me, and I would rouse from exhaustion to sleepily call back: "You're all right, darling, go to sleep, it's just a dream," and if she still called, in a sterner voice, "now go to sleep, Emily, there's nothing to hurt you." Twice, only twice, when I had to get up for Susan anyhow, I went in to sit with her.

Now when it is too late (as if she would let me hold and comfort her like I do the others) I get up and go to her at once at her moan or restless stirring. "Are you awake, Emily? Can I get you something?" And the answer is always the same: "No, I'm all right, go back to sleep, Mother."

They persuaded me at the clinic to send her away to a convalescent home in the country where "she can have the kind of food and care you can't manage for her, and you'll be free to concentrate on the new baby." They still send children to that place. I see pictures on the society page of sleek young women planning affairs to raise money for it, or dancing at the affairs, or decorating Easter eggs or filling Christmas stockings for the children.

They never have a picture of the children so I do not know if the girls still wear those gigantic red bows and the ravaged looks on the every other Sunday when parents can come to visit "unless otherwise notified"—as we were notified the first six weeks.

Oh it is a handsome place, green lawns and tall trees and fluted flower beds. High up on the balconies of each cottage the children stand, the girls in their red bows and white dresses, the boys in white suits and giant red ties. The parents stand below shrieking up to be heard and the children shriek down to be heard, and between them the invisible wall "Not to Be Contaminated by Parental Germs or Physical Affection."

There was a tiny girl who always stood hand in hand with Emily. Her parents never came. One visit she was gone. "They moved her to Rose Cottage," Emily shouted in explanation. "They don't like you to love anybody here."

She wrote once a week, the labored writing of a seven-year-old. "I am fine. How is the baby. If I write my leter nicly I will have a star. Love." There never was a star. We wrote every other day, letters she could never hold or keep but only hear read— once. "We simply do not have room for children to keep any personal possessions," they patiently explained when we pieced one Sunday's shrieking together to plead how much it would mean to Emily, who loved so to keep things, to be allowed to keep her letters and cards.

Each visit she looked frailer. "She isn't eating," they told us.

(They had runny eggs for breakfast or mush with lumps, Emily said later, I'd hold it in my mouth and not swallow. Nothing ever tasted good, just when they had chicken.)

It took us eight months to get her released home, and only the fact that she gained back so little of her seven lost pounds convinced the social worker.

I used to try to hold and love her after she came back, but her body would stay stiff, and after a while she'd push away. She ate little. Food sickened her, and I think much of life too. Oh she had physical lightness and brightness, twinkling by on skates, bouncing like a ball up and down up and down over the jump rope, skimming over the hill; but these were momentary.

She fretted about her appearance, thin and dark and foreign-looking at a time when every little girl was supposed to look or thought she should look a chubby blonde replica of Shirley Temple. The doorbell sometimes rang for her, but no one seemed to come and play in the house or be a best friend. Maybe because we moved so much.

There was a boy she loved painfully through two school semesters. Months later she told me how she had taken pennies from my purse to buy him candy. "Licorice was his favorite and I brought him some every day, but he still liked Jennifer better'n me. Why, Mommy?" The kind of question for which there is no answer.

School was a worry to her. She was not glib or quick in a world where glibness and quickness were easily confused with ability to learn. To her overworked and exasperated teachers she was an overconscientious "slow learner" who kept trying to catch up and was absent entirely too often.

I let her be absent, though sometimes the illness was imaginary. How different from my now-strictness about attendance with the others. I wasn't working. We had a new baby, I was home anyhow. Sometimes, after Susan grew old enough, I would keep her home from school, too, to have them all together.

Mostly Emily had asthma, and her breathing, harsh and labored, would fill the house with a curiously tranquil sound. I would bring the two old dresser mirrors and her boxes of collections to her bed. She would select beads and single earrings, bottle tops and shells, dried flowers and pebbles, old postcards and scraps, all sorts of oddments; then she and Susan would play Kingdom, setting up landscapes and furniture, peopling them with action.

Those were the only times of peaceful companionship between her and Susan. I have edged away from it, that poisonous feeling between them, that terrible balancing of hurts and needs I had to do between the two, and did so badly, those earlier years.

Oh there are conflicts between the others too, each one human, needing, demanding, hurting, taking—but only between Emily and Susan, no, Emily toward Susan that corroding resentment. It seems so obvious on the surface, yet it is not obvious. Susan, the second child, Susan, golden- and curly-haired and chubby, quick and articulate and assured, everything in appearance and manner Emily was not; Susan, not able to resist Emily's precious things, losing or sometimes clumsily breaking them; Susan telling jokes and riddles to company for applause while Emily sat silent (to say to me later: that was *my* riddle, Mother, I told it to Susan); Susan, who for all the five years' difference in age was just a year behind Emily in developing physically.

I am glad for that slow physical development that widened the difference between her and her contemporaries, though she suffered over it. She was too vulnerable for that terrible world of youthful competition, or preening and parading, of constant measuring of yourself against every other, of envy, "If I had that copper hair," "If I had that skin...." She tormented herself enough about not looking like the others, there was enough of the unsureness, the having to be conscious of words before you speak, the constant caring—what are they thinking of me? without having it all magnified by the merciless physical drives.

Ronnie is calling. He is wet and I change him. It is rare there is such a cry now. That time of motherhood is almost behind me when the ear is not one's own but must always be racked and listening for the child cry, the child call. We sit for a while and I hold him, looking out over the city spread in charcoal with its soft aisles of light. "*Shoogily,*" he breathes and curls closer. I carry him back to bed, asleep. *Shoogily.* A funny word, a family word, inherited from Emily, invented by her to say: *comfort.*

In this and other ways she leaves her seal, I say aloud. And startle at my saying it. What do I mean? What did I start to gather together, to try and make coherent? I was at the terrible, growing years. War years. I do not remember them well. I was working, there were four smaller ones now, there was not time for her. She had to help be a mother, and housekeeper, and shopper. She had to set her seal. Mornings of crisis and near hysteria trying to get lunches packed, hair combed, coats and shoes found, everyone to school or Child Care on time, the baby ready for transportation. And always the paper scribbled on by a smaller one, the book looked at by Susan then mislaid, the homework not done. Running out to that huge school where she was one, she was lost, she was a drop; suffering over the unpreparedness, stammering and unsure in her classes.

There was so little time left at night after the kids were bedded down. She would struggle over books, always eating (it was in those years she developed her enormous appetite that is legendary in our family) and I would be ironing, or preparing food for the next day, or writing V-mail to Bill, or tending the baby. Sometimes, to make me laugh, or out of her despair, she would imitate happenings or types at school.

I think I said once: "Why don't you do something like this in the school amateur show?" One morning she phoned me at work, hardly understandable through the weeping: "Mother, I did it. I won, I won; they gave me first prize; they clapped and clapped and wouldn't let me go."

Now suddenly she was Somebody, and as imprisoned in her difference as she had been in anonymity.

She began to be asked to perform at other high schools, even in colleges, then at city and statewide affairs. The first one we went to, I only recognized her that first moment when thin, shy, she almost drowned herself into the curtains. Then: Was this Emily? The control, the command, the convulsing and deadly clowning, the spell, then the roaring, stamping audience, unwilling to let this rare and precious laughter out of their lives.

Afterwards: You ought to do something about her with a gift like that—but without money or knowing how, what does one do? We have left it all to her, and the gift has as often eddied inside, clogged and clotted, as been used and growing.

She is coming. She runs up the stairs two at a time with her light graceful step, and I know she is happy tonight. Whatever it was that occasioned your call did not happen today.

"Aren't you ever going to finish the ironing, Mother? Whistler painted his mother in a rocker. I'd have to paint mine standing over an ironing board." This is one of her communicative nights and she tells me everything and nothing as she fixes herself a plate of food out of the icebox.

She is so lovely. Why did you want me to come in at all? Why were you concerned? She will find her way.

She starts up the stairs to bed. "Don't get me up with the rest in the morning." "But I thought you were having midterms." "Oh, those," she comes back in, kisses me, and says quite lightly, "in a couple of years when we'll all be atom-dead they won't matter a bit."

She has said it before. She *believes* it. But because I have been dredging the past, and all that compounds a human being is so heavy and meaningful in me, I cannot endure it tonight.

I will never total it all. I will never come in to say: She was a child seldom smiled at. Her father left me before she was a year old. I had to work her first six years when there was work, or I sent her home and to his relatives. There were years she had care she hated. She was dark and thin and foreign-looking in a world where the prestige went to blondeness and curly hair and dimples, she was slow where glibness was prized. She was a child of anxious, not proud, love. We were poor and could not afford for her the soil of easy growth. I was a young mother, I was a distracted mother. There were the other children pushing up, demanding. Her younger sister seemed all that she was not. There were years she did not want me to touch her. She kept too much in herself, her life was such she had to keep too much in herself. My wisdom came too late. She has much to her and probably little will come of it. She is a child of her age, of depression, of war, of fear.

Let her be. So all that is in her will not bloom—but in how many does it? There is still enough left to live by. Only help her to know—help make it so there is cause for her to know—that she is more than this dress on the ironing board, helpless before the iron.

1953–1955

The Fraychie Story

Harriet Rosenstein

THERE WERE, IN the beginning, seven children, each rising out of my great-grandmother's darkness every twelve or thirteen months like little full moons, following, even in birth, the quirky Jewish calendar. The sons came first: Mendel, Mischa, Isaac, and Schmuel. And then the pale and round-faced daughters: Sarah, Fraychie, and Sosiesther. My great-grandmother conceived and bore them, I am told, with bemused passivity, as tolerant as the moon must be of her own swellings and thinnings and equally unconscious. Four babies. Seven. A miscarriage or two. The number became finally a matter of indifference. For, of the Jews in Vischay, Lithuania, they were the least poor; my great-grandfather owned the *schvitzbod* (sweatbath), which usually kept the family in kopeks and spared the children the terrible winters. After the sons stoked the low

Harriet Rosenstein lives in Cambridge, Massachusetts, and teaches fiction writing at Tufts University. Her fiction and literary criticism have appeared in many publications, among them *The New Review* (London), *The New York Times Book Review*, *Ms.* magazine, and *Tri-Quarterly*. "The Fraychie Story," copyright © 1974 by Harriet Rosenstein, is reprinted from *Ms.* magazine (March 1974) by permission of the author.

brick bathhouse ovens with firewood for the night, they would
stretch out on them to sleep, contented from December
through March like no other boys in the village. Once the girls
were old enough not to topple, they too were accommodated on
the warm brick ledge. They ate well enough, always had a bit of
braid or ribbon to trim their coats, and knew that when the
peddler passed through town they could count on a whistle or
a top from his wagon. All year round plants hung in pots inside
the windows and in summer vines grew round the house. It
could have gone on indefinitely—summers, winters, whistles,
babies—except for two other facts of life: Cossacks and conscription. The Cossacks you've heard about, galloping giants
with fine uniforms and swinging sabers. They would fill themselves full of vodka, then plunge through the villages behind the
main road, one after the other, never stopping, whacking off
Jewish heads as if they were turnips. In less than a minute they
had made a clean sweep and vanished. A pastime, a sport. I
would not tell you about this without reason; the Cossacks killed
the first and last sons of my great-grandparents. Mendel and
Schmuel died on the same day, Mendel trying to protect his
little brother, whose howling must have enraged the men on
horseback.

You know that scientists ignore what is random; only if something happens often enough to be measured will they acknowl-
edge its reality by giving it a name. So it was with the Cossacks.
Pretty soon their raids became systematic; they didn't even
need the vodka to get them going; their casualties were no
longer haphazard. In other words, these massacres were admitted into the world of known phenomena and thus they got a
name: pogroms. And my great-grandparents' family suffered
still further. Now, like the rest of the villagers, they heard ru-
mors, advance warnings, and attempted to flee the streets and
the house and the *schvitzbod* before the sabers came. On one
occasion my great-grandmother, murmuring passages from
Lamentations as she pulled her apron over her head and her
cloak around her daughters, ran to the frozen riverbank to hide.
They covered themselves, all four, first with her cloak, then with
icy twigs and rushes, and burrowed into the ground, facedown.
There they lay from late morning until moonrise, too scared

and chilled even to whisper prayers. When it was safe, my great-grandmother, blue and almost paralyzed from the cold, managed to stand up, pulling away the cape and the reeds that shrouded her daughters' backs. All three seemed dead. She massaged and slapped and pounded them in turn, trying to beat the life back into her girls. Sarah and Fraychie survived. Sosiesther's body was purple, rigid as the glassy rushes clinging to her hair. They carried her in silence back to the town.

It was then they decided to come to America. In a year, my great-grandfather figured, he could save enough for steerage fare for his wife and four children. But, hard as it is to believe, the remaining sons were lost. Mischa and Isaac had hair on their faces and the voices of men. Elsewhere these facts might have been neutral; here they meant conscription. Friends of Mischa and Isaac, awaiting the Czar's officer who would carry them off forever, had gone out to the woods with axes and chopped off their own toes to save themselves from induction. Now the sons of my great-grandparents had four choices: to mutilate themselves or to give themselves to the Czar (and between them there was very little difference), to try to escape the country immediately, or to wait out the months till the whole family went, counting on sheer good luck to keep the officer from their door in the meantime. Luck they knew better than to trust. So my great-grandfather bribed a neighboring Gentile farmer to hide Mischa and Isaac under his hayrick and transport them to a border from which they would eventually make their way to America. Their parting was full of tears and promises. My great-grandfather improvised a prayer: "With the help of the Almighty, through Whom all things are possible, may we never again be parted after this parting. May we meet to live in safety in the new country in time to celebrate the next Purim." Then they went round the room, one by one, repeating my great-grandfather's words. Mischa and Isaac embraced their little round-faced sisters; their father, weeping, embraced the sons now taller than himself; but their mother could only sob without looking up—mourning her boys while they still stood in her kitchen. Finally, with purses tucked inside their sashes, Mischa and Isaac walked away from their parents and sisters in the middle of the August night. The farmer did his job. But Mischa and Isaac were never heard from.

When they were allowed to leave Ellis Island with the Anglicized name the official there had given them, the family went immediately to a Jewish agency. Before even asking for temporary shelter, they asked for their sons. Had Mischa and Isaac from Vischay in Lithuania, tall boys with thick black hair and gray-green eyes, seventeen and sixteen years old, come or written here in the past five months to say where they were and what name they now had? The lady at the desk spoke good Yiddish. The boys, she said, had not yet come; perhaps they were registered with a bureau in another part of the city or perhaps they were living in a different town. She would investigate. It would take time; there were many immigrants looking for relatives; surely, though, Mischa and Isaac would be found. And for seven years, from the time that my great-grandparents settled into a two-room flat, through the time that my great-grandfather, always a modest entrepreneur, opened a tiny dry-goods shop whose best customers were black and for whom, in his hoarse, cracked English, he would sing little package-wrapping songs— "Sam Brown he went to town," "Bill Jones he boughten cotton" —the family searched for Mischa and Isaac. They put ads in the *Forward;* every Jewish service bureau in the country and most of the Orthodox synagogues in the East knew to watch for the young men. At the end of the seven years, against the wishes of her husband, my great-grandmother lit *yahrzeit* candles (memorial candles for the dead) for her two lost boys. She, whose relation to maternity had been so passive, now took command of mortality. There had been enough waiting, she told him.

This was the story that Sarah, my grandmother, told me as I grew up. She told me it in summer as we spooned cold spinach borscht from tall glasses and in winter as we transferred her gold-brown *challahs* from the oven to a long mahogany sideboard in the dining room. There, lined up on the special sabbath cloth she had herself embroidered, they would cool. And we would talk. About the *shtetl* (Eastern European peasant village), about her brothers and her parents and her husband, all dearly loved, all dead. What she never talked about was her sister Fraychie. And I never dared to ask. Even my mother, her mother's favorite, could say very little. She knew only that there had been some rivalry or antagonism between the sisters when they were twenty or so. That they had argued bitterly and vowed never to do so much as nod at each other again. Their parents, by then well enough established, able to afford a house with two maple trees in the back and a toilet on the second floor, were helpless before their daughters. They pleaded; they scolded; they invoked the memories of the children who were dead and the mystery of those who were lost. But it was useless. The way they stared through each other, the sisters might as well have been windows.

My grandmother met a man named Sammy, an immigrant with a good heart who worked long hours selling wholesale produce at the market, who courted her with fresh peaches and my great-grandmother with luxuriant bouquets of beets. Even Sammy was enlisted in my great-grandparents' campaign to open the mouths and eyes of their daughters. He brought them green grapes, nectarines, melons, the sweetest of sweets. He might as well have brought lemons. When the couple became engaged, it seemed certain that the sisters would make up their differences, that love would soften Sarah and that she would ask Fraychie to be her bridesmaid. Perhaps Sarah tried. Perhaps Fraychie was envious. All my mother could tell me—and that she had pried from her grandparents when she was small—was that on the day Sarah and Sammy were to be married, Fraychie packed a handgrip with some underwear and a shift or two and she left. My great-grandparents went out of their heads with mortification and grief but the ceremony still took place. They lived long enough to receive a few cards from Fraychie, always postmarked from somewhere in the state, and to receive their first grandchildren, my uncle Willy and my mother, Annie. Sarah, I am told, refused even to utter her sister's name because she had cast such a blight on the family and, in particular, on her wedding day.

Yet she was not otherwise bitter. She had loved her husband with joy and pride and, like her own mother, had produced

seven children; they had the good fortune to live. She was de-
vout. She never entered her bedroom without first kissing her
fingers and pressing them to the mezuzah (a parchment, bearing twenty-two lines from the Bible, rolled in a metal or wooden
case) on the doorpost. Then she would station herself over the
heat register to undress. (I remember her always standing on
some heat register or other. Her circulation had gone bad,
perhaps because of the frostbite she had suffered as a girl.
Whatever the reason, she was always cold, she never sat—drawn
to warm air with the fidelity of a migrating bird. Whether it
flowed out of the oven or up from the register, there she would
alight; so when she was not baking, she was leaning against a
wall over an air duct. And, like the birds, she left tokens of
habitation. Her resting places were marked for all time by the
grease spots that her behind eventually pressed on walls above
every register in her house.) So—my grandmother Sarah,
braced by her grease spot, soothed from the bottom up by so
much heat, ended the day by uttering prayers from the instant
she started unlacing her corset until she had pulled the covers
up to her chin.

I used to watch this performance in amazement. The dress
and the nightgown traveled a parallel course, the dress stopping at her knees, the nightgown at her neck. Her head covered
in layers of flannel, her fingers seemed, nonetheless, to have
eyes of their own. They would unlace the corset—it seemed
always to be the same corset, although she must have had many
of the same pale orange color, the same stays made of whale-
bone, the same terrible dimensions. This corset stretched from
the invisible underside of my grandmother's breasts to the
equally invisible point where her hips met her thighs. Her flesh
was invisible because beneath the corset she wore one of her
husband's cotton undershirts, the kind with the skinny shoulder
straps, cut in deep ovals front and back, designed for sweaty
summers. But she wore them always, her great breasts swad-
dled in cotton, hoisted over the top of the corset, and then left
to plunge disastrously downward. In such a fashion my grandmother retained her waistline and her vanity and kept her naked
body forever a wonder and a secret to me. The corset undone,
it slipped down at the exact rate as her dress below and her

nightgown above—a perfect orchestration. Once this operation was completed, she managed, because her flowered flannel nightgowns were invariably enormous, to get the undershirt off while keeping the nightgown on. Throughout it all, she would pray like a woman possessed. Since I never learned Hebrew, I had no idea what she was talking about, and in my first years assumed that her sounds and the ritual of uncorseting had some mystical connection. Without this strange language, perhaps, there would be a failure: the dress too soon, the gown too late, the breasts that symbolized for me all the mysteries of the universe triumphantly, enormously revealed. But the prayers always worked. She would lie beside me in the cool double bed, praying still, and I would feel her flannel backside, and wonder.

I slept with her on those evenings that my parents deposited me in her house because her bed was half-empty. Her husband had died when I was only three. He had had great success with his fruits and vegetables and, my grandmother assured me, was very like her own father. He too would chant little ryhmes to his customers—a trick he had picked up to improve business and continued because it pleased him so. To his favorite black lady he would sing, "Esther Green, you are a queen," and his poetry made him loved, gave him honor. No one left his living room without a bag of apples and, when times were difficult, a bag of potatoes, too. As generous with his love as with his produce, he literally sang my grandmother's praises, even unto her pale orange corsets. If business was slow, he wrote courtly stanzas in black marking crayon on the backs of brown-paper sacks; her eyes dark as raisins, her skin white as milk, her face round as a melon, her mouth red and plump as a plum. It was grocer's verse. The grammar was bad. But my grandmother kept the brown bags. Of his children he was no less adoring: his three daughters were princesses and his four sons, every one a prince. He paid them tribute in rhyme, in kisses, in embraces and, one winter, in a bounty worthy of Romanoffs. At that time the youngest, Nomi, was three, and Willy, two years past Bar Mitzvah. The snows had been as dense, my grandmother said, as those she had endured in the old country, and the winds savage as a Cossack's blade. So my grandfather left his place early one afternoon and went to visit a friend, a wholesaler in furs. He came home with seven identical coats, thick-piled and white like Siberian bears, with matching muffs for the girls and flat-topped, steepsided hats for the boys. "Let the winter find us now!" he had laughed. That story I knew as a duet. My grandmother and my mother loved to tell it, my grandmother describing the opening of the boxes, my mother the trying on of the coats, my grandmother the hurtling of the children out of the house and into the twilight like oversize snowballs, and then, in unison, my grandfather's delighted cry.

The mourning for him, they told me, had been tremendous. More than a thousand people came to his coffin and to the home of his family, not because he was rich or powerful, but because he treasured life, because he made up little poems. People like Esther Green traveled from the other end of the city simply to let his wife know that they had cherished him.

My grandmother stayed on in the house for another ten years, no public figure, but a presence still. Small, pale, round-faced, even in old age remarkably beautiful. Her hair was pure white, pulled into a smooth circle at the base of her neck. Just leaning against the wall, despite the secret chill her bones held, she seemed a heat source in herself: her quick, dark eyes, her arms and fingers moving emphatically, then subtly, then quizzically to illustrate her stories or her meditations, her nostrils always flaring as if emotions had scents that she alone could recognize. Standing in her living room, surrounded by her children and her children's children, all of us slack in our easy chairs, she was the center, the life from which all this life had sprung. She knew more Torah than her sons, more prayers than her daughters, more Talmud than her rabbi. She knew from childhood the worst of loss and grief and terror and therefore did not fear them, would not capitulate to them. She knew that anger and love were next-door neighbors and with equal passion gave both to others. Women brought woes and confusions to her as they would to a Solomon and they left her light and easy, like the leaves after a rain. What she believed she believed absolutely; what she doubted she doubted silently, consigning her uncertainties perhaps to the cold places that hid inside her bones. When she laughed it was with such force that her undershirt and corset combined could not stop her breasts from laughing too.

At her death I wept for days. It was the springtime. She was beginning to set out flowers and hanging plants on her front

porch, preparing to leave her place by the wall and to move
outside where the warmth was real. Once *shivah* (seven-day
mourning period) was over, her daughters sorted her possessions. They found my grandfather's crayoned love poems and
found, too, poems that their mother had written to him. Over
these they wept with surprise: they had lost more through her
death than they had ever known they possessed. They found old
photographs, old documents, newspaper advertisements for
Mischa and Isaac. They placed in rows her corsets, her nightgowns, her aprons, her dresses—each daughter taking something as a remembrance. And they found a handful of yellow
postcards going back almost fifty years. The cards were ad-
dressed to their grandparents and were signed by Fraychie,
their mother's sister. It was decided first by my mother and my
aunts Dora and Nomi, and then agreed upon by my uncles
Willy, Norman, David, and Daniel, that Fraychie should be
found. That, for the sake of rightness and reconciliation, she
should be informed of her sister's death. None of them knew
whether Fraychie had married and thus what name she went by.
She could be anywhere. She could be dead. With nothing more
than these yellow cards to go on, they set about investigating.
God knows how they did it, but what they finally came up with
was this: there was a woman with the strange name of Fraychie
who lived on a small farm in the north of the state where she
kept chickens and where she sold eggs. In all likelihood, that
Fraychie was their mother's sister.

By now it was the middle of May; the trees had leapt overnight
from that sweet sad yellow-green of budding into the strong
deep green of leaves who know their rights. And we assembled,
Sarah's seven children, and their husbands and wives and children, crowding my grandmother's porch the way the leaves
were crowding the trees. My uncle Willy with his family was to
lead the caravan and in our cars, one after another, we were to
travel to that place where Fraychie lived. Among my parents, my
sister, and me there was more silence than talk, more staring
than looking. For three hours we drove, going higher, climbing
hills separating impossible pastures where the cows tilted and
the boulders showed, passing villages that lasted for a minute
then disappeared, and then, one by one, the cars slowed and

turned and stopped. My oldest uncle walked into a general store
and came out nodding. And everyone in the seven cars nodded
back. Again he started out and again we followed him. Past the
hamlet, down a dirt road that cut in half a forest, the first forest
I had ever seen. Through these woods, where suddenly it was
chill and damp and musky and dark, we slowly moved, finally
halted. There were thirty of us, going on tiptoe over the dead
leaves till we left the forest and the quiet it had imposed on us,
and found the sun once more. Before us was a tiny house,
whitewashed, slate-roofed, with vines that were just beginning
to color. Nobody had planned what to do when we arrived; we
simply stood there with the sun on us and the noises of chickens
coming from someplace unseen.

Then from that place, behind the house, walked a woman
carrying a crate of eggs. The woman could not have been Fraychie because she was my grandmother. The same face, the same
eyes, the same hair, even the same flaring nostrils. And when
she smiled, it was my grandmother smiling, inviting me and my
sister in for borscht and tales of the old country. She was no
more surprised at this congregation than my grandmother was
to see us arrive for Pesach or Purim. And this woman—Fraychie, Sarah, whoever she was—opened her mouth and out of it
came my grandmother's voice and, more mysterious still, my
grandmother's words. She looked at us and she said, "You are
Willy, yes? And you must be Annie. And you, with such a grin
on you, you are Daniel." And this woman went on, identifying
each of her nieces and nephews, and then, when I had stopped
breathing, each of us, their children. She asked us into her
house and we went. Into her small living room whose walls were
covered with photographs of bearded men and beardless boys
and corseted women and skinny girls and these were the photographs of my grandmother's stories. The vivid lines her hands
had drawn in telling them were fixed and mounted here. The
woman brought us tall glasses of tea. She smiled. The conversation was sweet and delicate. She knew us and all about us. And
there was no question of knowing her. We had known her all of
our lives. I knew the prayers she said at night and the way she
got into her nightgown. I knew the way she absorbed and erased
the suffering of anyone who brought it to her. I knew the way

she kneaded dough and grated beets till her fingers bled. I knew her pallor and the beauty of her white hair when she let it down to brush before bed. As we sat on the floor and in chairs in that little room while she stood there talking to us, all my grief at my grandmother's death left me. My senses said what was as obvious as the sun. Here was Sarah, going by the name of Fraychie, merely transported, tending chickens, cupping eggs in her palms, living in a whitewashed house at the edge of a forest.

For two hours we sat in her house. She explained that she had been told of her sister's death, as she had of the births of her nieces and nephews and of their children by an old friend of a still older relative. There was nothing new to say. There was nothing old to question. There had never been a breach and there was now no reason to heal it. As quietly, as sweetly, as we had begun, we rose to end our talk. We filed out of her house and into the cars smiling, touching her, kissing her, feeling her lips on our cheeks, her fingers on our hair, watching her grow smaller as we backed down the dirt road, still beautiful, still circled by sun, still holding one arm up whether in greeting or good-bye I could not have said, until the woods and the road were gone and we faced the known direction home.

Papa's Tea

Irena Narell

PAPA LIKED HIS tea strong and piping hot. He would come into the kitchen, his dignified, fastidious figure in utter contrast to the disorder that reigned all over the room. With a helpless glance at the large kitchen table on which, as usual, lay an infinite variety of objects of non-culinary character, he would ask:

"Well, where is Mama? I'd like some tea."

Where was Mama? Where was the wind, he could just as well have asked. She had flown off an hour, maybe two hours ago, no one knew precisely when. Where was she off to? The bakery maybe or the dry goods store? She was going to look at that piece of blue wool for my sister Bessie's new coat, so maybe that's where she went . . .

"Max, where did Mama go?"

Irena Narell is the author of *Joshua: Fighter for Bar Kochba*, winner of the 1979 National Jewish Book Award. The Polish-born historian, novelist, translator, and lecturer came to the U.S. in 1939. She is now working on a study of San Francisco's early Jewish settlers and speaks frequently on California Jewish history. "Papa's Tea," copyright © 1969 by Irena Narell, was first published by Brook Press of New Jersey.

"I don't know," came a disgruntled reply from my brother. "Don't bother me."

"Oh, for a glass of tea," sighed my father. "One glass, what am I saying? I could drink a dozen glasses."

What was the matter with Mama? She never could remember the time Papa was due home. Even if she did, she was sure to find some errand that couldn't wait and forget all about him.

Not that there was anything personal she had against Papa. Oh, no. Didn't she often forget when we were supposed to come home from school for a quick, half-hour lunch, and didn't we end up crying in the street dozens of times until some neighbor would feel sorry for us and let us in? And when we would berate her afterwards, she would say:

"I know, I know. I only went shopping for a short while. So why couldn't you wait five minutes?"

That was Mama. You couldn't change her and you couldn't make her understand certain simple facts of life, I thought, as I went into the kitchen, determined to take care of Papa. One just had to accept Mama as she was. And she was wonderful in so many ways! When she sang near the open window, it was as if all the sound and glory of a spring morning in the country had found its way into our Bronx apartment. The neighbors would hang their heads out of the windows to listen and comment:

"Mrs. Siegel, how you can sing! Like a regular opera star."

And Mama was always smiling. Sometimes there really wasn't anything to be cheerful about, but Mama invariably found some little thing to make her happy. Maybe it was a concert in the park, or a ticket to the opera, or the neighbor's fat new baby, or the pretty dress she had just made for me with her beautiful, clear stitches. I often wondered how a person so untidy in her household could sew so perfectly and be so painstakingly neat in this work. And she never, never hit us.

Her mind was always on beautiful things. And how she loved pretty clothes! Next to music, I guess she loved clothes just about the best. When the tailor got through making her a handsome new suit, Mama would go out and buy a twenty dollar silk blouse to wear with it.

We all thought she looked simply stunning. She was a little thing with a lovely head of brown hair, an elfish face, and a good figure, despite her lack of height. She carried her clothes well. But what happened to these clothes when she took them off!

Papa was fond of saying:

"Mama needs nice clothes so she can keep them under the kitchen sink."

And he wasn't far from wrong. Her things were everywhere except in the closet where they should have been. Once she got it into her head that she wanted a mink stole. Papa only said:

"Mama wants a mink stole so she can keep it underneath the washtub." And that was the end of that.

In the kitchen, I put my arms around Papa's neck.

"How is my Lily today?" he said, and smiled in that special way he reserved only for me. Even though there were four of us children, Papa's preference for me was acknowledged by the whole family and resented most by my brother Max.

"Papa's darling!" he would jeer at me when he got good and mad.

"Go in the living room, Papa," I said. "I'll make you some tea."

"Thank you, Lily dear, that would be very nice," Papa answered and he walked out.

The kitchen table was a real mess! There was the fabric for my skirt, and the pieces for Bessie's new hat, and two pots from last night's supper, and seven dirty spoons and forks, and the cookie jar, and the pot of jam from breakfast, and last Sunday's paper! The disarray was not exactly out of the ordinary. Only the items changed from time to time. Even when Mama happened to be home the table was so piled up with bundles that there was barely enough room for a plate or two.

I took off the two pots and put them in the sink and began moving the other things, one by one. For once Papa would have a completely clear table to drink his tea!

I found a pretty plate with rose clusters to put under the glass, and a white napkin. Where was there a clean spoon? I got the kettle going and prepared the tea. I took Mama's bundle of fabrics to her bedroom, the "dump" room. This was where we hastily dumped everything that lay all week long on chairs and couches and the floor, when a visitor was announced. Why did the house always have to be so disorderly? It would look exactly the same when we came back from school as when we had left it in the morning.

"But Mama, I'm ashamed to even bring a friend home," I would complain.

"If you don't like it, stay home and do it yourself. I got too many other things to do."

"But you know I have to go to school, Mama."

"So, is that my fault?"

What could you say?

The kettle was whistling. I ran back to the kitchen. What was that Papa had said?

"I could drink a dozen glasses." That was it!

He shall have a dozen glasses then! My heart was bursting with love for Papa who was good and kind. I knew how determined he was that we, his children, should have a better life than he himself had led, and how hard he labored to make it come true.

Papa's father was an innkeeper in a Russian town. His first wife, Papa's mother, came from a wealthy family and stayed with him just long enough to bear him two sons. Then she divorced him and married the town mayor. My grandfather promptly married a widow with two little girls. One of those girls was Mama! Grandfather was of sturdy stock and proceeded to outlive this wife of his, and then married twice more, each time outliving his much younger wives. Finally there were seventeen children in the house, and Papa, as the oldest, bore most of the responsibility for them. Mama was a very determined little girl even then. As Papa told it:

"When we were children, Mama decided that we would get married some day. As far as I was concerned, I could have stayed single all of my life!"

Mama had a good voice and wanted to go on the stage but instead was apprenticed to a dressmaker. Still, she managed to sneak out every now and then and sing in cabarets, until her stepfather would find out and drag her home virtually by the hair. But did this stop her? No. At the very next opportunity she was out, like a spark of flame, dancing, singing, enjoying herself. Life beckoned to Mama with irresistible force.

Papa felt responsible for her even then. For her, and the whole brood of children, until he was drafted into the czar's army. This was a calamity and Mama was in despair. She saved money from her earnings as a seamstress and it was arranged, over Papa's protests, to have him smuggled over the border the first time he came home on leave. Mama took care of getting him a passport and a change of clothes, bribing whomever was necessary, but Papa resisted to the very last. It wasn't legal, he said. It was not the proper way of doing things and Papa was a very proper person. Well, they got him over the border somehow and then onto a boat bound for England where an uncle lived.

There Papa who wanted to be an artist became a house painter so that he could earn a living. As soon as he had mastered the trade he was shipped off to America with a letter of recommendation to a "lantzman" on the Lower East Side of Manhattan. He worked and saved and sent for Mama. She too moved into a "lantzman's" railroad flat and went to work, sewing in a factory.

They didn't get married right away. How could they afford it, with so many brothers and sisters back home to send for? First, there was Aunt Esther. As soon as she came she fell in love with a cousin and the foursome worked to bring more relatives to America. Next came my Aunt Minnie. But that was after Mama and Papa got married and moved uptown to a five room apartment. Aunt Esther and Uncle Abe also moved in with them, and when Minnie came, naturally, she moved in as well.

Papa said to Minnie:

"Now it's your turn to go to work and send for your sisters."

But my Aunt Minnie wasn't that altruistic. Besides, she hated to work.

"I should work for them?" she said. "To hell with that!" Aunt Minnie didn't mince words.

"But Minnie, how can you behave like that?" Papa said. "Didn't we send for you?"

"So what!" was her answer. "I don't feel like it."

"Well, if that's the case, then maybe we'll let your sisters stay back in the old country," said Papa.

Aunt Minnie finally went to work for about a year but hated

it so much that as soon as Uncle Sam proposed to her, she married him, although she was only sixteen and he over twenty-five. From that moment on, she wiped her hands of her family in Russia. It took years for Papa to save enough money to try to bring more of them over, what with his own growing family to support.

By that time it was very difficult to locate them. They were scattered all over what was now the Soviet Union and had families and roots of their own. Besides, the government made it impossible for them to leave the country. Papa never saw them again.

I was rummaging in Mama's cupboard, trying to find twelve clean glasses. Then I tiptoed to the living room to steal a look at what Papa was doing. I didn't want him to discover my surprise a moment too soon!

Papa was sitting with his dictionary and a pad, writing down his daily quota of words. Papa read a lot, mostly Jewish books and Jewish newspapers. But he also made it a point to study Webster's dictionary, increasing his vocabulary by at least three words each day. He would write the definitions painstakingly on a little pad and never forget them.

"Why aren't you a businessman like Uncle Hymie, Papa?" I remember asking him once. Uncle Hymie lived in Brooklyn and had a fancy car.

"You really are so clever, Papa. You could make a lot of money, I'm sure!"

"Because, Lily darling, I'm just not made to be a businessman. A businessman, he has to be a little bit crooked. Don't let anybody tell you it isn't so. You can't make money in business being a hundred per cent honest. But your uncle Hymie, he is made to be a businessman. Even when we were children together in Russia, I knew he would be a businessman one day."

"Why, Papa?"

"Well, I'll tell you. On Saturdays when our father would go to shule, your uncle Hymie would set up a little business of his own. There was a window at the inn that went out onto a side street. And under this window was a high, long table. Your uncle Hymie would have a show right under that window, on top of that table, and he would charge money for it. A kopeck apiece to all the children in our town, and they could see the show from the outside. And business was good! Sometimes he would make a whole ruble on a Saturday!"

"But how, Papa?"

"Well, he would just pull down his pants and show his behind to the other children for a kopeck, that's how!"

"No, Papa!" I collapsed, convulsed with laughter.

"So, you see, Lily, that's how I knew he would be a businessman," Papa concluded triumphantly.

Here were the glasses at last. I counted an even dozen. Some of them didn't look any too clean, so I took them down from the shelf and reached under the sink for soap. I pulled out Mama's skirt instead, the one with the front pleat. She had only had it a month! Oh, well, the soap must be around somewhere. There was Bessie's slipper that she'd been looking for all week! Here was the soap, finally. I washed the glasses with care, making them shine for Papa. Where could Mama be all this time? I bet she went to the movies. There was a new musical at the Prospect, that's where she must be! Mama and her movies!

I smiled at the memory of all the movies she and we had seen together. We, the children, I mean. You see, Papa works very hard and during the week he likes to be in bed early. Nine o'clock and he is snoring away. But not Mama. Night does things to her. Her eyes begin to shine, her little feet begin to dance with impatience. She must be off and going somewhere. Sometimes I think that only with the advent of night does Mama really begin to realize fully her fierce joy of living. And it is not until the early hours of the morning that she begins to lose her nocturnal sparkle and makes ready to surrender herself to death-simulating sleep.

Well, the four of us children have to be put to bed. That is, four of us since a year and half ago, when Claire was born. Until then there was just Max, Bessie, and I. Papa needs his rest and Mama must go out to see a movie. Since we children make a lot of noise all alone by ourselves, Mama worked out a perfect compromise. She'd take us along!

As soon as Papa was asleep Mama would dress us all, including Claire, the baby, and off we would be, to the movies. We would settle ourselves as comfortably as we could, for we were good for the night. Mama had to see the picture several times over and often we would not go home until the movie house shut down for the night. Mama watched the movie and we slept until it was time to go home. She even got these nightly excursions down to a science. We would be wearing our pajamas underneath our clothes so that we could jump right into bed when we got home. Mama would open the door as quietly as she could, and would warn us as we staggered into bed:

"Shh! Don't wake Papa!"

It was nearly three years before Papa caught onto the fact that his whole family was missing, night after night. Claire at that point had been going with us for over a year. It seems that he had an attack of indigestion and got up at about 11 P.M., looked for Mama, then took a peek into our rooms. Nobody home. Well!

When we tiptoed in that night who should be sitting in the kitchen but Papa! What a rumpus there was! I have never seen Papa so mad. He took a plate and broke it right before our eyes! We all hid but we could hear his roaring.

"The children have to go to school! What do you mean by keeping them out so late? And a baby, too!"

He went on like this, fuming and shouting for quite a long time. Mama just sat there.

Finally she said, calm as calm could be:

"You're finished?"

"Yes, I'm finished!" Papa roared.

"What do you expect me to do? I'm not going to stay home night after night. If you want, I'll leave them home."

And that's just what she did. From then on our nightly escapades were over. All went well until one night Claire had a fit. She demanded Mama's presence and Papa couldn't calm her down. Finally, exasperated and worn to a frazzle, he gave her a good spanking. The next day, sheepishly, he said to Mama:

"From now on, you take *her* along." So Claire was now the only one of us children qualified to be a movie critic.

I had the gleaming glasses neatly arranged on the table. An even dozen! I brought over the sugar bowl, a little lemon. That's how Papa liked it. The tea smelled delicious. I poured it carefully, and didn't spill a drop.

"Papa, your tea is ready!" I called.

As he came into the kitchen, I pointed proudly.

"A dozen glasses, just like you wanted."

Papa looked surprised.

"But Lily, darling, I didn't really mean ..."

He reached for his eyeglasses and his handkerchief, and wiped them. Then he took me around and began to laugh. It was a happy kind of laughter, and I was relieved, because for a moment I thought he was going to cry. I guess he was pleased with his tea. But instead of drinking it, Papa kept laughing and laughing. I don't remember when I had heard Papa laugh like that before.

My, it was good to hear Papa laugh!

What Must I Say to You?

Norma Rosen

WHEN I OPEN the door for Mrs. Cooper at two in the afternoon, three days a week, that is the one time her voice fails us both. She smiles over my left shoulder and hurries out the words "Just fine," to get past me. She is looking for the baby, either in the bassinet in the living room or in the crib in the baby's room. When she finds her, she can talk more easily to me—through the baby. But at the doorway again, in the early evening, taking leave, Mrs. Cooper speaks up in her rightful voice, strong and slow: "I am saying good night." It seems to me that the "I am saying" form, once removed from herself, frees her of her shyness. As if she had already left and were standing in the hall, away from strangers, and were sending back the message "I am saying good night."

Maybe. I know little about Mrs. Cooper, and so read much into her ways. Despite the differences between us, each of us

Norma Rosen's work has appeared in *The New Yorker, Commentary, Ms.*, and other periodicals. She received a Radcliffe Institute fellowship and a New York State Creative Artist Public Service grant. Rosen is the author of *Joy to Levine, Green*, and *Touching Evil*. "What Must I Say to You?" copyright © 1963 by Norma Rosen, originally appeared in *The New Yorker* magazine, October 26, 1963.

seems to read the other the same—tender creature, prone to
suffer. Mrs. Cooper says to me, many times a day, "That is all
right, that is all right," in a soothing tone. I say to her, "That's
such a help, thank you, such a help." What can I guess, except
what reflects myself, about someone so different from me?

Mrs. Cooper is from Jamaica. She is round-faced and round-
figured. She is my age, thirty, and about my height, five-five.
But because she is twice my girth (not fat; if there is any
unfavorable comparison to be drawn, it may as well be that I am,
by her standard, meager) and because she has four children to
my one, she seems older. She is very black; I am—as I remember the campus doctor at the women's college I attended saying
—"surprisingly fair." Though, of course, not Anglo-Saxon. If
you are not Anglo-Saxon, being fair counts only up to a point.
I learned that at the women's college. I remember a conversation with a girl at college who had an ambiguous name—Green
or Black or Brown. She said in the long run life was simpler if
your name was Finkelstein. And I said it was better to be dark
and done with it.

Mrs. Cooper has been coming to us, with her serious black
bulk and her beautiful voice, for some months now, so that I can
get on with my work, which is free-lance editorial. The name is
lighthearted enough, but the lance is heavy and keeps me
pinned to my desk. Mrs. Cooper's work, in her hands, seems
delightful. Though she comes to relieve me of that same work,
it is a little like watching Tom Sawyer paint a fence—so attractive one would gladly pay an apple to be allowed to lend a hand.
Even the slippery bath, the howls as my daughter's sparse hairs
are shampooed, become amusing mites on the giant surface of
Mrs. Cooper's calm. They raise Mrs. Cooper's laugh. "Ooh,
my! You can certainly sing!"

I sneak from my desk several times an afternoon to watch the
work and to hear Mrs. Cooper speak. Her speech, with its trotty
Jamaican rhythm, brings every syllable to life and pays exquisite
attention to the final sounds of words. When she telephones
home to instruct the oldest of her children in the care of the
youngest, it is true that her syntax relaxes. I hear "Give she
supper and put she to bed." Or "When I'm coming home I am
going to wash the children them hair." But the tone of her voice

is the same as when she speaks to me. It is warm, melodious. Always the diction is glorious—ready, with only a bit of memorizing, for Shakespeare. Or, if one could connect a woman's voice with the Old Testament, for that.

"God is not a God of confusion." Mrs. Cooper says that to me one day while the baby naps and she washes baby clothes in the double tub in the kitchen. I have come in to get an apple from the refrigerator. She refuses any fruit, and I stand and eat and watch the best work in the world: rhythmic rubbing-a-dubbing in a sudsy tub. With sturdy arms.

She says it again. "God is not a God of confusion, that is what my husband cousin say." A pause. "And that is what I see."

She washes; I suspend my apple.

"It is very noisy in these churches you have here." She has been in this country for three years—her husband came before, and later sent for her and the children, mildly surprising her mother, who had other daughters and daughters' kids similarly left but not reclaimed—and still she is bothered by noisy churches. Her family in Jamaica is Baptist. But when she goes to the Baptist church in Harlem, she is offended by the stamping and handclapping, by the shouted confessions and the tearful salvations. "They say wherever you go you are at home in your church. But we would never do that way at home."

She lifts her arms from the tub and pushes the suds down over her wrists and hands. "But I will find a church." The purity of her diction gives the words great strength. The tone and timbre would be fitting if she had said, "I will build a church."

Again she plunges her arms in suds. "Do you ever go," she asks me, "to that church? To that Baptist church?"

Now is the time for me to tell her that my husband and I are Jewish—and so, it occurs to me suddenly and absurdly, is our three-month-old daughter, Susan.

It is coming to Christmas. I have already mentioned to my husband that Mrs. Cooper, who has said how her children look forward to the tree, will wonder at our not having one for our child. "I don't feel like making any announcements," I tell my husband, "but I suppose I should. She'll wonder."

"You don't owe her an explanation." My husband doesn't know how close, on winter afternoons, a woman is drawn to another woman who works in her house. It would surprise him to hear that I have already mentioned to Mrs. Cooper certain intimate details of my life, and that she has revealed to me a heartache about her husband.

"But I think I'll tell her," I say. "Not even a spray of balsam. I'd rather have her think us Godless than heartless."

My husband suggests, "Tell her about Chanukah"—which with us is humor, because he knows I wouldn't know what to tell.

Mrs. Cooper stands before my tub in the lighted kitchen. I lean in the doorway, watching her. The kitchen window is black. Outside, it is a freezing four o'clock. Inside, time is suspended, as always when the baby sleeps. I smell the hot, soaped flannel, wrung out and heaped on the drainboard, waiting to be rinsed in three pure waters. "We don't attend church," I say. "We go—at least, my husband goes—to a synagogue. My husband and I are Jewish, Mrs. Cooper."

Mrs. Cooper looks into the tub. After a moment, she says, "That is all right." She fishes below a cream of suds, pulls up a garment, and unrolls a mitten sleeve. She wrings it and rubs it and plunges it down to soak. Loving work, as she performs it—mother's work. As I watch, my body seems to pass into her body.

I am glad that my reluctance to speak of synagogues at all has led me to speak while Mrs. Cooper is working. That is the right way. We never, I realize while she scrubs, still seeming to be listening, talk face to face. She is always looking somewhere else—at the washing or the baby's toy she is going to pick up. Being a shy person, I have drilled myself to stare people in the eyes when I speak. But Mrs. Cooper convinces me this is wrong. The face-to-face stare is for selling something, or for saying, "Look here, I don't like you and I never have liked you," or for answering, "Oh, no, Madam, we never accept for refund after eight days."

The time Mrs. Cooper told me her husband had stopped going to church altogether, she was holding Susan, and she uttered those exquisite and grieved tones—"He will not go with me, or alone, or at all any more"—straight into the baby's face, not mine.

Mrs. Cooper now pulls the stopper from the tub and the suds

choke down. While she is waiting, she casts a sidelong look at
me, which I sense rather than see, as I am examining my apple
core. She likes to see the expression on my face after I have
spoken, though not while I speak. She looks back at the sucking
tub.

When Mrs. Cooper comes again on Friday, she tells me, as
she measures formula into bottles, "My husband says we do not
believe Christmas is Christ's birthday."

I, of course, do not look at her, except to snatch a glance out
of the corner of my eye, while I fold diapers unnecessarily. Her
expression is calm and bland, high round cheekbones shining,
slightly slanted eyes narrowed to the measuring. "He was born,
we believe, sometime in April." After a bit, she adds, "We
believe there is one God for everyone."

Though my husband has told me over and over again that this
is what Jews say, Mrs. Cooper's words move me as though I
have never heard them before. I murmur something about my
work, and escape to my desk and my lance again.

Mrs. Cooper has quoted her husband to me several times. I
am curious about him, as I am sure she is about my husband.
She and my husband have at least met once or twice in the
doorway, but I have only seen a snapshot of her husband: a
stocky man with a mustache, who is as black as she, with no
smiles for photographers. Mrs. Cooper has added, in the winter
afternoons, certain details important to my picture.

Her husband plays cricket on Staten Island on Sundays and
goes on vacations in the summer without her or the children,
sometimes with the cricketers. But to balance that, he brings
her shrimps and rice when he returns at 1:00 A.M. from cricket-
club meetings on Friday nights. His opinion of the bus strike
in the city was that wages should go up but it was unfair to make
bus riders suffer. About Elizabeth Taylor he thought it was all
just nonsense; she was not even what he called pretty—more
like skinny and ugly.

In most other respects, it seems to me, he is taking on the
coloration of a zestful America-adopter. There are two kinds of
immigrants, I observe. One kind loves everything about America, is happy to throw off the ways of the old country, and
thereafter looks back largely with contempt. The other kind

dislikes, compares, regrets, awakens to *Welt-* and *Ichschmerz* and feels the new life mainly as a loss of the old. Often, the two marry each other.

Mr. Cooper, though he still plays cricket, now enjoys baseball, the fights on television, his factory job and union card, and the bustle and opportunity of New York. I mention this last with no irony. Mr. Cooper's job opportunities here are infinitely better than in Jamaica, where there aren't employers even to turn him down. He goes to school two nights a week for technical training. He became a citizen three years ago, destroying his wife's hopes of returning to Jamaica in their young years. But she dreams of going back when they are old. She would have servants there, she told me. "Because there aren't enough jobs, servants are cheap." Her husband, in her dream, would have a job, and so they would also have a car. And a quiet, gossipy life. She likes to move slowly, and this, as she herself points out, is very nice for my baby.

Christmas Week comes, and we give Mrs. Cooper presents for her children. And since Christmas Day falls on the last of her regular three days a week, we pay her for her holiday at the end of the second day. "Merry Christmas, Mrs. Cooper," I say. "Have a happy holiday."

Mrs. Cooper looks with interest at the baby in my arms, whom she had a moment before handed over to me. Suddenly she laughs and ducks her knees. Her fingers fly with unaccustomed haste to her cheek and she asks, "What must I say to you?"

"You can wish me the same," I say. "We have a holiday. My husband gets the day off, too."

I am glad that Mrs. Cooper has not grown reticent, since her embarrassment at Christmas, in speaking to me of holidays. Soon she is telling me how her children are looking forward to Easter. The oldest girl is preparing already for her part in a church play.

I fuss with the can of Enfamil, helping Mrs. Cooper this way when what I want is to help her another way. "Will your husband come to the play?" I ask casually.

"I am not sure," she says. After a while, "We haven't told him yet." Another little while. "Because it seems also he is against these plays." Then, with just enough of a pause to send those tones to my heart, she says, "I think he will not come."

Because the Judaeo-Christian tradition will have its little joke, Passover Week sometimes coincides with Easter Week, overlaying it like a reproach. It does the year Mrs. Cooper is with us. First, Good Friday, then in a few days is the first day of Passover.

"This year," my husband says, "because of Susie, to celebrate her first year with us, I want us to put a mezuzah outside our door before Passover."

"I'm not in favor." I manage to say it quietly.

"You don't understand enough about it," my husband says.

"I understand that much."

"Do you know what a mezuzah is? Do you know what's in it?" Taking my silence as an admission of ignorance, my husband produces a Bible. "Deuteronomy," he says. He reads:

"Hear, O Israel: The Lord our God, the Lord is one Lord:
And thou shalt love the Lord thy God with all thine heart, and with all thy soul, and with all thy might.
And these words, which I command thee this day, shall be in thine heart:
And thou shalt teach them diligently unto thy children, and shalt talk of them when thou sittest in thine house, and when thou walkest by the way, and when thou liest down, and when thou risest up. . . ."

All this and more is written on a parchment that is rolled up tight and fitted into the metal or wooden mezuzah, which is no more than two inches high and less than half an inch across and is mounted on a base for fastening to the doorframe. My husband finishes his reading.

"And thou shalt write them upon the door-posts of thine house, and upon thy gates:
That your days may be multiplied, and the days of your children, in the land which the Lord sware unto your fathers to give them, as the days of heaven upon the earth."

The words might move me if I allowed them to, but I will not allow them to.

My husband closes the Bible and asks, "What did your family observe? What was Passover like?"

"My grandfather sat on a pillow, and I was the youngest, so I found the matzos and he gave me money."

"No questions? No answers?"

"Just one. I would ask my grandfather, 'Where is my prize?' And he would laugh and give me money."

"Is that all?" my husband asks.

"That was a very nice ceremony in itself," I say. "And I remember it with pleasure, and my grandfather with love!"

"But besides the food, besides the children's game. Didn't your grandparents observe anything?"

"I don't remember."

"You sat at their table for eighteen years!"

"Well, my grandmother lit Friday-night candles, and that was something I think she did all her life. But she did it by herself, in the breakfast room."

"Didn't they go to a synagogue?"

"My grandmother did. My grandfather did, too, but then I remember he stopped. He'd be home on holidays, not at the services."

"Your parents didn't tell you anything?"

"My parents were the next generation," I say. "And I'm the generation after that. We evolved," I say—and luckily that is also humor between my husband and me.

But my husband rubs his head. It's different now, and not so funny, because this year we have Susan.

My husband was born in Europe, of an Orthodox family. He is neither Orthodox nor Reform. He is his own council of rabbis, selecting as he goes. He has plenty to say about the influence of America on Jewishness, Orthodox or not. "The European Jew," my husband says, "didn't necessarily feel that if he rose in the social or economic scale he had to stop observing his Jewishness. There were even a number of wealthy and prominent German Jews who were strictly observant."

"I'm sure that helped them a lot!" This is as close as I come to speaking of the unspeakable. Somewhere in the monstrous testimony I have read about concentration camps and killings are buried the small, intense lives of my husband's family. But why is it I am more bitter than my husband about his own experiences? And why should my bitterness cut the wrong way?

It is the word "German" that does it to me. My soul knots in
hate. "German!" Even the softening, pathetic sound of "Jew"
that follows it now doesn't help. All words fail. If I could grasp
words, I would come on words that would jump so to life they
would jump into my heart and kill me. All I can do is make a
fantasy. Somewhere in New York I will meet a smiling German.
In his pocket smile the best export accounts in the city—he is
from the land of scissors and knives and ground glass. Because
I am surprisingly fair, he will be oh, so surprised when I strike
at him with all my might. "For the children! For the children!"
My words come out shrieks. He protests it was his duty and,
besides, he didn't know. I am all leaking, dissolving. How can
a mist break stone? Once we exchange words it is hopeless; the
words of the eyewitness consume everything, as in a fire:

> "The children were covered with sores. . . . They screamed and
> wept all night in the empty rooms where they had been put. . . .
> Then the police would go up and the children, screaming with
> terror, would be carried kicking and struggling to the courtyard."

How is it my husband doesn't know that after this there can be
no mezuzahs?

"It's too painful to quarrel," my husband says. He puts his
hands on my shoulders, his forehead against mine. "This is
something I want very much. And you feel for me. I know you
feel for me in this."

"Yes, I do, of course I do." I use Mrs. Cooper's trick, and
even at that close range twist my head elsewhere. "Only that
particular symbol—"

"No, with you it's all the symbols." My husband drops his
hands from my shoulders. "You don't know enough about them
to discard them."

I don't have the right to judge them—that is what I feel he
means. Since I was not even scorched by the flames of their
futility. As he was, and came out cursing less than I.

"But besides everything else"—I take hasty shelter in practi-
calness—"a mezuzah is ugly. I remember that ugly tin thing
nailed to the door of my grandmother's room. If I spend three
weeks picking out a light fixture for my foyer, why should I have
something so ugly on my door?"

Then, as my husband answers, I see that this shabby attack has fixed my defeat, because he is immediately reasonable. "Now, that's something else. I won't argue aesthetics with you. The outer covering is of no importance. I'll find something attractive."

The next night my husband brings home a mezuzah made in the East. It is a narrow green rectangle, twice the normal size, inlaid with mosaic and outlined in brass. It does not look Jewish to me at all. It looks foreign—a strange bit of green enamel and brass.

"I don't like it," I say. "I'm sorry."

"But it's only the idea you don't like?" My husband smiles teasingly. "In looks, you at least relent?"

"It doesn't look bad," I admit.

"Well, that is the first step." I am happy to see the mezuzah disappear in his dresser drawer before we go in to our dinner.

When Mrs. Cooper comes next day, she asks, "What have you on your door?"

I step out to look, and at first have the impression that a praying mantis has somehow hatched out of season high on our doorway. Then I recognize it. "Oh, that's . . ." I say. "That's . . ." I find I cannot explain a mezuzah to someone who has never heard of one.

While Mrs. Cooper changes her clothes, I touch the mezuzah to see if it will fall off. But my husband has glued it firmly to the metal doorframe.

My husband's office works a three-quarter day on Good Friday. I ask Mrs. Cooper if she would like time off, but she says no, her husband will be home ahead of her to look after things. I have the impression she would rather be here.

My husband comes home early, bestowing strangeness on the rhythm of the house in lieu of celebration. I kiss him and put away his hat. "Well, that was a nasty thing to do." I say it lazily and with a smirk. The lazy tone is to show that I am not really involved, and the smirk that I intend to swallow it down like bad medicine. He will have his way, but I will have my say—that's all I mean. My say will be humorous, with just a little cut to it, as is proper between husband and wife. He will cut back a little, with a grin, and after Mrs. Cooper goes we will have our peaceful dinner. The conversation will meander, never actually pricking sore points, but winding words about them, making pads and cushions, so that should they ever bleed, there, already softly wrapped around them, will be the bandages our words wove. Weave enough of these bandages and nothing will ever smash, I say. I always prepare in advance a last line, too, so that I will know where to stop. "When mezuzahs last in the doorway bloomed," I will say tonight. And then I expect us both to laugh.

But where has he been all day? The same office, the same thirty-minute subway ride to and from each way, the same lunch with the same cronies. . . . But he has traveled somewhere else in his head. "Doesn't anything mean anything to you?" he says, and walks by me to the bedroom.

I follow with a bandage, but it slips from my hand. "I know a lot of women who would have taken that right down!" It is something of a shout, to my surprise.

He says nothing.

"I left it up. All I wanted was my say."

He says nothing.

"I live here, too. That's my door also."

He says nothing.

"And I don't like it!"

I hear a loud smashing of glass. It brings both our heads up. My husband is the first to understand. "Mrs. Cooper broke a bottle." He puts his arms around me and says, "Let's not quarrel about a doorway. Let's not quarrel at all, but especially not about the entrance to our home."

I lower my face into his tie. What's a mezuzah? Let's have ten, I think, so long as nothing will smash.

Later, I reproach myself. I am in the living room, straightening piles of magazines, avoiding both kitchen and bedroom. A woman, I think, is the one creature who builds satisfaction of the pleasure she gets from giving in. What might the world be if women would continue the dialogue? But no, they must give in and be satisfied. Nevertheless, I don't intend to take back what I've given in on and thereby give up what I've gained.

I am aware of Mrs. Cooper, boiling formula in the kitchen, and of my baby, registering in sleep her parents' first quarrel since her birth. "What must I say to you?" I think of saying to my daughter—Mrs. Cooper's words come naturally to my mind.

I go to the kitchen doorway and look at Mrs. Cooper. Her face indicates deaf and dumb. She is finishing the bottles.

When Mrs. Cooper is dressed and ready to leave, she looks into the living room. "I am saying good night."

"I hope you and your family will have a happy Easter," I say, smiling for her.

I know in advance that Mrs. Cooper will ask, "What must I say to you?"

This time she asks it soberly, and this time my husband, who has heard, comes in to tell Mrs. Cooper the story of Passover. As always in the traditional version, there is little mention of Moses, the Jews having set down from the beginning not the tragedy of one but their intuition for the tragedy of many.

When my husband leaves us, Mrs. Cooper takes four wrapped candies from the candy bowl on the desk, holds them up to be sure I see her taking them, and puts them in her purse. "I do hope everything will be all right," she says.

"Oh, yes," I say, looking at the magazines. "It was such a help today. I got so much work done. Thank you."

I hear that she is motionless.

"I will not be like this all the days of my life." It is a cry from the heart, stunningly articulated. I lift my head from the magazines, and this time I do stare. Not be like what? A Jamaican without a servant? A wife who never vacations? An exile? A baby nurse? A woman who gives in? What Mrs. Cooper might not want to be flashes up in a lightning jumble. "I am going to find a church," she says, and strains her face away from mine.

I think of all the descriptions of God I have ever heard—that He is jealous, loving, vengeful, waiting, teaching, forgetful, permissive, broken-hearted, dead, asleep.

Mrs. Cooper and I wish each other a pleasant weekend.

II
SEEKING

Where Moth and Rust

Gertrude Friedberg

1

IN RECENT YEARS there have been many precautions one has had to take against disaster. The disaster that menaced Mrs. Fortrey was not the obvious one that frightened all others. It was the destruction and ruin that would engulf her home were she to fail in her performance of the many small tasks of protection and repair that custom, direction leaflets, and her vigilant sister prescribed.

No sooner was a new acquisition, whether a furnishing, an ornament, or merely a child, brought proudly into the home than it began to succumb to a thousand effects of use, age, and chemistry, which might be held in unwilling abeyance only by the indicated rituals. So seductively did the written prescriptions belittle the amount of time needed for each particular care that Mrs. Fortrey for a long time failed to feel deprived as she

A New Yorker and a graduate of Barnard College, *Gertrude Friedberg* is the author of *The Revolving Boy*, a science fiction novel. Her short stories have appeared in *The Atlantic, Harper's, Esquire,* and elsewhere. "Where Moth and Rust," copyright © 1957 by The Atlantic Monthly Company, Boston, Massachusetts, is reprinted with permission.

raced in a treadmill of small palliative measures which produced nothing, improved nothing, but merely retarded the processes of inevitable decay or returned things to a state that was surely not as good as new.

So every Monday morning Mrs. Fortrey started out bravely with a pitcher of water and a can of 3-in-1 oil to perform eight measures of prophylaxis in one grand round from kitchen to front room. The electric fan, the vacuum cleaner, and the sewing machine needed a paltry libation of only three drops of oil (after every ten hours of use) to keep their motors from burning out or worse. It took but a few minutes more to oil the wall can opener, the knife sharpener, the children's roller skates, the flute keys, and the drapery pulley tracks.

On the return trip from front room to kitchen Mrs. Fortrey poured a little water into the philodendron plants, moistened the rubber plant and the ivy, put a bit in the parakeet's cup, poured some into the radiator pan to keep the air from drying the furniture, and put a little in a pan under the broiler to keep the stove from smoking up the white kitchen. Then she usually stopped to empty the pencil sharpener. She once told her sister that she oiled all the way from the back of the apartment to the front and watered from the front to the back.

Mrs. Fortrey knew of four kinds of rot and how to avoid them. The chrome fixtures, if not shined with a special cream, would succumb to green rot; the mahogany tables, if not rubbed with polish, would yield to dry rot; clothes left too long in a hamper would get wet rot; dead batteries left in a flashlight produced chemical rot. And a leaflet that the children brought home from school cautioned Mrs. Fortrey that if the frayed electric cords were not taped up, her family would be electrocuted.

Every month or so a bit of Vaseline had to be spread on the washing machine spindle to keep the agitator from sticking, and a bit of black stuff had to be rubbed on Mr. Fortrey's electric razor to sharpen it while the electricity hummed and Mrs. Fortrey counted to sixty in a loud voice as bidden. She rubbed ashes on the glass rings left on table tops, leather conditioner on the desk top, and, almost with a sense of wanton mischief, soap on the edges of all the doors.

When the carpets were brand-new, Mrs. Fortrey's sister made

the family take their shoes off as soon as they entered the house. This zeal did not survive one week, for as small unavoidable spots gathered despite their care, their hearts hardened and their feet stepped more boldly. At last only Mrs. Fortrey frowned at the dark patches before each door. To avoid increasing dirt and wear on the most traveled paths of the carpet, she took to sidling close against the walls and leaping from a point about two feet before each threshold to a point two feet within the room. She took great pleasure in the thought that in this way the carpet was spared perhaps hundreds of extra scuffs. Once Mr. Fortrey, coming back for a moment for an umbrella, saw her sidling and leaping about the apartment. He thought it best to say nothing, but quietly let himself out again.

Finally she contented herself with brushing a glamorizing powder into the dark patches twice a month. This usually reminded her to sprinkle talcum powder on the slide rule where it customarily slid, and fuller's earth on the food spots on the dining-room chairs.

2

Mrs. Fortrey's sister always had many useful suggestions for the preservation of things. It was she who pointed out that all the ash trays, lamps, and bric-a-brac which stood on the fine tables would leave dreadful scratches each time they were moved if Mrs. Fortrey did not line their bases with some gentle stuff. Looking for scraps of felt for this purpose, Mrs. Fortrey was happy to find in the children's room a great pile of round felt pieces of exactly the right conformation. They were camp awards which, accumulated for six years or more of earnest athletic endeavor, presented at last a grave problem of storage. It was therefore doubly satisfying to Mrs. Fortrey when each morning, for many mornings (work divided into time in this way gave her the illusion of being somehow diminished), she pasted to the base of a lamp or vase a bright yellow patch. Only the truly curious would ever lift them to read "Camp Katchewan —For Proficiency in Intermediate Archery."

Shoes had to be reheeled and resoled. Hems fell and needed to be raised. Trouser cuffs drooped and were retacked. Elbows

wore out and were patched, and everybody in the family
dropped buttons and stood still while Mrs. Fortrey sewed them
on again. She sewed the little ribbon tape back on the umbrella,
the fringe back on the chaise longue, and the hanger tape back
on Mr. Fortrey's overcoat, and restitched three brief cases with
a handy little leather stitcher.

It seemed quite clear from the start that a bright new uphol-
stered chair ought not to be sat on. When Mr. Fortrey, who
sometimes forgot the rules, plunked down in the beige chair,
she ran at him with a lace doily to put under his head.

"Darling, nobody uses such things any more," her sister said.
"You have your upholsterer make false covers for the backs and
arms out of the leftover pieces of material."

Soon every chair, and even the couch, had extra pieces of
matching material over the original coverings. They were
merely tacked in place and were not too noticeable. Mr. Fortrey
never got the knack of sitting properly in the living room. He
managed to sit on each piece in turn and always disarranged the
protective disguise pieces, so that after an evening the carpet
would be littered with pages of newspaper and pieces of backs
or arms.

When summer came, all the true coverings and false coverings had to be covered with covers which were neither true nor
false but just slip. You slipped the chairs and cushions into them
much as you slipped a heavy woman into a girdle, and zipped.
They were very attractive and her sister thought it a pity that
they should be ruined so quickly by the dust which rained in
through the windows all day. "I'd just put a plastic covering
over the very tops," she said, and Mrs. Fortrey added, "And
maybe just where your hands rest."

Every night a plastic cover had to be put over the parakeet
cage, and every winter a plastic cover had to be put over the air
conditioner, and every summer plastic covers were put on all
the lamp shades. Mrs. Fortrey once considered making a plastic
cover for Mr. Fortrey, who habitually spilled soup on his tie and
sloshed his cuffs around in the gravy, but she ended by rubbing
him down instead with Renuzit.

The stapling machine and the ball-point pens had to be reloaded, the filters replaced in the air conditioner, a fresh throwaway bag inserted into the vacuum cleaner, a fresh ribbon put into the typewriter, and fresh fuel oil dripped into the cigarette lighters.

Every summer the drapes had to be taken down, cleaned, folded away, and in the fall put up again. This large familiar effort each year stung the wound of passing time.

"Why couldn't I just let them hang?" Mrs. Fortrey asked her sister.

"You'll have to throw them out in the fall," said her sister. "It's not only the dust. It's the sun too."

She took them down.

Her coat needed periodic reglazing, the rubbertile foyer needed periodic rewaxing, her graying hair needed periodic retinting, the springs of the couch needed retying, the mirrors needed resilvering, the silver pieces needed reglazing to protect their resilvering, the bathroom wallpaper needed repasting, the kitchen needed repainting, the library steps needed revarnishing, the dictionary needed rebinding, and one of the children, changing schools, needed extensive readjusting.

Moths were a constant threat. Mr. Fortrey had once told her very firmly that it unnerved him if during an evening in which they had been quietly reading, leaning with only half their weight on the false backs of their living-room chairs and dangling their hands unsupported three inches above the chair arms, she would suddenly leap up with a loud cry and clap her hands together directly above his head.

"It's too noticeable," he complained.

After that Mrs. Fortrey tried to be more discreet in her pursuit, but she continued to feel that to be mothproof was to achieve virtue. She sprayed every woolen suit, coat, and dress, put them in clothes bags, hung moth gas containers in all the closets, and put the children's mittens in the little cellophane bags which she saved from bunches of carrots.

She used Easy-off on the stove, Soil-off on the walls, Dust-off —full of static electricity—on the coffee table, Slipit on the window tracks, Weldit on the loose tile in the kitchen wall, Kaukit on the spot under the hot-water pipe where the plaster had come off, and Exit under the sinks. She used Jubilee on the enamels, Pride on the kitchen linoleum, Cheer in the clothes washer, Joy in the sink, and had death in her heart.

One winter the handle came off the door of the refrigerator, the drawers stuck, a piano key broke, a radio knob cracked, the screws fell out of the stove, the ironing board collapsed, the plates chipped, the magnetic can holder let the cans drop, the hair drier smoked, the wire recorder raveled a whole spool of wire, all the tubes on the horizontal circuit of the television set burned out, and one of Mrs. Fortrey's own tubes was a bit inflamed.

When she got back from the hospital, she found that the agitator in the washing machine was wobbly, there were moth holes in the suit that Mr. Fortrey had been saving until he got thinner, and the children had spots. There were cracks in the window shades, feathers were coming out of the pillows, the eight-day clock went only three and a half days, there was a steady hum on the record player, and the ceiling drier had fallen.

It was not long after this that Mrs. Fortrey stopped. She told Mr. Fortrey while he was having breakfast.

"I'm not going to do anything any more," she said. "It's all too much trouble for me."

"Name me one thing," said Mr. Fortrey, "that's too much for you to do."

Mrs. Fortrey thought a moment. "I don't want to reload the stapling machine," she said.

Reloading the stapling machine was really a small thing, but Mrs. Fortrey didn't want to mention all the other things to Mr. Fortrey while he was having his breakfast. Actually she stopped everything that very day.

At first nobody noticed, and Mrs. Fortrey didn't say any more. She started to play the piano, learn Spanish, and practice tumbling tricks. As she walked through the apartment she stepped boldly on the middle of the carpet and wiped her feet on the dark spot at the threshold.

The calendar leaves weren't torn off, and since nobody knew when October was over, the library books were overdue. As if despoiled by an autumn trapped unexpectedly indoors with all its colors ready to flow, her furnishings started to turn color. The silver turned brown. The chrome fixtures turned green. The copper casserole turned pink. The blue chair turned gray. The white bedroom drapes turned yellow.

One day Mr. Fortrey pushed back his dining chair, took off his plastic cuffs, and told Mrs. Fortrey that he was leaving her.

"I refuse to be seen in public with a woman in an unglazed mink coat," he said firmly. He would have left that day, but the zipper on his valise got stuck midway and he had to wait two weeks to have the zipper teeth realigned by a woman whose business it was to realign zipper teeth. When he left, Mrs. Fortrey turned off the air conditioners.

The parakeet was the next to leave. His cage had no carpet to darken at the threshold, but the gravel paper which served him instead had not been changed for three weeks and was piled high with empty seed shells. He found an open window and headed toward Park and 56th Street, where he felt he might find a tidier home.

The children put up with her for a few months longer, but relations broke down at last when they found that Mrs. Fortrey had given up using the pliers on the rings of their loose-leaf notebooks to ply them into tight embrace, and had neglected to Scotch-tape the edges of the music books, which were now beginning to rain bits of dried yellow paper all over the piano, the carpet, and their hands as they practiced. This was too much and both children went to join their father, taking the Erector set with them.

Mrs. Fortrey moved into one room and lived, on the small allowance she received, not at all as she should. She found out how umbrellas started, did lots of geometry, and learned Speedwriting, which she wrote slowly, embellishing each capital letter with extraordinary flourishes and tiny clever pictures. She set up a basketball net over her front door, looked up how to pronounce *disheveled,* and practiced bad posture.

She ate only foods that came ready-baked in heat-and-throw-away containers. Rather than wash each item of her no-iron dip-and-hang clothing separately, she bathed with her clothes on and sat on the radiator, reading, while she dried. Late at night when the city was quiet she could hear the moths feeding in the closet. From time to time she opened the closet door and threw them a sweater.

When Mrs. Fortrey died, it was after a period of six months during which nobody had seen or spoken to her. Two men broke down her door and took a good two hours to cart away rubbish piled ceiling high before they reached her bed.

She had died of what is still called a natural cause. A small valve in her heart, diseased from a childhood illness, had become rigid, its sides had fused, and the closure had provoked a gradual deterioration of her circulatory system and finally death. A surgeon, with the gentlest pressure of his index finger, might have split the fused valve open and restored her to a state almost as good as new. It was the sort of small mechanical repair that Mrs. Fortrey had once performed on a stenosed perfume atomizer in the days of her greatest zeal.

The Long-Distance Runner

Grace Paley

ONE DAY, BEFORE or after forty-two, I became a long-distance runner. Though I was stout and in many ways inadequate to this desire, I wanted to go far and fast, not as fast as bicycles and trains, not as far as Taipei, Hingwen, places like that, islands of the slant-eyed cunt, as sailors in bus stations say when speaking of travel, but round and round the county from the sea side to the bridges, along the old neighborhood streets a couple of times, before old age and urban renewal ended them and me.

I tried the country first, Connecticut, which being wooded is always full of buds in spring. All creation is secret, isn't that true? So I trained in the wide-zoned suburban hills where I wasn't known. I ran all spring in and out of dogwood bloom, then laurel.

Grace Paley is the author of two short-story collections: *The Little Disturbances of Man* and *Enormous Changes at the Last Minute.* A recipient of grants from the Guggenheim Foundation and the National Council on the Arts, and an award from the National Institute of Arts and Letters, she teaches at Sarah Lawrence College. "The Long-Distance Runner," from *Enormous Changes at the Last Minute* by Grace Paley, copyright © 1974 by Grace Paley, is reprinted with the permission of Farrar, Straus and Giroux, Inc.

People sometimes stopped and asked me why I ran, a lady in silk shorts halfway down over her fat thighs. In training, I replied and rested only to answer if closely questioned. I wore a white sleeveless undershirt as well, with excellent support, not to attract the attention of old men and prudish children.

The summer came, my legs seemed strong. I kissed the kids goodbye. They were quite old by then. It was near the time for parting anyway. I told Mrs. Raftery to look in now and then and give them some of that rotten Celtic supper she makes.

I told them they could take off any time they wanted to. Go lead your private life, I said. Only leave me out of it.

A word to the wise . . . said Richard.

You're depressed Faith, Mrs. Raftery said. Your boy friend Jack, the one you think's so hotsy-totsy, hasn't called and you're as gloomy as a tick on Sunday.

Cut the folkshit with me, Raftery, I muttered. Her eyes filled with tears because that's who she is: folkshit from bunion to topknot. That's how she got liked by me, loved, invented and endured.

When I walked out the door they were all reclining before the television set, Richard, Tonto and Mrs. Raftery, gazing at the news. Which proved with moving pictures that there *had* been a voyage to the moon and Africa and South America hid in a furious whorl of clouds.

I said, Goodbye. They said, Yeah, O.K., sure.

If that's how it is, forget it, I hollered and took the Independent subway to Brighton Beach.

At Brighton Beach I stopped at the Salty Breezes Locker Room to change my clothes. Twenty-five years ago my father invested $500 in its future. In fact he still clears about $3.50 a year, which goes directly (by law) to the Children of Judea to cover their deficit.

No one paid too much attention when I started to run, easy and light on my feet. I ran on the boardwalk first, past my mother's leafleting station—between a soft-ice-cream stand and a degenerated dune. There she had been assigned by her comrades to halt the tides of cruel American enterprise with simple socialist sense.

I wanted to stop and admire the long beach. I wanted to stop in order to think admiringly about New York. There aren't many rotting cities so tan and sandy and speckled with citizens at their salty edges. But I had already spent a lot of life lying down or standing and staring. I had decided to run.

After about a mile and a half I left the boardwalk and began to trot into the old neighborhood. I was running well. My breath was long and deep. I was thinking pridefully about my form.

Suddenly I was surrounded by about three hundred blacks.

Who you?

Who that?

Look at her! Just look! When you seen a fatter ass?

Poor thing. She ain't right. Leave her, you boys, you bad boys.

I used to live here, I said.

Oh yes, they said, in the white old days. That time too bad to last.

But we loved it here. We never went to Flatbush Avenue or Times Square. We loved our block.

Tough black titty.

I like your speech, I said. Metaphor and all.

Right on. We get that from talking.

Yes my people also had a way of speech. And don't forget the Irish. The gift of gab.

Who they? said a small boy.

Cops.

Nowadays, I suggested, there's more than Irish on the police force.

You right, said two ladies. More, more, much much more. They's French Chinamen Russkies Congoleans. Oh missee, you too right.

I lived in that house, I said. That apartment house. All my life. Till I got married.

Now that *is* nice. Live in one place. My mother live that way in South Carolina. One place. Her daddy farmed. She said. They ate. No matter winter war bad times. Roosevelt. Something! Ain't that wonderful! And it weren't cold! Big trees!

That apartment. I looked up and pointed. There. The third floor.

They all looked up. So what! You blubrous devil! said a dark young man. He wore horn-rimmed glasses and had that intelligent look that City College boys used to have when I was eighteen and first looked at them.

He seemed to lead them in contempt and anger, even the littlest ones who moved toward me with dramatic stealth singing. Devil, Oh Devil. I don't think the little kids had bad feeling because they poked a finger into me, then laughed.

Still I thought it might be wise to keep my head. So I jumped right in with some facts. I said, How many flowers' names do you know? Wild flowers, I mean. My people only knew two. That's what they say now anyway. Rich or poor, they only had two flowers' names. Rose and violet.

Daisy, said one boy immediately.

Weed, said another. That *is* a flower, I thought. But everyone else got the joke.

Saxifrage, lupine, said a lady. Viper's bugloss, said a small Girl Scout in medium green with a dark green sash. She held up a *Handbook of Wild Flowers.*

How many you know, fat mama? a boy asked warmly. He wasn't against my being a mother or fat. I turned all my attention to him.

Oh sonny, I said, I'm way ahead of my people. I know in yellows alone: common cinquefoil, trout lily, yellow adder's-tongue, swamp buttercup and common buttercup, golden sorrel, yellow or hop clover, devil's-paintbrush, evening primrose, black-eyed Susan, golden aster, also the yellow pickerelweed growing down by the water if not in the water, and dandelions of course. I've seen all these myself. Seen them.

You could see China from the boardwalk, a boy said. When it's nice.

I know more flowers than countries. Mostly young people these days have traveled in many countries.

Not me. I ain't been nowhere.

Not me either, said about seventeen boys.

I'm not allowed, said a little girl. There's drunken junkies.

But *I! I!* cried out a tall black youth, very handsome and well dressed. I am an African. My father came from the high stolen plains. *I* have been everywhere. I was in Moscow six months, learning machinery. I was in France, learning French. I was in

Italy, observing the peculiar Renaissance and the people's sweetness. I was in England, where I studied the common law and the urban blight. I was at the Conference of Dark Youth in Cuba to understand our passion. I am now here. Here am I to become an engineer and return to my people, around the Cape of Good Hope in a Norwegian sailing vessel. In this way I will learn the fine old art of sailing in case the engines of the new society of my old inland country should fail.

We had an extraordinary amount of silence after that. Then one old lady in a black dress and high white lace collar said to another old lady dressed exactly the same way, Glad tidings when someone got brains in the head not fish juice. Amen, said a few.

Whyn't you go up to Mrs. Luddy living in your house, you lady, huh? The Girl Scout asked this.

Why she just groove to see you, said some sarcastic snickerer.

She got palpitations. Her man, he give it to her.

That ain't all, he a natural gift giver.

I'll take you, said the Girl Scout. My name is Cynthia. I'm in Troop 355, Brooklyn.

I'm not dressed, I said, looking at my lumpy knees.

You shouldn't wear no undershirt like that without no runnin number or no team writ on it. It look like a undershirt.

Cynthia! Don't take her up there, said an important boy. Her head strange. Don't you take her. Hear?

Lawrence, she said softly, you tell me once more what to do I'll wrap you round that lamppost.

Git! She said, powerfully addressing *me*.

In this way I was led into the hallway of the whole house of my childhood.

The first door I saw was still marked in flaky gold, 1A. That's where the janitor lived, I said. He was a Negro.

How come like that? Cynthia made an astonished face. How come the janitor was a black man?

Oh Cynthia, I said. Then I turned to the opposite door, first floor front, 1B. I remembered. Now, here, this was Mrs. Goreditsky, very very fat lady. All her children died at birth. Born, then one, two, three. Dead. Five children, then Mr. Goreditsky said, I'm bad luck on you Tessie and he went away. He sent $15 a week for seven years. Then no one heard.

I know her, poor thing, said Cynthia. The city come for her summer before last. The way they knew, it smelled. They wropped her up in a canvas. They couldn't get through the front door. It scraped off a piece of her. My uncle Ronald had to help them, but he got disgusted.

Only two years ago. She was still here! Wasn't she scared?

So we all, said Cynthia. White ain't everything.

Who lived up here, she asked, 2B? Right now, my best friend Nancy Rosalind lives here. She got two brothers, and her sister married and got a baby. She very light-skinned. Not her mother. We got all colors amongst us.

Your best friend? That's funny. Because it was *my* best friend. Right in that apartment. Joanna Rosen.

What become of her? Cynthia asked. She got a running shirt too?

Come on Cynthia, if you really want to know, I'll tell you. She married this man, Marvin Steirs.

Who's he?

I recollected his achievements. Well, he's the president of a big corporation, JoMar Plastics. This corporation owns a steel company, a radio station, a new Xerox-type machine that lets you do twenty-five different pages at once. This corporation has a foundation, The JoMar Fund for Research in Conservation. Capitalism is like that, I added, in order to be politically useful.

How come you know? You go over their house a lot?

No. I happened to read all about them on the financial page, just last week. It made me think: a different life. That's all.

Different spokes for different folks, said Cynthia.

I sat down on the cool marble steps and remembered Joanna's cousin Ziggie. He was older than we were. He wrote a poem which told us we were lovely flowers and our legs were petals, which nature would force open no matter how many times we said no.

Then I had several other interior thoughts that I couldn't share with a child, the kind that give your face a blank or melancholy look.

Now you're not interested, said Cynthia. Now you're not gonna say a thing. Who lived here, 2A? Who? Two men lives here now. Women coming and women going. My mother says, Danger sign: Stay away, my darling, stay away.

I don't remember, Cynthia. I really don't.

You got to. What'd you come for, anyways?

Then I tried. 2A. 2A. Was it the twins? I felt a strong obligation as though remembering was in charge of the *existence* of the past. This is not so.

Cynthia, I said, I don't want to go any further. I don't even want to remember.

Come on, she said, tugging at my shorts, don't you want to see Mrs. Luddy, the one lives in your old house? That be fun, no?

No. No, I don't want to see Mrs. Luddy.

Now you shouldn't pay no attention to those boys downstairs. She will like you. I mean, she is kind. She don't like most white people, but she might like you.

No Cynthia, it's not that, but I don't want to see my father and mother's house now.

I didn't know what to say. I said, Because my mother's dead. This was a lie, because my mother lives in her own room with my father in the Children of Judea. With her hand over her socialist heart, she reads the paper every morning after breakfast. Then she says sadly to my father, Every day the same. Dying . . . dying, dying from killing.

My mother's dead Cynthia. I can't go in there.

Oh . . . oh, the poor thing, she said, looking into my eyes. Oh, if my mother died, I don't know what I'd do. Even if I was old as you. I could kill myself. Tears filled her eyes and started down her cheeks. If my mother died, what would I do? She is my protector, she won't let the pushers get me. She hold me tight. She gonna hide me in the cedar box if my Uncle Rudford comes try to get me back. She *can't* die, my mother.

Cynthia—honey—she won't die. She's young. I put my arm out to comfort her. You could come live with me, I said. I got two boys, they're nearly grown up. I missed it, not having a girl.

What? What you mean now, live with you and boys. She pulled away and ran for the stairs. Stay way from me, honky lady. I

know them white boys. They just gonna try and jostle my black
womanhood. My mother told me about that, keep you white
honky devil boys to your devil self, you just leave me be you old
bitch you. Somebody help me, she started to scream, you hear.
Somebody help. She gonna take me away.

She flattened herself to the wall, trembling. I was too frightened by her fear of me to say, honey, I wouldn't hurt you, it's
me. I heard her helpers, the voices of large boys crying. We
coming, we coming, hold your head up, we coming. I ran past
her fear to the stairs and up them two at a time. I came to my
old own door. I knocked like the landlord, loud and terrible.

Mama not home, a child's voice said. No, no, I said. It's me!
a lady! Someone's chasing me, let me in. Mama not home, I
ain't allowed to open up for nobody.

It's me! I cried out in terror. Mama! Mama! let me in!

The door opened. A slim woman whose age I couldn't invent
looked at me. She said, Get in and shut that door tight. She took
a hard pinching hold on my upper arm. Then she bolted the
door herself. Them hustlers after you. They make me pink.
Hide this white lady now, Donald. Stick her under your bed, you
got a high bed.

Oh that's O.K. I'm fine now, I said. I felt safe and at home.

You in my house, she said. You do as I say. For two cents, I
throw you out.

I squatted under a small kid's pissy mattress. Then I heard the
knock. It was tentative and respectful. My mama don't allow me
to open. Donald! someone called. Donald!

Oh no, he said. Can't do it. She gonna wear me out. You know
her. She already tore up my ass this morning once. Ain't *gonna*
open up.

I lived there for about three weeks with Mrs. Luddy and Donald
and three little baby girls nearly the same age. I told her a joke
about Irish twins. Ain't Irish, she said.

Nearly every morning the babies woke us at about 6:45. We
gave them a bottle and went back to sleep till 8:00. I made coffee
and she changed diapers. Then it really stank for a while. At this
time I usually said, Well listen, thanks really, but I've got to go
I guess. I guess I'm going. She'd usually say, Well, guess again.

I guess you ain't. Or if she was feeling disgusted she'd say, Go
on now! Get! You wanna go, I guess by now I have snorted
enough white lady stink to choke a horse. Go on!

I'd get to the door and then I'd hear voices. I'm ashamed to
say I'd become fearful. Despite my wide geographical love of
mankind, I would be attacked by local fears.

There was a sentimental truth that lay beside all that going
and not going. It *was* my house where I'd lived long ago my
family life. There was a tile on the bathroom floor that I myself
had broken, dropping a hammer on the toe of my brother
Charles as he stood dreamily shaving, his prick halfway up his
undershorts. Astonishment and knowledge first seized me
right there. The kitchen was the same. The table was the enam-
eled table common to our class, easy to clean, with wooden
undercorners for indigent and old cockroaches that couldn't
make it to the kitchen sink. (However, it was not the same table,
because I have inherited that one, chips and all.)

The living room was something like ours, only we had less
plastic. There may have been less plastic in the world at that
time. Also, my mother had set beautiful cushions everywhere,
on beds and chairs. It was the way she expressed herself, artisti-
cally, to embroider at night or take strips of flowered cotton and
sew them across ordinary white or blue muslin in the most
delicate designs, the way women have always used materials that
live and die in hunks and tatters to say: This is my place.

Mrs. Luddy said, Uh huh!

Of course, I said, men don't have that outlet. That's how
come they run around so much.

Till they drunk enough to lay down, she said.

Yes, I said, on a large scale you can see it in the world. First
they make something, then they murder it. Then they write a
book about how interesting it is.

You got something there, she said. Sometimes she said, Girl,
you don't know *nothing*.

We often sat at the window looking out and down. Little tufts
of breeze grew on that windowsill. The blazing afternoon was
around the corner and up the block.

You say men, she said. Is that men? she asked. What you
call—a Man?

Four flights below us, leaning on the stoop, were about a dozen people and around them devastation. Just a minute, I said. I had seen devastation on my way, running, gotten some of the pebbles of it in my running shoe and the dust of it in my eyes. I had thought with the indignant courtesy of a citizen, This is a disgrace to the City of New York which I love and am running through.

But now, from the commanding heights of home, I saw it clearly. The tenement in which Jack my old and present friend had come to gloomy manhood had been destroyed, first by fire, then by demolition (which is a swinging ball of steel that cracks bedrooms and kitchens). Because of this work, we could see several blocks wide and a block and a half long. Crazy Eddy's house still stood, famous 1510 gutted, with black window frames, no glass, open laths. The stubbornness of the supporting beams! Some persons or families still lived on the lowest floors. In the lots between, a couple of old sofas lay on their fat faces, their springs sticking up into the air. Just as in wartime a half-dozen ailanthus trees had already found their first quarter inch of earth and begun a living attack on the dead yards. At night, I knew animals roamed the place, squalling and howling, furious New York dogs and street cats and mighty rats. You would think you were in Bear Mountain Park, the terror of venturing forth.

Someone ought to clean that up, I said.

Mrs. Luddy said, Who you got in mind? Mrs. Kennedy?—

Donald made a stern face. He said, That just what I gonna do when I get big. Gonna get the Sanitary Man in and show it to him. You see that, you big guinea you, you clean it up right now! Then he stamped his feet and fierced his eyes.

Mrs. Luddy said, Come here, you little nigger. She kissed the top of his head and gave him a whack on the backside all at one time.

Well, said Donald, encouraged, look out there now you all! Go on I say, look! Though we had already seen, to please him we looked. So the stoop men and boys lounged, leaned, hopped about, stood on one leg, then another, took their socks off, and scratched their toes, talked, sat on their haunches, heads down, dozing.

Donald said, Look at them. They ain't got self-respect. They got Afros *on* their heads, but they don't know they black *in* their heads.

I thought he ought to learn to be more sympathetic. I said, There are reasons that people are that way.

Yes, ma'am, said Donald.

Anyway, how come you never go down and play with the other kids, how come you're up here so much?

My mama don't like me do that. Some of them is bad. Bad. I might become a dope addict. I got to stay clear.

You just a dope, that's a fact, said Mrs. Luddy.

He ought to be with kids his age more, I think.

He see them in school, miss. Don't trouble your head about it if you don't mind.

Actually, Mrs. Luddy didn't go down into the street either. Donald did all the shopping. She let the welfare investigator in, the meterman came into the kitchen to read the meter. I saw him from the back room, where I hid. She did pick up her check. She cashed it. She returned to wash the babies, change their diapers, wash clothes, iron, feed people, and then in free half hours she sat by that window. She was waiting.

I believed she was watching and waiting for a particular man. I wanted to discuss this with her, talk lovingly like sisters. But before I could freely say, Forget about that son of a bitch, he's a pig, I did have to offer a few solid facts about myself, my kids, about fathers, husbands, passers-by, evening companions, and the life of my father and mother in this room by this exact afternoon window.

I told her for instance, that in my worst times I had given myself one extremely simple physical pleasure. This was cream cheese for breakfast. In fact, I insisted on it, sometimes depriving the children of very important articles and foods.

Girl, you don't know nothing, she said.

Then for a little while she talked gently as one does to a person who is innocent and insane and incorruptible because of stupidity. She had had two such special pleasures for hard times she said. The first, men, but they turned rotten, white women had ruined the best, give them the idea their dicks made of solid gold. The second pleasure she had tried was wine. She

said, I do like wine. You *has* to have something just for yourself
by yourself. Then she said, But you can't raise a decent boy
when you liquor-dazed every night.

White or black, I said, returning to men, they did think they
were bringing a rare gift, whereas it was just sex, which is
common like bread, though essential.

Oh, you can do without, she said. There's folks does without.

I told her Donald deserved the best. I loved him. If he had
flaws, I hardly noticed them. It's one of my beliefs that children
do not have flaws, even the worst do not.

Donald was brilliant—like my boys except that he had an
easier disposition. For this reason I decided, almost the second
moment of my residence in that household, to bring him up to
reading level at once. I told him we would work with books and
newspapers. He went immediately to his neighborhood library
and brought some hard books to amuse me. *Black Folktales* by
Julius Lester and *The Pushcart War,* which is about another
neighborhood but relevant.

Donald always agreed with me when we talked about reading
and writing. In fact, when I mentioned poetry, he told me he
knew all about it, that David Henderson, a known black poet,
had visited his second-grade class. So Donald was, as it turned
out, well ahead of my nosy tongue. He was usually very busy
shopping. He also had to spend a lot of time making faces to
force the little serious baby girls into laughter. But if the subject
came up, he could take *the* poem right out of the air into which
language and event had just gone.

An example: That morning, his mother had said, Whew, I just
got too much piss and diapers and wash. I wanna just sit down
by that window and rest myself. He wrote a poem:

> Just got too much pissy diapers
> and wash and wash
> just wanna sit down by that window
> and look out
>   ain't nothing there.

Donald, I said, you are plain brilliant. I'm never going to
forget you. For God's sakes don't you forget me.

You fool with him too much, said Mrs. Luddy. He already

don't even remember his grandma, you never gonna meet someone like her, a curse never come past her lips.

I do remember, Mama, I remember. She lying in bed, right there. A man standing in the door. She say, Esdras, I put a curse on you head. You worsen tomorrow. How come she said like that?

Gomorrah, I believe Gomorrah, she said. She know the Bible inside out.

Did she live with you?

No. No, she visiting. She come up to see us all, her children, how we doing. She come up to see sights. Then she lay down and died. She was old.

I remained quiet because of the death of mothers. Mrs. Luddy looked at me thoughtfully, then she said:

My mama had stories to tell, she raised me on. *Her* mama was a little thing, no sense. Stand in the door of the cabin all day, sucking her thumb. It was slave times. One day a young field boy came storming along. He knock on the door of the first cabin hollering, Sister, come out, it's freedom. She come out. She say, Yeah? When? He say, Now! It's freedom now! Then he knock at the next door and say, Sister! It's freedom! Now! From one cabin he run to the next cabin, crying out, Sister, it's freedom now!

Oh I remember that story, said Donald. Freedom now! Freedom now! He jumped up and down.

You don't remember nothing boy. Go on, get Eloise, she want to get into the good times.

Eloise was two but undersized. We got her like that, said Donald. Mrs. Luddy let me buy her ice cream and green vegetables. She was waiting for kale and chard, but it was too early. The kale liked cold. You not about to be here November, she said. No, no. I turned away, lonesomeness touching me and sang our Eloise song:

> Eloise loves the bees
> the bees they buzz
> like Eloise does.

Then Eloise crawled all over the splintery floor, buzzing wildly.

Oh you crazy baby, said Donald, buzz buzz buzz.

Mrs. Luddy sat down by the window.

You all make a lot of noise, she said sadly. You just right on noisy.

The next morning Mrs. Luddy woke me up.

Time to go, she said.

What?

Home.

What? I said.

Well, don't you think your little spoiled boys crying for you? Where's Mama? They standing in the window. Time to go lady. This ain't Free Vacation Farm. Time we was by ourself a little.

Oh Ma, said Donald, she ain't a lot of trouble. Go on, get Eloise, she hollering. And button up your lip.

She didn't offer me coffee. She looked at me strictly all the time. I tried to look strictly back, but I failed because I loved the sight of her.

Donald was teary, but I didn't dare turn my face to him, until the parting minute at the door. Even then, I kissed the top of his head a little too forcefully and said, Well, I'll see you.

On the front stoop there were about half a dozen mid-morning family people and kids arguing about who had dumped garbage out of which window. They were very disgusted with one another.

Two young men in handsome dashikis stood in counsel and agreement at the street corner. They divided a comment. How come white womens got rotten teeth? And look so old? A young woman waiting at the light said, Hush . . .

I walked past them and didn't begin my run till the road opened up somewhere along Ocean Parkway. I was a little stiff because my way of life had used only small movements, an occasional stretch to put a knife or teapot out of reach of the babies. I ran about ten, fifteen blocks. Then my second wind came, which is classical, famous among runners, it's the beginning of flying.

In the three weeks I'd been off the street, jogging had become popular. It seemed that I was only one person doing her thing, which happened like most American eccentric acts to be the most "in" thing I could have done. In fact, two young men ran alongside of me for nearly a mile. They ran silently beside me and turned off at Avenue H. A gentleman with a mustache, running poorly in the opposite direction, waved. He called out, Hi, senora.

Near home I ran through our park, where I had aired my children on weekends and late-summer afternoons. I stopped at the northeast playground, where I met a dozen young mothers intelligently handling their little ones. In order to prepare them, meaning no harm, I said, In fifteen years, you girls will be like me, wrong in everything.

At home it was Saturday morning. Jack had returned looking as grim as ever, but he'd brought cash and a vacuum cleaner. While the coffee perked, he showed Richard how to use it. They were playing tick tack toe on the dusty wall.

Richard said, Well! Look who's here! Hi!

Any news? I asked.

Letter from Daddy, he said. From the lake and water country in Chile. He says it's like Minnesota.

He's never been to Minnesota, I said. Where's Anthony?

Here I am, said Tonto, appearing. But I'm leaving.

Oh yes, I said. Of course. Every Saturday he hurries through breakfast or misses it. He goes to visit his friends in institutions. These are well-known places like Bellevue, Hillside, Rockland State, Central Islip, Manhattan. These visits take him all day and sometimes half the night.

I found some chocolate-chip cookies in the pantry. Take them, Tonto, I said. I remember nearly all his friends as little boys and girls always hopping, skipping, jumping and cookie-eating. He was annoyed. He said, No! Chocolate cookies is what the commissaries are full of. How about money?

Jack dropped the vacuum cleaner. He said, No! They have parents for that.

I said, Here, five dollars for cigarettes, one dollar each.

Cigarettes! said Jack. Goddamnit! Black lungs and death! Cancer! Emphysema! He stomped out of the kitchen, breathing. He took the bike from the back room and started for Central Park, which has been closed to cars but opened to bicycle riders. When he'd been gone about ten minutes, Anthony said, It's really open only on Sundays.

Why didn't you say so? Why can't you be decent to him? I asked. It's important to me.

Oh Faith, he said, patting me on the head because he'd grown so tall, all that air. It's good for his lungs. And his muscles! He'll be back soon.

You should ride too, I said. You don't want to get mushy in your legs. You should go swimming once a week.

I'm too busy, he said. I have to see my friends.

Then Richard, who had been vacuuming under his bed, came into the kitchen. You still here, Tonto?

Going going gone, said Anthony, don't bat your eye.

Now listen, Richard said, here's a note. It's for Judy, if you get as far as Rockland. Don't forget it. Don't open it. Don't read it. I know he'll read it.

Anthony smiled and slammed the door.

Did I lose weight? I asked. Yes, said Richard. You look O.K. You never look too bad. But where were you? I got sick of Raftery's boiled potatoes. Where were you, Faith?

Well! I said. Well! I stayed a few weeks in my old apartment, where Grandpa and Grandma and me and Hope and Charlie lived, when we were little. I took you there long ago. Not so far from the ocean where Grandma made us very healthy with sun and air.

What are you talking about? said Richard. Cut the baby talk.

Anthony came home earlier than expected that evening because some people were in shock therapy and someone else had run away. He listened to me for a while. Then he said, I don't know what she's talking about either.

Neither did Jack, despite the understanding often produced by love after absence. He said, Tell me again. He was in a good mood. He said, You can even tell it to me twice.

I repeated the story. They all said, What?

Because it isn't usually so simple. Have you known it to happen much nowadays? A woman inside the steamy energy of middle age runs and runs. She finds the houses and streets where her childhood happened. She lives in them. She learns as though she was still a child what in the world is coming next.

from Riverfinger Women

Elana Nachman

DISOWN THEM AS she may try, Mr. & Mrs. Bramanoi and their youngest child, Albert (re-christened Al Bear Riverfingers by Inez, ten years his senior), write a few words to their only daughter as she travels. They love her, they try to love her, they try anyway to give her a sense that she has a family background.

August, 1963

Dear Inez,

Albert is now going to type a few words to you all by himself.

sally runs tothe car.Dick play ball.

Thank uyou very much for therecord. Itis a nice record.I love

ey you very much.

Jane fell down.Spot bit Puff.

Albert

Elana Nachman has traveled extensively in the Northwest, and lived there for a time. In addition to her novel, *Riverfinger Women,* she is the author of a short story collection, *They Will Know Me by My Teeth.* This excerpt from *Riverfinger Women,* copyright © 1974 by Elana Nachman, is reprinted by permission of Daughters Publishing Co., Inc.

May, 1964

Dearest daughter,

It was so good speaking to you on the phone. Things here follow their usual course. Mommy is usually in pain but bears up well. And I go on working. Now that I have given up psychiatry, I am lost. Instead of weird dreams, I have nightmares. No one ever knows the private hells that exist in the minds of others or the loneliness. When I had my kidney stone all I could think about besides the pain was you and how awful it would have been if this happened when I was alone. I started to worry about your being alone. I am concerned that man because of his frailty and lack of physical ability to cope with his environment is a gregarious animal. He *needs* people to help him live. We all live needing other people. Enough philosophy. How's kicks? Can't wait to see you. All my love,

Daddy

June, 1966

Dear Inez,

I love you very much. School is very good and my report card is best and I got all A's and B's, too. I'm doing very good in school but school is out now and we have a summer vacation. School is out, play begun.

Mike just had his birthday party and he's 11 years old and he had a picture of two bats and a ball on his cake. I'm doing very good in my swimming. I went to the beach yesterday and Mike got a fishing rod for his birthday from his dad and I gave him Flubber but that was nothing much. I think that's all.

Love,
Albert

June, 1967

Dear Inez,

I only wish I could express myself as well as you do, could put thoughts and feelings on paper in the magic, meaningful ways you do. I'm slowly getting back to my typewriter (your father insists I should write more) but still the mechanical instrument fights back. But I shall try to tell you what reactions your letter brought, what latent feeling and emotions within me.

First of all, your letter about you and Abby clarified, in a way, what I was mulling over in my heart and mind these past months and I tried to express to you during your visit here spring vacation: all of us here love you very much—if a child does well she should be happy and of course mother and father will be at ease. But, as your mother, perhaps greatly aided by five years of my own psychiatry and gaining more insight thereby, I came to realize that I have always loved you (fat, thin, bright, stupid, responsive, withdrawn, etc.) and I don't even know exactly if it's because you are my daughter, though I know it may be trite to repeat the old cliches of "mother's love is a birthright" and "even a beetle is beautiful in the eyes of its mother." I say these things to you now for several reasons. perhaps I myself have been too "hung up" to express them before to you and you have been out of the family environment for so long that you cannot really know that you would have actually felt this love constantly had you lived with all of us, even in the midst of fights, yellings, scenes, worries and problems.

Your relationship with Abby, as you described it so well, comes as no great shock or surprise to me or would to those who have known you best through these years. I know that you have been kind of wavering back and forth about homosexuality for a long time (forgive my nonscientific language) and that was evident often from other graspings for relationships you had; that whatever you feel you must do to maintain your happiness and dispel the fears that go bump in the night can only bring happiness to me, too . . . I have long since learned that all is not black or white and mine is not to "approve" or "disapprove" but just try to understand and accept—this I do, in all good spirit and love (should add that, in my role of mother and omnivorous reader, I shall continue to caution against anything but brief, limited, experimental activities involving "mind-blowing" drugs and the like, including traveling around without using extreme caution and sense, which I think you have developed better than most—not that my cautions will prevent anything but it makes me feel better that I haven't been entirely remiss in "parental advice").

As for Abby herself, she did immediately strike me as a warm, sensitive, yearning person, the kind I instinctively like and want to be with, and I'm very glad now that you gave us the opportunity to meet her at your graduation. I wonder, not actually knowing them personally, if her parents are not aware somehow of your situation, if only subconsciously, and of course, most parents do not want to recognize any "divergencies" unless directly confronted. At any rate, I hope, for both of you, that your relationship is as warm and good as you make it sound.

You asked me to accept your life and you for what it is and you are. This you can count on always. We are here to be counted on and to be of help and to love you.

But also, there will be times when neither I nor your old friends will be available to you in Portland. I have mulled this over and feel it is fair enough to ask, in return for my understanding (not for my love—that is not on the "bargain" table), you contact, at the *very first* opportunity when you get to Portland, a "good" psychiatrist, and try to make a start at regular appointments with him (or her)—believe me, Inez dear, this suggestion is not made because I have any notions that you are "sick" or that your relationship with Abby is "evil" or "unhealthy"—I just feel that there will be times, certainly, when you will need absolutely someone with whom you can talk and work things out.

I have never known many women—or men, for that matter—who were homosexuals, perhaps there were some who never "let it out," but it will be difficult, I imagine, for you to adjust to college life with this extra facet, and I want to make sure you can get whatever help you might need.

Daddy had not been feeling well for a couple of weeks and he desperately needs some rest. Frankly, Inez, I don't really know how *he* was hit emotionally by your letter because he doesn't talk much about these things (I used to think it was just him who was so reticent, but I am beginning to feel most men don't have the same facility for talking about their emotions as women do; that's nature, I guess). But you are his love—that you know without my rhetoric.

My arm is dropping off! Write (or rite, as Albert says)! All my love,

                                        Mother

January, 1968

Dearest Inez,

I realize that it has been too long since my last letter (I can plead work, of which there is always so much I don't know what to do) or my own father's death, but these things are my worries —and you are my joy. Possibly that's why I have not written in so long—the Puritan in me keeps me from those I most enjoy.

But you worry me sometimes too. I never answered/responded to your summer letter about you and Abby partially because I thought Mommy did such a good job and partially because I did not then, nor now, know what it is I should say, or want to say.

In some sense there is a parental feeling of failure—I know that is a social hang-up but it exists. The only homosexuals I ever knew were when I was in college, they were all men and seemed to me caught up in a trap of self-centered, egotistical (and brief) relationships to each other and the world, characterized chiefly by their vanity. I certainly hope that you will not become like that and I realize that these were only what they call the visible homosexuals. As I have always told you, I only want that you should be happy; if this is how you want to live your life, I accept it so long as it does not hurt you or anyone else and does not hold back or freeze your capacity as a productive person.

More than that I don't know what to say. I hope you are enjoying school and not working as hard as I have to, to keep you there. Seriously, I know the competition is rough, but I'm sure you're doing well. You're my daughter, after all. I miss you all the time and wish you were here. You'll always be the girl of my dreams.

                                        Love,
                                        Daddy

Mom, I'm Glad You're Not a Scorpio

A mother is a strange object in my mind, one who scrapes out the lining of my intestines with a furcovered fork, whom I would please, whom I would be patient for, through the time when the

question is asked and considered: When will you admit to knowing something about me? But there was never anything—a
space you tried to cover with the cards of your boredom (boredom?).

mother

I have no comfort to give you, only shame. Mother, so many
impossible gestures built into the blood because I can say to
you, "I love you, I am trying to" and you can tell me that a
mother always loves its child; but the lioness in the wood and
the bear by the stream full of their appetites love nothing but
themselves, with a tedious and lumbering instinct, and not with
the knowledge of what it is to die and what precautions must be
taken in the human state to keep the children of knowledge
from going crazy, wandering the earth in small bands waking
in the night for fear of noises and afraid of the water and the
sky. It takes more than a blind rat gnawing at the trap door to
tap the hidden spring of what people can do for each other.

mother

This is a letter from me to you which I didn't start out at. The
Investigating Committee has my name now because I joined the
L.A. G.L.F. not to mention Gay Women's Liberation in San
Francisco and other things I can't tell you about. They are afraid
because we are no longer separating out our private lives from
our public lives and they use always the tools of the liberals to
lobotomize the revolutionaries. To be a lesbian is to be implic-
itly revolutionary and I am just beginning to find out what that
means and so the slick men question and where they can they
jail or hospitalize. I'm not making this up, mother, I've seen it.

Mother I am not sure where I am. I think I am in love again
but sometimes it slips from me while I am out walking after
sundown and I look at the stars and feel as if no one will ever
look up and see me. The distances are too great, the buildings
are too long. There is a certain span where one hopes and after
that time of being able to hope one must give in to being
disappointed. One cannot reach in voids every day, day after
day, when day after day the silver fish that flashes in the bright
waters, which our fingers touch, is gone. She does not hear and
I walk sometimes, over my body a kind of ache after which the
time of hope is gone. The pain, once one has shrugged finally

and said "I hear nothing either," remains a kind of bitterness, a tearing hunger, final impoverishment, and that is what comes to me sometimes though I am still hoping as yet and not really preparing for rejection. But I am afraid and if I am going to be hurt again a year since Abby's going I want it to be simple, clean anesthetic

mother

what could I teach you but how to look gently beyond your own sorrow and fear into how human that is, and how to move past our terrible isolation. My dreams are of you by the sea and large buildings and elevators and the impossibility of it all, about misunderstandings and betrayals and fleeing and not being able to find the right apartment and lost in the alarm clock lost in the work.

mother

these things granted: that you will never speak to me and will never listen to my voice or the stories I mean to tell you and the understanding and the shield, the refuge, sanctuary, will never be given me, nor clemency—you will not know what I mean because you will answer "well, you have a way with words" and gradually the letters will drift back to being about how well you did in the last tennis tournament and my letters will be about nothing. With all of that it is enough you are a Sagittarius and not Scorpio because the women with their black hair, their fresh-bread-smelling breasts and their spider-lady eyes are almost always those (intertwined with the gentle Tauruses who come to rescue me when it becomes too hard). With the Scorpio women it is always life or death (but mother understand I have been hurt so by women because I am an intense asking person. I am always asking and if they had been men instead it would have been much much worse. What I am saying is do not harbor a reserve, a pity, because what a shame it is that she can't be making these motions with the opposite sex. If it had been Scorpio men, mother, I would be dead). And if you had been, had had that hooked jaw behind the careless breath, the accidental brushing of hips at dinner and the denial always of your intentions I would have been mad long past. It is well you are a Sagittarius and tried to do your best and although nothing came of it at least it is not rape itself having to be faced each

time you march across my memory, but only the sense of loss,
a certain kind of long moon sadness, a fading Japanese print of
it, with the sun going down and its red beams like searchlights
over the highways
              mother open this letter
              I cannot bring myself to write it

   Naomi Riverfingers turned to Inez in the Gay Liberation
Office and hugged her, having read this letter. Naomi had only
come to see how Inez was, to talk about a project Inez was
planning, in Tangier. Naomi was not altogether comfortable in
the Gay Liberation office; it was just to see Inez that she had
come. They would sit and talk together, Naomi and Inez, about
writing and revolutions, how the world is changing. Naomi
liked the idea of strong women coming together to make a
women's revolution. She liked it as an idea she might want to
put into a dance. Naomi quickly saw that there were not many
women in the Gay Liberation Front office. Inez was slowly coming to the same conclusion.
   Naomi was seventeen, she was a dancer, and she lived with
men. She had violet eyes and long black hair. They heard things
about a women's movement, but for Naomi it would mean
reconsidering the men. She wasn't ready. To Inez it meant
calling Naomi her sister, which wasn't true. Naomi was a friend
who had a strong taste for adventure. For Naomi knowing Inez
was an experiment.
   "I'm sorry. I can't," Naomi said after she read the letter.
Naomi was not a Scorpio, but she knew she would do as well;
she did not mean to get entangled in the part that was not an
adventure, in the part that is about: will we be working for a
good common life? She hugged Inez, and walked out. They
would meet next week.
   Inez folded the letter carefully into her notebook. Inez
watched from the window, Naomi and her hair walking down
the street.

The Phantom Child

Aviva Cantor

SEVEN YEARS AGO I became pregnant and had to decide whether or not to have an abortion.

The circumstances were these: I was thirty-one, not overage, and physically healthy. I'd been married five years. I was not poverty-stricken; financially, we could probably afford a child if we cut down on some of the material goodies.

I knew I was pregnant even before the second test verified it, knew it by a kind of sharp sucking-in feeling in the belly. I was only a week late, but I Knew. Still, I was not prepared for the shock I felt upon getting the official confirmation. I couldn't breathe. I could barely move. I was frozen with terror.

Yes or no? Day and night, I cried interminably. The only

Aviva Cantor, the daughter of Russian Jewish immigrants, graduated from Barnard College, having also attended the Hebrew University. Since receiving her master's degree in journalism from Columbia, she has served on the staff of the *London Jewish Chronicle*, *Israel Horizons*, and *Hadassah* magazine. A Socialist Zionist, she worked for the Jewish radical movement and edited the *Jewish Liberation Journal*. She is a founding editor of *Lilith*, the Jewish feminist magazine. She lives in Manhattan with her husband and two cats.

previous anxiety attack of such magnitude and scope I'd experienced was when my mother was dying piece by piece. Except that then, I escaped into work, into sleep, into eating, and into an intense romance (despite my guilt). This time, those escape routes were closed. My husband withdrew into a self-protective shell, sicklied o'er with the pale cast of pseudo-feminist rhetoric: "It's your body, you decide," he said. My terror was compounded by his withdrawal.

Yes or no? Back and forth like a tortured laboratory animal in an impossible maze: there are two exits, but both give the animal an electric shock.

Yes or no? Could I handle being responsible for another human being? And yet, could I actually destroy this life? And for such ... frivolous reasons? Could I be so selfish, so petty? When one of my cats gave birth to a kitten who couldn't walk without falling over, I could not bring myself to "put him to sleep."

Could I kill my own *child*? Excise it from my body like a cancer?

There is no doubt in my mind that part of me wanted a child.

For the preceding three years I had been involved body and soul in work for the Jewish radical movement. I'd had the feeling that all my previous experience and education were but a *hachshara*, a preparation for this great moment in history of which I was a part. At last, I thought, at last I found my Destiny. But now the movement was collapsing ... my Destiny had eluded me, it was a phantom. With the movement gone, the thought teased: "Well, if it happens, it happens."

Had I fallen, then, into the typical woman's trap of becoming pregnant because I perceived other paths to be blocked? Was it because everything was collapsing around me that I sought "refuge" in (creating a new) family? For I had no family: my parents were dead, my aunts and uncles far away in Canada and Russia, my siblings nonexistent. My husband was not "family": a couple is not a family.

Yes or no? As the thoughts swirl in my head, the fetus digs

its claws deeper into my uterus. I try not to think of this thing growing in me: growing means like a growth. Growing uncontrollably. I have no control over it. It will grow and grow and take over. Take over my body and my life.

What, oh what would my mother have said had she been alive—and thank God she was dead. This would have killed her—and me, too, had she known. But while my mother had been buried in 1966, she was alive inside my head, exhorting, begging, pleading, threatening, inducing guilt: nagging. How can you do this? You'll always regret it, always. You remember your Aunt Dora, how poor they were when they got married, it was the Depression? Well, she thought she was pregnant and took hot baths and her period came and she never got pregnant again. Some women only have one chance. (Remembering this, I immerse myself in super-hot baths and emerge faint and breathless but still pregnant. I also contemplate throwing myself down the stairs as Ava Gardner did in *The Snows of Kilimanjaro* but am too cowardly.) And didn't Simone de Beauvoir once say that the one thing she regretted was never having a child?

Not to speak of my mother herself, who lost the baby she was carrying three years after I was born. And who was still weeping over it when I was nine and she told me how babies are born (an appropriate confluence of information-sharing, of course). And whose passionate desire was to have another baby because she saw herself first and foremost as a Mother: who went to numerous doctors who stuck painful objects up her womb to Find Out Why she couldn't get pregnant again, but who never discovered The Secret. My mother who considered the childless to be victims of a cruel fate from which she was but one step removed. I was not to speak of children, *any* children, in front of Aunt Dora, it was too painful. Do you know, she almost went *crazy* when she found out she couldn't get pregnant?

Yes, women were always going Crazy when they couldn't get pregnant and here I was going crazy when I did. Our Fourmothers (foremothers) were constantly tearing their hair out when they had a prolonged nonintentional breather between children. (Of course, since the birth of daughters was never recorded, they may have been popping out unwanted girl-children, we'll never know.) And remember that scene in *The Wall* when Symka tries to tell Berson "It's impossible" for her to have children but he's busy discussing philosophy with a friend and tosses off a nonchalant "That's too bad, dear ... come and discuss Kant with us" and she flings herself into the bedroom to sob (while the men continue discussing philosophy).

At last I understand the look on my mother's face in the picture album I'd made at the age of nine in imitation of the one on *I Remember Mama* and as a talisman to transform us into a "happy family," American-style. Before she'd had the miscarriage, her face is all trusting smiles, love. Afterward, a look of hard determination, of steely stubbornness. A Never Again look. She blamed my father for the miscarriage and resolved never to trust him again. From now on, *she* would make the important decisions in the family, she would be Boss. And so it was.

How I hated her for it! How I wanted us to be a "happy family," i.e., where the man was boss. How I longed for Daddy, a gentle and peaceful man (whom I saw then as weak), to put his foot down when she began nagging. And yet ... maybe she was as she was because she knew that men cannot be counted on, that the basic unit in society has always been the mother and her children, that men are not dependable, men collapse, men withdraw, men abandon.

My mother had learned about abandonment a long, long time before this. She was born in Dubno (then Russian Poland) several years before World War I, the second of four girls. When she was only six, her father Lazar died of gangrene; her mother Esther of typhoid. Superimposed on this primal abandonment was a secondary one: the rest of the family, the uncles and aunts and grandparents, did not take in the four little girls, they left them to fend for themselves all alone, to dig for potatoes and to steal apples in the middle of the night. Why they abandoned the children is a family mystery. (Many, many years later, when one of the aunts survived the Holocaust and came to North America, she begged forgiveness of my mother, but had no explanation for the family's behavior.) And finally, the third abandonment. A committee of well-meaning Jews in Montreal decided to bring war orphans to Canada. They were farmed out to foster homes. The "people I lived with" (as my mother called them) treated her like a servant, forcing her to leave high school to take care of the children and the store. Another abandonment. Finally, she and her two younger sisters ran away.

The oldest sister, Gittel, had remained in Dubno because she was already in love with Shmuel, whom she later married. There's a picture in the album of their two sweet little boys who wrote my mother from Dubno how they were going to "make something of themselves." Fertilizer the whole family became. Shmuel, his arms torn off during a deportation. Gittel shot trying to reach him. And the little boys, nobody knows what happened to them, I don't even know their names. . . .

When I was twelve, my mother's first cousin came to New York to seek other survivors. He sat in the kitchen at night telling my parents horror stories by the hour. He and his mother had survived because a peasant hid them in a pit with other Jews for two years. You couldn't stand in the pit, only lean. Little did they know that I was listening. After that I graduated to my own extensive Holocaust research.

I remember how in *The Wall* Rutka and Mordechai decide to have a baby and how that baby makes it impossible for her (but not him) to be in the Resistance. (What if, God forbid, there's another Holocaust? If I have a child I'll have to worry about her getting killed or tortured, having to hide her, give her away. Without a child, the worst that can happen is that I'd be tortured.) Someone asks Rutka why did they deliberately have the baby in such brutal times and she tells them how Chaim, a worker in Vilna, had told her, "Rutka, you'll never know what it means to be a Jew until you're the parent of one."

For the preceding five years, I had written and lectured passionately about "Jewish values" and how we had to rediscover them and preserve them and develop them. Now I sought to find one Jewish reason to have this child when the idea so terrified me and I could not.

I thought of great scholars, thinkers, leaders. What if Ber Borochov's mother had had an abortion? Or Moshe's mother? Or Emma Goldman's? What if this baby is destined to do great deeds, to be a light unto the world?

What if my baby is the Messiah?

(I don't have enough to feel guilty about, I also have to lacer-
ate myself for denying Redemption to the world.)

My friend Fanya, who is well along in years, listens to the
whole story. Like all my women friends, she is warm and sup-
portive. She tells me this is not a world to bring a child into.

But wasn't it always thus? Didn't people in every period of
history think their times the worst? My mother told me how
she'd convinced my father that it was time to become parents.
My father, having married at forty-two after an enjoyable bache-
lorhood, hadn't given children much thought; moreover, he was
underemployed. "Let's wait for the right time," said Joseph.
"There'll never *be* a right time," from Naomi. So I was conceived and brought into the world, loved and welcomed. The
pictures of my mother in the album have a "hey, I actually did
it" look on her thin girlish face. My father looks pleasantly
surprised and vastly relieved: it wasn't so bad, after all.

Fanya doesn't feel guilty about her nine illegal abortions, she
tells me. And yet, had she also aborted her only child, a daughter, who would be taking care of her now? If I abort this child,
I'll be alone in my old age. I'll be a shopping-bag lady on the
streets of New York, a prey of muggers. I'll be helpless, a
prisoner in a Bergman nursing home. I'll be dying of cancer in
great pain with no one to even bring me exit pills.

My mother, though, did have a daughter and that was as good
as having none at all. My mother died of cancer in great pain,
and I didn't help her. I hadn't known what to do, I was afraid
of the doctors and nurses, afraid to pester them again and again
for more morphine lest they vindictively cut it off entirely. Why
didn't I scream at the doctor? find another one? ten other doctors? fifty other treatments? Why did I abandon her as she'd
been abandoned so many times before?

So I blew my last chance to reconcile, to atone. To make up
for having been an insensitive and inconsiderate daughter. For
having tormented her with words of rage when we fought, telling her how worthless her life was because she didn't have more
children and how glad I was that she'd had a miscarriage and
lost the baby because she would have made my sister suffer as

she made me suffer. Every word a poisoned dart. But somehow, this revenge had no sweetness, no relief. She would cry. And then I would feel my guts turning over with pity and guilt, and I would cry. And we'd swear never to fight again ... until the next time.

There in the hospital, she lies dying and I can't talk to her. We are playing a Game. I don't tell her she's dying to "protect" her; she doesn't tell me she knows she's dying to "protect" me. The doctors have told me this is the best way. One night I dream we are shopping and she buys me a coat because, she says, she'll never be able to buy me anything ever again. I wake up sobbing: I realize she knows. . . . But I do nothing. I am paralyzed. I cannot accept that she is dying.

If I'd had a good relationship with my mother, wouldn't I want to be a mother myself? Am I afraid of repeating with *my* child the relationship I had with my mother? Do I want to have an abortion to spite my mother (even though she will never know)? Or do I want to have the baby to placate her? to diminish my guilt (it can never be removed) by doing something that she considered the Right Thing? To do something *for* her? To do this thing that I don't want to do as punishment for killing her so that I can stop punishing myself in other ways? Do I see having a child as a punishment? ("May your children treat you as you treat me," was one of her favorite curses.) As penance?

Although I can find no Jewish reason to have the child, I find plenty of Jewish reasons for having an abortion. Consulting my trusty resource *Birth Control and Abortion in Jewish Law,* I confirm that abortion is permitted when the mother's physical *or mental* health is in danger. Then it's a matter of self-defense and the mother's life comes first. Didn't the rabbis permit abortions during the Holocaust because a pregnant mother's life was automatically in danger? And further, doesn't the Talmud say that if two people are in a desert and one has a bottle of water, and if sharing it with his companion would save neither, he (the bottle owner) has the right to drink it all himself, because his life is worth just as much as his friend's. Isn't my life worth saving just as much as the baby's? I wouldn't go so far as saying more, but as much. . . . See, all those years of studying Talmud and learning *pilpul* have not been in vain.

After a month of agonizing, it comes to this: it's either me or the child. And I have a right to live.

I have to sacrifice the child in self-defense.

February 4, 1972. A bright crisp morning eight days before my thirty-second birthday (makes it easy to remember, as if I needed that *zets* every year). My husband drives me to the doctor's office. Getting out of the car, I have a brief flash of running away screaming, "No, I won't do it!" like April in *The Best of Everything* (the movie not the book).

But I didn't run away.

The operation takes all of twenty minutes, only about five of which are painful. I'm willing to endure the pain: I deserve it. During these endless minutes, I see myself in Block X in Auschwitz, being sterilized by Dr. Mengele or a cohort, without anesthesia or other medication. And Dr. Brewda (the brave woman doctor there: not for naught have I done my Holocaust research) holds my hand and says, "Be brave, my child, just a little longer." I hold the nurse's hand very tight and she actually squeezes back. I love her like a mother, a real mother, who is tender and loving, not nagging, pushing, yelling, rejecting.

It's all over.

I resolve not to ask or think about what they do with the fetuses after the "procedure" as they call it, otherwise I'll weep forever.

As I walk out, I feel I've made the first adult decision of my entire life.

P. S.: Five years later. I go to a NOW-New York abortion rap. A woman there talks of the illegal abortion she had thirty years ago. "You never forget," she said. "Every year you think of its birthday, how old it would be now.

"It's a phantom child."

First Love

Andrea Dworkin

> Yet if I care to care
> force loving into being, then I pry open
>
> all memory's charnal house of sores
> —Robin Morgan, "Credo"

E,

It is so hard to write you. Why am I doing it this way, not
intending ever to send this letter, still with one eye to publication, a grand concept for a book in some sense, and still with
one eye, that poets conscience, to a future which becomes in-
creasingly impossible to imagine. It seems the only way I can
bear the passion behind the language, the memory, the desire,

"First Love," copyright © 1978, 1980 by Andrea Dworkin, is from Dworkin's
epistolary novel-in-progress, Ruins. Her published works include Woman Hating,
Our Blood: Prophecies and Discourses on Sexual Politics, and the new womans broken
heart. She is currently writing a feminist analysis of pornography. Lines from
"Credo," copyright © 1972, are from Monster: Poems by Robin Morgan, Random
House and Vintage Books (1972), and are used with permission.

the only way not to be burnt up by what I feel. You come over me in waves of memory, especially when I sleep, and I wake up in sweat and trembling, not knowing where I am, not remembering the years that separate us.

So often I wanted to write, dear E, now I am this person, I look this way (you wouldnt like it), I do this, I feel this, lists, details, it was warm or cold on that day when that happened and then my life changed in this way and that—but I cant, I never could, and I cant now. In writing this letter, not to be sent, perhaps I can find the signs that will tell you who I have become.

Dearest E, I loved you. Now that love is memory, sometimes haunting, sometimes buried, forgotten, as if dead. I see yr face, yes, I know, as it was, I remember you as I remember the sun, always, burned in my brain; somehow you are part of me, mixed up in me, for all the days of my life. I left you when you were life to me, when to be physically separated from you was sheer and consuming pain, as if a limb had been cut off, amputated. Leaving you was the hardest, and perhaps the bravest, thing I have ever done.

Dearest E, I want to describe in some way the *drive to become* that impelled me to go to you and to go from you, that has driven me from person to person, place to place, bed to bed, street to street, and which somehow coheres, finds cogency and true expression, when I say, I want to write, or I want to be a writer, or I am a writer. I want to tell you that this *drive to become* is why I left you and why I never returned as I had promised.

I was 19 when I knew you. I wanted to be a writer. I didnt want to go mad or suffer or die. I was 19. I wasnt afraid of anything, or, as I sometimes thought, I was equally afraid of everything so that nothing held a special terror and no action that interested me was too dangerous. I wanted to do everything that I could imagine doing, everything I had ever read about, anything any poet or hero had ever done. I loved Rimbaud. I loved Plato and through him Socrates. I loved Sappho. I loved Dostoevsky, and sweet Shelley, and Homer. I loved cold Valery, and warm D.H. Lawrence, and tortured Kafka, and raging tender Ginsberg.

I didnt have questions in words in my mind. I had instead

these surging impulses that welled up and were spent. I had a hunger to know and to tell and to do everything that could be done. I had an absolute faith in my own will to survive.

What I didnt want to do was to say, look Im this height, and I went to school here and there, and then that year I did this and that, and then I knew so and so, and then the next one was so and so, and then this situation occurred, and then that one, and the room was red and blue and three by four, and then I was that old and went there and did that and then that and then, naturally, that.

I wanted instead to write books that were fire and ice, wind sweeping the earth. I wanted to write books that, once experienced, could not be forgotten, books that would be cherished as we cherish the most exquisite light we have ever seen. I had contempt for anything less than this perfect book that I could imagine. This book that lived in my imagination was small and perfect and I wanted it to live in person after person, forever. Even in the darkest of human times, it would live. Even in the life of one person who would sustain it and be sustained by it, it would live. I wanted to write a book that would be read even by one person, but always. For the rest of human time some one person would always know that book, and think it beautiful and fine and true, and then it would be like any tree that grows, or any grain of sand. It would *be*, and once it was it would never not be.

In my secret longings there was another desire as well, not opposite but different, not the same but as strong. There would be a new social order in which people could live in a new way. There would be this new way of living which I could, on the edges of my mind and in the core of my being, imagine and taste. People would be free, and they would live decent lives, and those lives would not be without pain, but they would be without certain kinds of pain. They would be lives untouched by prisons and killings and hunger and bombs. I imagined that there could be a world without institutionalized murder and systematic cruelty.

I imagined that I could write a book that would make such a world possible.

So my idea of my book that I would write sometimes took another turn. It had less to do with the one person who would always, no matter how dark the times, somewhere be reading it, and it had more to do with here and now, change, transformation, revolution. I had some idea of standing, as one among many, my book as my contribution, at one point in history and changing its course and flow. I thought, imagine a book that could have stopped the Nazis, imagine a life strong and honest enough to enable one to make such a book. I began to think of writing as a powerful way of changing the human condition instead of as a beautiful way of lamenting it or as an enriching or moving way of describing it.

I had wanted to make Art, which was, I had been led to believe, some impeccable product, inhuman in its process, made by madmen, inhuman in its final form, removed from life, without flaw, perfect, crystal, monumental, pain turned beautiful, sweat turned cold and stopped in time, suffering turned noble and stopped in time.

But I also wanted to write a book that could be smelled and felt, that was total human process, the raw edges left as raw as any life, real, with a resolution that took one to a new beginning, not separate from my life or the lives of the multitudes who were living when I was living. I wanted to write a book that would mean something to people, not to dead people past or future, but to living people, something that would not only sustain them but change them, not only enhance the world in the sense of ornament, but transform, redefine, reinvent it.

When I knew you I was 19. I did not know many things. How could I? I wanted to make Art, and I had a passion for life, and I wanted to act in the world so that it would be changed, and I knew that those things nourished one another but I did not know how. I did not know that they could be the same, that for me they must be the same, for they all had to live in this one body as one or they could not live at all.

The teachers I had had did not know or tell the truth. They did not care about how artists lived in the world. They seemed to find the lives of artists shoddy and cheap, even as they found works of art marble and pure. They never talked about art as if it had anything at all to do with life. They thought that the texts were there to be analyzed, or memorized, one after another. They thought that art was better than life, better than the artists who made the art and lived their lives. They had no notion of process, how one made something out of the raw impulses of the imagination, how one ransacked or chiseled experience in search of meaning, how one cried out or mourned or raged in images, in language, in ideas. So they taught that ideas were fixed, dead, sacred or profane, right or wrong, to be studied but not created, to be learned but not lived. They did not seem to know that the whole of human literature is a conversation through time, each voice speaking to the whole of human living.

And I did not understand so much. I did not understand, for instance, that people really die. I did not understand that death is irrevocable. I did not understand the grief of those who remember the dead. I did not understand that the horrors of history, those textbook cases of genocide, rape, and slaughter, would happen in my lifetime to people I knew. And so I did not understand that the earth is real, and that what happens on it happens to real people just like me. I did not understand that as I grew older my life would continue with me. I thought instead that each event in my life was discrete, each person of that moment only. I did not understand that the people I knew I would always know, one way or another, for the rest of my life. I did not know that one never stops knowing anything, that time continues to pass relentlessly, though without any particular vengeance, taking each of us with it. I did not understand then that there is no choice, that one always writes for the living, that there is no other way to create the future or to redeem the past. I also did not know that each human life is precious, brief, an agony, filled with pain and struggle, sorrow and loss.

I love books the way I love nature. I can imagine now that someday there will be no nature, at least not as we knew it together on Crete, no mysterious ocean, no luminous sky, no stark and unsettled mountains. I can imagine now that a time will come, that it is almost upon us, when no one will love books, that there will be no people who need them the way some of us need them now—like food and air, sunshine and warmth. It is

no accident, I think, that books and nature (as we know it) may
disappear simultaneously from human experience. There is no
mind-body split.

I never think of you without remembering the ocean. It is an
emblem for me of that time in my life, of the depth and tumult
of my feelings, of how my life broke out of my skin and beyond
itself into an unknown, primal realm. The ocean does not signi-
fy anything whimsical, cheap, romantic, or self-indulgent. It
signifies the true mysteries, not the mystifying ones. It signifies
the light years between galaxies, as well as ones tie to everything
on earth. It signifies ones tie to the enormity of being, to the
mystery of this universe—stars, moon, sun, black holes, rings
around Saturn. It makes one aware that this universe is a tapes-
try of the most awesome magnificence. It does compel awe.

It has always been to me, the ocean, overwhelming, monstrous, deep, dark, green and black, so foreign that it requires
respect, silence, humility. It is boundless and deep, no human
sense of time can circumscribe it, it rumbles with cavernous
sounds, it is filled with grotesque forms, luminous colors,
shapes that defy imagination. All of the life in it is menacing,
compelling, exquisite, with nothing consoling.

I love books too in the same way. They are the human ocean,
life before and through and beyond this self, footsteps on the
sand in the largest desert, the wind blows, the tracks are sometimes obscured, covered over, hidden, waves of human experience in which one drowns, which carry one, against which one
struggles with every life force, forced sometimes under, struggling for any breath, the weight of that water bearing down
mercilessly on one, or floating, effortless, calm, at the precise
point between earth and sky. They are the human ocean of our
time, the quest of people through time to know, ask, feel, survive, to survive beyond the limits of an awful, or insignificant,
or invisible, or painful or ordinary life, beyond the limits of this
mortal body, sick, needful, the vessel of so much suffering and
despair. They are the meaning of life as fully as we can render
it. They are the human ocean of everything that has been
experienced, thought, felt, wondered, suffered, recognized,
realized, imagined, affirmed—messages sent through time

from one finite human who asked questions, attempted answers, described, felt, needed, wanted, endured, resisted, to
another who is different yet the same.

A book is at once connected to eternity and to one persons
mortal flesh. It is whatever this flow is that connects us one to
the other throughout human time, but it is also the fruit of one
persons specific moment. It is the present, just as the ocean,
whatever it was before, whatever it will be later, exists for the
one who sees it when she sees it. Think of it, each book is what
it is for one person to be alive, in her particular present, what
it is, anguish, joy, fear, duration, process, hope. Each person
asks the question of her time and place. Each persons life inhab-
its and informs every word written. Sitting somewhere, ancient
Greece or Manhattan 1974, hoping that the words will come and
make the feeling in the body bearable, fill the need, make the
day or night endurable, that one will be able to give shape to the
chaos of feeling, needing, not knowing. The world takes form
when one writes, for the writer. The world becomes knowable,
its meaning revealed and affirmed. Struggling with the present,
with death, with pain, with love, articulating the present, ima-
gining it as it is and as it might be, asking every question but
also taking time itself and giving it shape, substance, weight:
revealing it to those who share it.

Ive been reading Kafka, his letter to his father, his diaries, his
letters to his woman friend Felice. Discovering the person behind those monuments of consciousness, discovering the tortured man who subsumed the person. Discovering the fragile,
vulnerable, terrified being behind those monuments of ravaged
and ravaging male consciousness. What is it about genius that
it can inhabit the body of a tubercular, frightened, insignificant
German Jew and that he can then force the world into a new
shape so profound, so recognizable, its vision so deeply rooted
in the nature of things as they are, so tangled in the gut and
psyche of life as we experience it, that one says, I dont know
where this story ends and life begins, I dont know the difference
anymore between this story and life, I dont know at what point
I became part of this story and forgot that it is print on a page,
I dont know how these words were ever put together this way,

or how these images were formed, but I know that this writing embodies the world as profoundly as a male could embody it in words.

To me, the real mystery is, what made him a writer, how did he become a writer, what in his life determined it, how was it even possible. He was a writer, how can I say it, the way that a fish is a fish. Not fragmented, a bit here, a bit there, sometimes choosing this, sometimes doing that, not with other ways of being, e.g. sometimes we walk and sometimes we sit and sometimes we run. He was a writer as a fish is a fish, always, all the time, knowing nothing else, without any other possibility. Imagine being a writer like that. (In a footnote I read: "Kafka was survived by three sisters. All three sisters, including Kafka's favorite, Ottla, and the larger part of their families, were killed by the Nazis.")

The first book I remember reading was *Squanto and the Indians.* The Pilgrims, an austere religious group, came to Amerika from England where they were persecuted for their religious beliefs. The voyage was long and hard and many died and many more were gravely ill. In the new land life was no easier. Winters were freezing and hard, the soil was barren and nothing they planted grew. They suffered terribly, starving and dying. Then an Indian named Squanto befriended them. He showed them how to plant corn and how to live off the land. He helped them to plant their crops. They reaped a good harvest which Amerikans commemorate as Thanksgiving. Then they slaughtered Squanto and his tribe.

On the one hand, the genius, the kindness, the fragile, single human being who can, through an act of being, a simple act of simple giving—writing, teaching, planting—do so much more than endure, who can transform, who can make life both possible and meaningful. Then, always, on the other hand, vicious slaughter, insane, impossible, relentless slaughter.

Squanto, Kafka, the Nazis, those first English interlopers, the tanks entering Athens, my friends, fragile human beings every one, rounded up like cattle, herded into jails, there tortured, there their bodies broken, terror, violation, killings and ravag-

ings on a grand scale, always the grand scale, mad ambition,
hundreds or thousands or millions, victims, tanks, rifle butts,
machine guns, searches, seizures, arrests, terror, death. I am
always asking, will it never end. I am always vowing, we will end
it.

I remember one letter you wrote me after the colonels took
over. You said that yr life was bitter, that the earth had turned
to poison. You said, what do you know about any of this? And,
after all, what did I know? I didnt know then most of what I have
had to learn—slow, dimwitted, dull, fighting always the romantic self-indulgences into which I was born. I didnt know then
that I wont be spared anything. I didnt know then that none of
us will be spared anything. Anyway, there is really no way to
describe white Amerikan ignorance (and it is not only middle-
class, it is *Amerikan,* an ignorance democratically distributed).
Who would believe that this ignorance is real as villages burn
and people die? And there is really no way to talk about white
Amerikan innocence, except to say that some of us have lost it.
Except to say that years later I learned that I was a woman, and
so learned most of everything.

I came to Crete. I was 19. I was running from Amerika. I was
dislocated, wounded, confused.
  I had spent four days in jail, yes, only four days, New York
Citys Womens House of Detention, a brutal, dirty, archaic jail.
I had been arrested for demonstrating at the United States
Mission to the United Nations. Adlai Stevenson, then the conscience of liberal Amerika, walked by us into the building as the
police dragged us away. Inside the jail I was given a brutal
internal examination by two male doctors. As a result I bled for
15 days after that, terrified, afraid to go to a doctor, afraid of
doctors, afraid to tell my parents, afraid to ask anyone for help.
At that time I was living with two men, and they had what Ive
since learned to appreciate as a typical male reaction to Blood
Down There, a kind of *his*terical stiffening of every muscle, a
stony indifference, a strained withdrawing of mind and body.
But at the time I thought that they, two particular persons, were
horrified by me, one particular person, who was bleeding,

bleeding, bleeding. At that time, I also had another lover, an older black man named Arthur. I liked him a lot, and so on the phone he said, where you been, and I said, the House of D, and they did that and that and that to me, and he said, white girl, thats what they do. I felt his contempt for me, and also knew more than I could stand to know about his real life, and so I never saw him again. Wherever I turned trying to say what had happened to me, I met that same contempt, or silence, or indifference—but of course, I always turned to men. When finally, choked and enraged, filled with fury and confusion, I did turn to two women (I barely knew them), they knew viscerally, absolutely, what had happened to me, they knew what it had been. But then, in those years, I didnt turn to women very often or understand that men could not dare to know.

I felt alone, enraged, furious, violated, hurt, and so afraid. I did not know how to contain or to understand what had happened to me. I didnt know how to contain or to understand what I had seen happening in that jail to other women. There was no language to describe it.

There are themes in ones life, themes which resonate. One theme in my life, an important piece of who I am, the Nazi slaughter, resonated then. What had happened to me, the blood, my fear, the brutality, conjured up the Nazi doctors who had tortured flesh of my flesh and blood of my blood, and an aunt who had survived to tell me, retching in terror and memory. The doctors in that jail when they were abusing me—my aunts Nazi violation resonated then; in the nightmares I had after—it resonated then. It was what it was, the violation of one woman by two particular men, but it also conjured up that near history of my living flesh and so it had a resonance beyond itself—a sound, an echo, through 6,000,000 bodies.

I didnt know then about the 9,000,000 witches burned alive, or the billions of women raped, abused, bloodied, and abandoned all over this planet. I didnt know then. I felt it, womans fury, but I couldnt name it, or call it out, and so I anguished, isolated, confused, unable to name, the very power of speech, and so of knowing, taken away from me. I didnt know then that we women were a sisterhood united in blood and toil on this earth, each one speechless, experiencing the unspeakable, robbed of the power of naming and so of speaking and so of knowing. I knew then only about the several hundred women in that one jail, each speechless, each experiencing the unspeakable, robbed of the power of naming and so of speaking and so of knowing. This is happening to *us*, I remember was the phrase that turned over and over again in my mind those days in jail, this is happening to *us*.

A Jew, a woman, my ties to the dead, my commitment to the living. There is no place on earth, no day or night, no hour or minute, when one is not a Jew or a woman. There is no time or place on this earth that does not resonate through 6,000,000 bodies tortured and gassed, through 9,000,000 bodies tortured and burned.

In all the years Ive been involved with leftist politics, in Greece, Holland, England, and Amerika, you were the only man who ever told me this story: "I was a member of the young communists, an illegal group in Greece since the Civil War; there was a woman comrade, and we had all done actions with her, and slept with her, and then she had a political difference with the others and they, who had been her lovers, refused to speak to her or to associate with her, she was ostracized and cursed; and I quit because I thought, *if these are the people who are making the revolution and if this is the way they act, then I dont want to live in the kind of world they would make.*"

I didnt understand this story until many years later. When I knew you, I was a committed leftist. I had seen many women used then abandoned, I had been used then abandoned myself; still, I could not make sense of what I had seen or of my own experience, I did not make sense of it for several more years. The story you told me stayed with me, embarrassed me somewhat because I didnt entirely understand what you had done or why you had done it. Still, I liked you for it.

I learned from you, from my landlady, that ancient ruined woman, that the Nazis had come to Crete because (as reasons go) they wanted a small airstrip on the island. In the course of their occupation, they did carnage, annihilated whole villages— sometimes they killed all of the men and boys and left the women and girls (when they finally did leave, after rape) to mourn, to go hungry, to survive mutilated as if each husband

and boy child killed were a limb that had been severed and she, the woman, was left with the stumps bleeding.

I did not mistake where I was or what had happened there. Each day there was an echo, almost hissing in the air, the Nazi slaughter. Each day that slaughter was sounded in the bodies of the old women, dressed in black, mourning still, remembering still, faces older than this old earth, faces weighted down with the years of loss and murder. And before that, the Cretans were murdered by the Turks, 400 years of occupation and tyranny. And the Cretans murdered the Jews—each year over the centuries pogroms on Easter avenged the death of that other Jew, Jesus. And of course the women belonged to the occupied or to the occupiers, the living or the dead. The women were murdered and the women were raped and the women were left to mourn their dead. It was the human family, bound together in a web of murder and pain, and each member of that family had murders mark on her.

Living on Crete brought me to a new sensitivity, acute and intolerable. I felt the resonances of those dead, all of them, and the lives of those living, all of them, in my own body, and I came to know who I was—that self tied to the past which was ever present in a way that was not melancholy or romantic. In Amerika, each person is new, like hemp before the rope is made. On Crete the rope was used, bloodstained, it smelled of everything that had ever touched it.

And so we, you and I, in ways so different, each were suffused with Crete. You loved the land, the mountains and what they held, the sea and what it brought and took away. Amerikans for the most part dont know what that means. The land moved you, you knew its story, and you were bound to it. I was Amerikan, Jew, female, who knew nothing at first of the land and what it held—I grew up first in a city, cement, telephone poles, and then in a suburb, boxlike houses, small plotted lawns, an occasional tree. But yr land and its people entered into me and in me I began to discover the memory, passion, and experience of all the peoples of whom I was a part. In that way we touched each other, and in that way we were brother and sister.

But now comes the harder part, how we were lovers. Who was

I then, I barely remember her, that woman. She doesnt live in me very much anymore.

I was in Greece (Athens, Piraeus, Crete). I was 19. I wrote. I saw, for the first time, the mountains, the light, that luminous Greek light, the ocean which from the shore was filled with bright strips of color. I had many lovers, all men.

I was a person who always had her legs open, whose breast was always warm and accommodating, who derived great plea-sure from passion with tenderness, without tenderness, with brutality, with violence, with anything any man had to offer.

I was a person who always had her legs open, who lived entirely from minute to minute, from man to man. I was a person who did not know that there was real malice in the world, or that people were driven—to cruelty, to vengeance, to rage. I had no notion at all of the damage that people sustain and how that damage drives them to do harm to others.

I was a person who was very much a woman, who had internal-ized certain ways of being and of feeling, ways given to her through books, movies, the full force of media and culture— and through the real demands of real men.

I was a person who was very much a woman, accommodating, adoring of mens bodies, needful, needing above all to be fucked, to be penetrated, loving that moment more than any other.

I was a person who was very much a woman, who loved men, who loved to be fucked, who gloried in cock, who called every sexual act, tender, violent, brutal, the same name, "lovemak-ing."

I thought, how can I even explain it now, that life was what Miller and Mailer and Lawrence had said it was. I believed them. I thought that they were creative and brilliant truth tellers. I thought that the world was as they said it was, that to be a hero, one must be as their heroes were. I wanted to be a hero-writer, outside the bounds of stifling convention. I thought that I was becoming as they were by doing that which they admired and advocated. I did not know, or feel, or realize what was being done to me by those who were as they were. I did not experience myself or my body as my own.

I did not feel what was being done to me until, many years

later, I read Kate Milletts *Sexual Politics*. Something in me moved then, shifted, changed forever. Suddenly I discovered something inside me, to feel what I had felt somewhere but had had no name for, no place for. I began to feel what was being done to me, to experience it, to recognize it, to find the right names for it. I began to know that there was nothing good or romantic or noble in the myths I was living out; that, in fact, the effect of these myths was to deprive me of my bodily integrity, to cripple me creatively, to take me from myself. I began to change in a way so fundamental that there was no longer any place for me in the world—I was no longer a woman as I had been a woman before. I experienced this change as an agony. There was no place for me anywhere in the world. I began to feel anger, rage, bitterness, despair, fury, absolute fury, as I began to know that they, those writers and their kind, had taken cruelty and rape and named it for me, "life," "sex," "lovemaking," "freedom," and I hated them for it, and I hate them for it still.

There was a particular part of *Sexual Politics* that began this change in me, a small moment in a vast book. Millett described Henry Millers depictions of sex acts in a voice I had never heard before. She said, simply it seems now, *look at this, this is what he does and then this is what he calls it.* Then I saw it—the cruelty of it—as what it was, no matter what others, the whole world, called it. No one who has ever had this experience denies the revolutionary power of language or the absolute importance of naming, or the violation which inheres in being robbed of speech even as one experiences the unspeakable.

E, you see, this is what is so hard to describe to those who have not experienced it: that as a woman, ones body is *colonialized,* ones flesh is actually taken from one, named and owned by others, all experience *their* experience, all value *their* value. The process for a woman of becoming whole, herself, cannot even be described as reclaiming ones flesh (ones land), ones personality (ones land), ones own integrity (ones land), because one has been deprived of both core and vessel for too long, over too many generations and centuries. One can say that the French colonialized Algeria, and conjure up a vision of a free Algeria, because one has a memory that the French did not always own Algeria. But Algerian women have no memory of a time when they were not owned by Algerian men. Algerian women, and all women, have been robbed of any memory of freedom. Our bondage is so ancient, so absolute, it is every inch of the past that we can know. So we cannot reclaim, because no memory of freedom animates us. We must invent, reinvent, create, imagine the scenarios of our own freedom against the will of the world. At the same time we must build the physical and psychic communities that will nourish and sustain us. For in reality, as the Three Marias of Portugal have written, "there is no bread for us at the table of man," that is, unless we are first willing to prepare and serve the meal. And, of course, the men own the bread and the table and the women who serve and the beds we must sleep in at night.

I am saying that my body was colonialized, owned by others, imperialists who robbed it of its richest resources—possessed, taken, conquered, all the words those male writers use to describe ecstatic sexuality. And I am saying that I was that slave woman, that caricature of a human being, that servant whose core and vessel belonged to those who had conquered it. I was that slave woman who accepted the conquerors naming of my experience and called it, their dreadful brutality, their possessing and taking, "lovemaking," "ecstasy," "freedom." That was the woman you knew.

I tremble when I know that you loved her, and only her. I am afraid, cynical, bitter, when I want to believe that you were also better than that, as I was in some not yet living part of myself; when I think, over these 10 long years, this is a man who could know me now, who could love me now, whom I could know and love. In some part of me—a part I do not dare trust or respect— I believe, but am also afraid to believe, and also do not believe, that in you there lives one who is not committed to oppressing women. I dare allow myself, sometimes, to imagine (or is it remember) that we did touch each other in those hidden parts.

I arrived in Athens on my 19th birthday. I was very lonely. There had been riots in Athens, Papandreou Senior had been ousted from the government by King Constantine; the people rioted in protest. I met an officer in the Greek Army, we drank ouzo on a mountain top, we looked down on the thousands in the

streets, then we went to some crummy hotel and he fucked me.
It was a horrible moment afterwards, when I looked at him and
saw him and said, you really hate women you know. I saw the
muscles in his arm tighten, and the impulse to strike animate
his body, and his insane vanity, and then the decision that it
wasnt important after all. I had never known that, that there
were men who hated women, and yet at that moment I knew that
I had just been fucked by one. It was the gift of my 19th birthday.
I never forgot that man or that moment.

There seemed to be only two possibilities. To be a housewife
like my mother, limited, boring, irritating. How we have been
robbed of our mothers, I knew only the narrowness of her life,
nothing of its depths. She was kept from me, cloistered,
covered from my gaze by impenetrable layers of cultural lies.
She was kept from me. We were set against each other, every
mother Clytemnestra, every daughter Electra. I did not want to
be her. I wanted to be Miller, or Mailer, or Rimbaud, my Rimbaud, a hero, nothing of the world closed to me, an initiator, an
inventor, a creator. No one said the truth: phallic initiator,
phallic inventor, phallic creator. Those were the false, vicious
choices.

There were so many, and each was the one I was with. One after
another, over and over.
    I had been on Crete maybe three months when I first saw you.
Glorious, golden moment. I was drinking vermouth at an out-
door café. The day was dark and drizzly. You stepped out of a
doorway, looked around, stepped back in out of sight. You were
so beautiful, so incredibly beautiful, radiating light, yr eyes so
huge and deep and dark. I dont remember how we began to talk
or when we first made love, but it really did happen that way,
I saw you and the earth stood still, everything in me opened up
and reached out to you. Later I understood that you were too
beautiful, that yr physical beauty interfered with yr life, stood
between you and it, that it created an almost unbridgeable distance between you and others, even as it drew them to you.
    I was happy. I loved you. I was consumed by my love for you.

It was as if I breathed you instead of the air. Sometimes I felt a peace so great that I thought it would lift me off the earth. I felt in you and through you and because of you. Later, when you were so much a part of me that I didnt know where you ended and I began, I would still sometimes step back and marvel at yr physical beauty. Sometimes I would think that my life would be complete if I would always be able to look at you.

I dont know what you felt. I never questioned it or thought about it. What was admitted of no other possibility. What was had no words, no language. I remember that a time came when we no longer made love all day and all night, but only twice each day, once in the night and once in the morning, and I asked a woman I knew if she thought you still loved me.

I was ecstatic with you. What are the words? I loved you, I breathed you. What does that mean? What does it mean that two people, a man and a woman, who share no common language, come together and for almost a year share every day in an erotic ecstasy, die in each other, are born in each other, rise and fall and intertwine and cry out, breathe in and through each other, are nourished and sustained by mutual touch, are one in the way that the sun is one, when the coming together of those two people embodies every possible feeling, sound, silence?

And towards the end, before I left, when we began to fight, to have those monstrous wordless fights composed of a passion as large as the love we were—what was that? What does it mean that two people, a man and a woman, who require each other for the sake of life itself, like water or food or air, who do not share a common language, who speak only pidgin bits of French, English, Greek, but know each other completely, understand whole sentences and speeches composed in three languages at a time, begin to tear and rend each others insides—using gestures, fragments, emblems, signs. What does it mean when these two people, a man and a woman, have a fight, a monstrous fight, that lasts all night, through every fury and silence (but he will not leave her, he will not go from her house), a fight that begins when she tries to kill him, literally to tear the life out of him with her bare hands because he dares to touch her (and she would die without that touch), and their pain is so great, so physically unbearable, that still they have only each other, because only they in all the world share that pain and grief? What is that?

I swear I dont know, all these years later I still dont know. When I left you I thought that the pain would kill me, literally, physically. I felt a physical pain so acute, all through my body, in every part of it, for well over a year I felt this pain, it kept me awake, it filled my sleep, nothing around me was as real as the pain inside me, and still, ten years later, sometimes I wake up from a dream that has forced me to feel it again.

I have always wanted to know why I left you. I have wanted to know what in me was stronger than my love for you—what nameless drive, in me but not claimed by me as part of me, moved me to decide to leave you, to make the arrangements necessary to leave you, to walk to the boat, to get on the boat, to stay on the boat even as you called to me from the shore.

I remember that you hated it that I was a writer. It was all right as long as it meant that I had been at home all day, nothing more. But when a small collection of my poetry was privately printed by some friends, on the day I held that book in my hands, you hated me. You were jealous as you never would have been of another lover. (I remember that one night I woke up to find you rifling through my papers, searching fiercely, not able to read English—searching for what?—searching, I think, for the strength that did not breathe in you and because of you.)

I dont know exactly when or why yr anger took explicit sexual forms. You began fucking me in the ass, brutally, brutally. I began to have rectal bleeding. I told you, I implored you. You ignored my screams of pain, my whispers begging you to stop. You said, a woman who loves a man stands the pain. I was a woman who loved a man; I submitted, screamed, cried out, submitted. To refuse was, I thought, to lose you, and any pain was smaller than that pain, or even the contemplation of that pain. I wondered even then, how can he take such pleasure when I am in such pain. My pain increased, and so did yr pleasure.

Once you stopped speaking to me (had I resisted in some way?).

When finally (was it a day or two?) you came to me I waited for an explanation. Instead you touched me, wanting to fuck me, as if no explanation were necessary, as if I was yrs to take, no matter what. Had I been strong enough, I would have killed you with my bare hands. As it was, you were weak in yr surprise, and I hurt yr neck badly. I was glad (Im still glad). We fought the whole night long, with long stretches of awful silence and a desperate despair. In the course of that night you told me that we would marry. It was towards morning, and after you had raped me as is the way with men who are locked in a hatred which is bitter and without mercy, you said, thats all thats left, to get married, isnt that what people do, isnt this the way that married people feel. Bored and dead and utterly bound to each other. Miserable and sick and without freedom or hope. Yr body moving above me during that rape, my body absolutely still in resistance, my eyes wide open staring at you in resistance, and you said, now Ill fuck you the way I fuck a whore, now youll know the difference, how I loved you before and how I hate you now. I said, numb and dead and dying, no, I wont marry you, I cant stand this, its worse than anything. You said, we cant be apart, youll see, it wont be so bad. I remember that then you lay between my legs, both of us on our backs, and we didnt move until dawn. Then you left.

The next day I took my razor blades to a woman friend and I said, keep these, I dont want to be silly but I think that at any minute I wont be able to stand it anymore, to stand this excruciating pain, to take one more second of this being alive without him, and I will be happy to be dead before the next second comes, but I dont want to be dead, and I need help not to be. She knew that it was the truth and my friends didnt leave me alone for one minute after that. I was in despair. I had no hope. Time was anguish. I learned how many seconds there were in a day.

I left Crete a few weeks later. Somehow we endured. Somehow we survived that agony. Somehow only we had suffered it and all the others were outside of it. Somehow we became tender with each other again. Somehow we made love again, with such great sadness and softness that it was new. It was as if either of us might break into a million pieces at any minute, as if there was nothing to save or to hide or to redeem either, as if the only parts of us still living were as fragile as dust in the wind.

And it was very important, I think, that our last week together was spent celibate. You had, after that terrible night, gone to Athens and there gotten the clap from some young man, and me from you, and so our last week together we didnt make love. We went to Athens in yr fathers truck full of tomatoes to take the tomatoes to the market. I cried the whole time, hysterically, doubled up on the car seat, from market to market, howling, wailing, screaming like a banshee, the tears never stopped. You were very kind, tender, and so we began to laugh together again, and on the day I left we were closer than we had perhaps ever been.

If you loved him, why did you leave him? My friends asked me that often, and it was strange that I had left, that any woman would leave a man she loved the way I loved you. I answered in many ways. Sometimes I said that I had become sick. It was true. I had gonorrhea, and my ass had been torn apart. I had an operation on my rectum and as I lay in the hospital wracked with pain, I received letters from you which were completely indifferent to my physical condition. You did not want to know. A woman who loves a man accepts the pain. I did accept it, but not gracefully. Sometimes I told people that I had left because we had begun to fight. That too was true, though when I left I knew that I could stay, that you would not leave me, that we could even marry, if I wanted.

The decision to leave was not rational. It was made, in fact, long before the worst happened. It was a feeling, an impulse, that inhabited my body like a fever. Once I felt it I knew that I would leave no matter what. I describe it to you now as the *drive to become* that lives in the part of me that did not breathe in you, that is a writer, and that even my identity as a woman could not entirely silence. It is that part of me that enraged you even as it enthralled you, the part that could not be subsumed by seduction or anal assault or any sort of domination. It is that part that could not even be conquered, or quieted, by tenderness. It is the part of me that was, even then, most alive, and that no man,

not even you who were for me the air I breathed, could ever take
from me.

If you had truly loved him, you never would have left him. Some have
said that to me, but I say no, I loved you, and I left you. I had
a drive to become, to live, to imagine, to create, and it could not
be contained in what took place between us.

I wanted to come back. I expected to come back. I planned to
come back. I started to come back. But I never did return to you.
    Two years after I had left, as I had promised, I started on my
way back to you. I went to Amsterdam. I wrote you, Im coming
back. I received a letter from you that said, my life is bitter, you
dont know whats happening here, Amerikans are stupid and
you are an Amerikan, tanks and death are everywhere, my
friends are being imprisoned and tortured and killed, come if
you can bear it, I cant promise you anything. You said that you
yourself knew only bitterness, and, indeed, yr letter was bitterness.

I had exactly enough money for fare one way, nothing more.
I had wanted you to say, come, come now, I need you now, now
in this time of desperate trouble I need you.

I did not return. A few months later I married.

I was married for three years. During those years, I dreamed
of you. I would wake up in a cold sweat, desperate just to hear
the sound of yr voice. I never understood why I had not gone
to you.

A year after my marriage ended, talking with a friend, I understood why I had not gone to you. Whatever the false (male-
determined) values that still infuse my judgment of myself—e.g.
I betrayed you, abandoned you, deserted you, had no right not
to return to you given yr desperate situation—I discovered, in
my failure to return, the dimensions of my own cowardice. I had
been so afraid, E, so afraid of the reality of what had happened/
was happening to you. The real guns. The real police. The real
torture. The real dying. I had stayed in Amsterdam to pursue
a life of "radical" pleasure—smoking dope, fucking, the romance of radical ideas without the reality of dangerous opposi-
tion. And I realized too that I had not been able to accept the
letter you had written me—"I am only bitter"—no image of

romantic love was there to propel me toward you, toward self-sacrifice, toward bravery.

I wrote to you then, after my marriage ended, saying, I am living alone, writing a book, and in November I would like to come see you if you are still willing to see me. Miraculously, you wrote back, saying where you would be, warm, saying to come.

But as I worked on my book and struggled with this new clarity, I saw that in Greece I could do nothing, and that my struggle was in Amerika. I saw that I had to come back here, to Amerika, to hone my book into an instrument of revolution. I had to confront the real danger here—not give myself in service to the romance of Amerikas male "radicals," but instead to confront the hatred of women, male power over women, from which, I believe, all other illegitimate power is derived. Here, knowing the language, I could take responsibility. Elsewhere, I would still be running, still hiding. I saw that this assumption of responsibility must be at the center of my life. I saw that I could not be any mans woman, not even yours; that I myself must act in the world directly, develop and use all my strength in the pursuit of my vision, a vision no male could have birthed. I knew that I had discovered my true faith.

I wrote you again, saying, E, I am returning to Amerika, when I finally do come to Crete will you see me? No answer from you. I ask our Greek friends in Paris for news of you, but there is none.

Now, more time has passed. I dont think that I will ever come back to you or see you again. Sometimes I wish that were not so. But I have one choice to make in life, to make and to keep making—will I seek freedom, or will I dress myself in chains? I am on a journey long forbidden to women. I want the freedom to become. I want that freedom more than I want any other thing life has to offer. I no longer believe that yr freedom is more important than mine, that yr pleasure or pain is more important than mine. I no longer believe that the torture of a man in prison is worse than the torture of a woman in bed.

I began this letter in desire; I end in anger. I dream that love without tyranny is possible.

A.

The Woman Who Lost Her Names

Nessa Rapoport

S HE WAS NAMED after her grandmother, Sarah, a name no one else had then because it was considered old-fashioned. Eight days after the naming her father's brother died, and they gave her a middle name. The brother was Yosef—Joseph—so her mother went down to City Hall, Bureau of Births and Deaths, and Josephine was typed in the space after Sarah. "A name with class," her Aunt Rosie said. Sarah hated it.

When she got to school the kindergarten teacher sent home a note. The family read it together, sitting around the kitchen table. "Dear Mrs. Levi, we have decided to call the child Sally for the purpose of school as it will help integrate her and make the adjustment easier."

"What's to adjust?" the brother next to her asked.

"Shah," her father said.

Her father was a gentle man, remote, inaccessible. The books that covered the tables and chairs in his small apartment were the most constant factor in his daily life, and the incongruity of

Nessa Rapoport is a writer and editor living in New York. She is currently working on a novel. "The Woman Who Lost Her Names," copyright © 1979 by Nessa Rapoport, originally appeared in *Lilith* magazine and is reprinted by permission. All rights reserved.

raising seven Orthodox children in the enlightened secularism of the Upper West Side never penetrated his absorption in Torah. Sarah grew up next to the families of Columbia intellectuals who were already far enough from Europe to want to teach their children civilization. The girls in her class had radios, then TVs, then nose jobs and contact lenses. They grew more graceful in their affluence, and she grew a foot taller than all of them, early. There were many blond girls in her class each year, and she'd stare at their fair delicate arms whose hair was almost invisible. "Sally, how does your garden grow?" the boys would pass her in the hall, staring at her breasts, the thick dark hair covering her arms to her wrists, the wild hair that sprung from her head independent of her. She'd look down at herself, her bigness, ungainly, and think "peasant, you peasant" to herself and the grandmother who'd bequeathed her these outsized limbs. No one would fall in love with her.

Her mother was fierce, intense, passionately arguing, worrying about people, disdainful. "She married for money," "he could have been a scholar," indicting these neighbors who were changing their names, selling their birthright. "Sarele," she'd suddenly gather her in her arms late at night when her brothers were sleeping, "remember who you are and you'll have yourself. No matter what else you lose—" She never finished the sentence. Sarah would look into her mother's face, full of shadows, ghosts, and touch the cheek that was softer than anything. "You're a big girl, Sarah," her mother shook herself free, always, "go to bed." Her mother would sit at the kitchen table alone, head in her hands, thinking. Once long past midnight Sarah saw her that way, shaking her head between her clenched fingers, and tiptoed in to say, "Mama, I understand." Her mother looked up, uncomprehending.

When she was seventeen and had given up hope she suddenly bloomed. Her hair calmed down, and a kind of beauty emerged from under her skin. The boys in her youth movement started to talk to her after meetings, inviting her places. First she said no, then she believed them and went gladly to rallies, campfires, lectures to raise money for the new state of Israel. She dreamed of Israel often, dancing the folk dances in the orange groves of her imagination, fighting malaria, drowning in jasmine. None of the boys touched her heart.

At school boys were thinking of college, and girls were thinking of boys. Graduation came on a hot day in June, and her parents watched her get a special award in poetry, poems she had written that no one but the teacher would ever read. "Poetry, Sarele," her father was pleased. "My dreamer," her mother whispered. "We have a surprise for you. From Israel," the word was still strange to her mother's tongue.

Yakov Halevi was her cousin, a first cousin from Jerusalem she'd never met. He got up to greet her from the couch in her parents' living room, the room reserved for company, and she watched his thin energized frame spring forward. He was meant to be dressed in black like the rest of her cousins whose pictures she'd seen in her mother's hand, sidecurls swaying in an overseas wind. But his hair was short, startling, red, and the hair of his chest showed in his open-neck shirt. He spoke seriously, with a heavy accent, and she loved to watch the words form in his mouth before he released them. Yakov was a poet, only twenty and known already for his fervent lines. Great things were expected of him, and he carried their weight on his narrow Hebrew shoulders. Her Bible knowledge wasn't enough, and she struggled with the new language to read his book, tracing the letters of the title page, alarmed: Jerusalem Fruit, by Yakov Peniel.

"Who's Peniel?" she asked him. "Why did you change your name?"

"I didn't change it, I lost it," he laughed. "When the editor wrote to me accepting my poems he had to ask my name, for I hadn't sent it. 'Hagidah na shmekha,' he wrote, what Yakov our forefather asked when he wrestled the angel. 'Why is it that you ask my name?' I wrote back, as the angel answered, and he published me under the name Yakov gave that place—Peniel."

"But your letters come to you in that name. How did it happen?"

He shrugged. "People wanted to meet the bright young poet, Peniel. Then I was asked to talk, introduced that way. On the street they would say 'That's Peniel,' and so it came to be."

"But you're the tenth generation of Jerusalem Halevis. You can't give it up, it's your name."

"Just a name," he smiled. "The soul underneath is the same, in better and worse."

She loved that humility, and the heart of Eretz Yisrael she heard pounding in his chest when he held her. He loved her and loved her America. "It's not mine," she'd insist, "I don't belong here." But he stood in the middle of New York looking up. "So big," he would cry in his foreign tongue. "So big."

He wanted to cross the country sea to sea, to marvel at mountains and chasms. She had waited so long to go home, to Israel, she could wait a little longer. Then he was her home, she became him, she loved every bone of his self, every line. The words of his mouth were her thoughts, what he touched she found worthy. It thrilled her, their sameness, and she'd wake in the mornings eager for the coming confirmations. They would say the same things at one time, and reach for each other, marveling. She wasn't alone anymore, she had found a companion. When she tried to explain about the Upper West Side and the girls in her class he would say, "Every one is alone. Man is alone before God, that's our state." Hearing him say it bound her even more. She wanted to breathe his breath, use his language, and searched through his poems, word after word, for her hidden presence.

"My muse," he sorted her hair. "Sarele," saying it the old Jewish way as he'd heard his mother, also a Sarah, being called.

They knew they would marry, she floated for months on that knowledge, walking down Broadway to the rhythm of Solomon's Songs. "Sarele," Yakov drew her to him one night. "We must talk of the name."

"It's OK. I don't mind Peniel. It's better in a way than Halevi, which is almost my name. No one would know I was married."

"It's the other name—Sarah. My mother's name. A man cannot marry a woman with his mother's name."

She turned white. "A man cannot marry?"

He noticed her face. "Oh no no, he can marry, but she, she must change the name."

She said in relief, "But what name? Sarah was my name."

"Do you have a middle name?"

She scowled. "Josephine."

"A *goyische* name, Josephine. So what do we do?"

She thought for a while. "I don't know. Josephine is Josie, but that's no good."

"Jozzi," it was clumsy, "Jozzi. There is no Jozzi in Hebrew."

She had no suggestion.

"Wait," he told her. "Jozzi is Joseph, Yosef, is that right?"

She nodded.

"Well then it's Yosefah. Yosefah," he tried it on. The Hebrew sounds spun in the air. "Yosefah," he turned her around and around till the trees flew in front of her, dizzy.

They married in spring and all summer they traveled as he fell in love with America. He loved New York City, the place where they'd started, he fingered the wheat of Midwestern fields, and stood on a rock high over the ocean as if he'd discovered the water. In the evenings and as she woke up he was scribbling. Poems, letters, stories poured from his hands. She sat amazed as the papers grew and multiplied in hotel rooms, in the trunk of the car. The strange Hebrew letters leaped from the pages, keeping their secrets against her straining will. "Are you writing of me?" she wanted to know. He smiled, "They are all of you." He told her he sometimes took phrases she said and transplanted them into his work. She was grateful and mystified, peering through the foreign marks for herself, not finding resemblance.

Yearning for Israel they moved to New York. He studied small Talmudic matters on which great things depended. She had a son, then another. The boys laughed and cried with her all day, alone in the house, surrounded by papers, and books of ancient cracked binding. When he finished his doctorate they would live in Israel, and she counted the days as they lengthened to months, alone with her children and the fierceness of her desire. She was America to him, aspiring to be free, and he envied her readiness to leave such abundance behind. "It's your home," he tried to soften her, frightened by her single burning.

"It has nothing to do with me," she'd deny. He trembled in the face of seduction—the grandness of America's gestures, hundreds of plains crossed by rivers whose opposite shores were too far to see.

"We must leave," he said. "We must go."

She stopped her daydream of years and started to pack. The boat left in winter, and the grey piers of New York, city of her birth but not her death, she was sure, were left behind her, unmourned. He stood watching the gap of water widen, then turned to her and was thankful.

There were cypress and palm trees, traveling in, and a perfume heavier than air. Jerusalem approached them at twilight, her gold roofs and domes aching for heaven. She recognized the city as a lover, missing past time, a shock of remembrance that stirred her body like a child. The boys were crying, tired, afraid, and she sheltered them under the sleeves of her coat, "We are home."

Jerusalem was designed for the world to come more than for now, and she washed, cleaned, shopped, scrubbed over and over again, as the dust blew in the summer and the winter wind seeped through the cracks. The boys got sick, and well, and she was sick in the morning, pregnant with the next child. Yakov laughed as he smoothed her hair. "A girl, a *maidele* next."

From America letters came. A brother was hired, her mother was sick, Aunt Rosie was worried, family troubles, her mother was sick, Papa retired, a nephew converted, her mother was going, dying, gone. There was no money for planes, and the pregnancy was hard, so half a world away she guarded her pain, talking to her mother in dreams about the coming daughter. Her mother, sitting now at a kitchen table that was not of the earth, holding her head in her hands. Night after night she lay on her back, her stomach a dome in her arms.

When the child was born she could hardly know, groaning in a voice unknown to herself, stuffed between Arabs and old men in this not-American hospital. Outside the war in Sinai was sending soldiers into her ward, and sending her into the hall and then home, almost before she could stand. She bore the child alone, Yakov at the front, and when she looked down at her daughter, resting on her breast, she was full and at peace with this breathing body of her secret prayers, in love with the child, flesh of her flesh, bone of her bone, not a stranger. Yakov came home, exhausted, off for three days to see her and rejoice in his daughter. When he finally was there she stared from her bed unbelieving, two ones loved so dearly, both whole in limb. It was wondrous to her, and she ran her fingers up and down those tiny arms and legs hundreds of times. And Yakov, unmutilated, only tired, spoke to her saying, "We must give the child a name."

"But I know the name," and she did, waiting for him to come home from the war, reading the Book of Psalms. "She is Ayelet Hashachar—the dawn star."

Yakov smiled over her, indulgent, "This is not a name."

"This is the name," she said firmly. "Ayelet, Ayelet Hashachar, it's beautiful."

"Yes," he said gravely. "It is beautiful. But it's not the child's name. Yosefele," the smile, "your mother."

"My mother would love the name. She would love it," remembering her mother alone at the table dreaming her dreams long past midnight.

"Your mother was Dinsche," he told her, "and the child must be Dina. It is the Jewish way."

She looked at him, trying to find in herself some agreement, even a small accord and she'd bend to his will. But there was nothing.

"Yakov," she pleaded, "my mother won't care. I represent her, I know." Her mother holding her head in her hands. "It cannot be Dina. It can't be." Her voice was rising, new sounds that surprised her. "There's blood on that name."

She rose from the bed, "Look," and held out the Bible, shaking, to him. "Read," she tore through the page in her haste. " 'And when Schechem the son of Hamor the Hivite, the prince of the land, saw her, he seized her and lay with her and humbled her.' "

He stood before her in silence. "Rape," she said. "You want a daughter named for a rape."

"It is out of respect," he said. "For your mother. I don't understand what you want. A *goyische* name like Diana?" he asked. "If it's better we'll call her Diana."

"Ayelet Hashachar," she whispered in mourning, swaying like a rebbe in prayer.

"So what is it?" he asked.

"I don't care what you do," came the words in that voice, the one she had heard from herself giving birth. "Do what you want," turning her face to the wall.

He stroked her hair straight back from her forehead until finally she was asleep.

When the day of the naming arrived she was numb, jabbing the pins of her headcovering into her hair. She walked with her sons and her husband to the synagogue, and left them to climb the steps to the balcony for women. Below her the men were lifting the Torah, opening and closing it, dressing, undressing it, reading the day's portion. The people in the synagogue were singing quite loud, and some of the women sang too. The women around her moved their lips to the words. She stood still. She stood in her place, the place where the mothers always sat for their children. She closed her mouth, her lips pressed together, one on top of the other, and waited to hear her daughter's name.

III
FINDING

My Mother's Story

Roberta Kalechofsky

"TELL US A story," the children said.

My mother turned at the door with her night-time look of weariness. I, being older by nine years than the other two, understood her longing to be finished with the day.

"Jim," she said to me, "you read to the children tonight."

"No, no," they said, "*you* tell us a story." They spoke like imperious rulers and my mother took her hand off the door-knob and sat down on the edge of their bed.

"Well," she said, twisting her wedding band as she always did when she was driven to think something out against her will, "what shall I tell you about? I am quite empty tonight." She laughed about her confession to the small children, yet pleasure came into her eyes as Bobby, who was eight, curled his boyhood into her lap and Lucille, seven, draped her arms around her

Roberta Kalechofsky's work has appeared in *Epoch, Western Humanities Review, The Jewish Advocate,* and other publications, including *The Best American Short Stories* 1972; in the 1975 volume "My Mother's Story" was listed as a distinctive short story. A teacher and lecturer, Kalechofsky lives in Marblehead, Massachusetts, where she founded Micah Publications in 1975. "My Mother's Story," copyright © 1974 by Ball State University Forum, is reprinted with permission.

neck, and my mother was held captive by what she longed to escape and what she hoped to rescue.

"Tell us a story about when you were a child," Bobby said.

"Oh, my," my mother laughed, "and who told you I was ever a child?" She looked at me sitting in the rocking chair in the corner with my science manual in my lap. "This was Jim's night to tell you about space ships and rockets and how you can fly away from this world. Wouldn't you rather hear about that?"

"Tell us a story," Lucille whispered sternly, knowing that this banter was wasting time because Mother rarely refused them anything, least of all a story.

"Very well," she said. "A story. About my own childhood." I dimmed the light over my shoulder and smiled at her with the understanding that she enjoyed this more than she would admit. She smiled back at me vacantly, frowning, reaching into her mind for something to tell them. She stretched out her hands over Bobby's head and looked at them in that complex way I knew better than the children, as if she were struggling to repossess something she had lost, struggling and losing. I sat under my dim light and watched her, not sure of the sympathy I felt for her, because I knew she wanted sympathy and understanding from me. She looked back at me, resenting my determination to be a child and keep her in her place. Then her eyes and her hands fluttered down to Bobby, little boy rightfully in his mother's lap, and she found her voice.

"Well, you know, Mommy used to take piano lessons a long time ago. That's why she knows so many songs to play to you. At that time I lived in a city far north of here and it used to be cold almost all the year round. Somehow I remember always going for my lessons in the snow, although I am sure there must have been months when there was no snow. But it seems to me," she smiled, "that I was always walking in the snow and that it was miles and miles to my teacher's house. It was an old-fashioned stone house with a stone wall and green awnings, but I never saw the awnings unrolled because there was never enough sunshine for that.

"The house was old, older than my piano teacher. There were eight stone steps to the front door, and some of the steps were cracked. There was a little garden in front of the house and a

pine tree in the middle of it. When I sat at the piano in front of
the bay window I used to watch the snow shape the branches of
the tree, until my teacher would rap on the piano top with her
pencil and call me back to attention. Not kindly, either. She had
no patience with dreaming or with mistakes. I'm not even sure
she liked me."

She took her hands off Bobby's head and clasped them under
her chin. "No, I'm sure she didn't like me," she said in a voice
as if an old question had suddenly been answered. "But she
gave me such careful attention that it sometimes confused me.
I paid for an hour's lesson three times a week and she often gave
me two hours and sometimes more, while I played and played
and watched the snow grow shaggy on the pine tree. She gave
me more than I wanted." My mother stretched her hands out
and laughed. "More than I've known what to do with. She gave
and I took, and I'm not sure why I took so much." She looked
at me sitting in the dim light. "Children so often have such a
sense of obligation, so often feel obliged to stay where they are
put, forgetting they have legs under them." She looked down
at her wedding band again. "I was most unhappy in her house,
but I took all she had to give."

Bobby twisted his head in her lap and assumed a thoughtful
expression. "Was she a witch?" he whispered.

My mother looked at him blankly for a moment. Then catching the light in his eyes, she said, "Quite. Yes, she must have
been a witch and she cast a spell on me. She took the tongue
out of my head so that I could not tell her when my time was
up and that I'd rather play in the snow, and she took my legs
away so that once I sat down on the piano bench I could not get
up again. All that she left me was my hands that played on and
on like the red slippers that danced by themselves."

"What did she look like?" Lucille said, apparently pleased that
my mother was getting down to fundamentals.

But my mother was confused by the question. I saw her struggling between her memory and my sister's imagination. "Well,
like a witch, I suppose," she said. "Certainly not at all like a
piano teacher. She had a small, plump, bustling body that
seemed as impatient as I was to be doing something else. She
had short, thin legs. She had tiny feet that led me from the door

to the piano bench with a quick, sharp step as if they were always saying, quickly, quickly, before we think of something else. She took my coat, hung it away, and usually said, 'Very well, begin.' Sometimes she held her hand out the door and said, 'Snowing? Again? Well, well.' Certainly she had a sharp, witchlike nose and she kept rhythm with it. Her nose was as sharp and as perfect as the metronome that clicked on the piano top, tick-tock, tick-tock, for two hours or more until I forgot the sound of the snow and the sound of the fire in the fireplace. Tick-tock, tick-tock, cheerlessly and perfectly.

"Her ears were very large. She sat on a chair next to my bench with one ear turned to me, and I could see that her ear was most witchlike. It was as large as a tunnel and all the melody was running into it like a river. She listened with her eyes too, for she never closed them and dreamed like people sometimes do when they have to listen to music for a long time. She watched the air with her small, brown eyes as if each note was before her.

"It might interest you to know," my mother said, "that as sharp and as small and as witchlike as this teacher was she had a husband who was large and slow and who sat in a wheelchair and dreamed by the fire."

"I never heard of a witch who was married," Bobby said with suspicion.

My mother saw that she had taken a wrong turn. "He was a witch too, and maybe they weren't married. I think they weren't. They lived together because they had bewitched one another. He lived in his wheelchair by the side of the fire and she lived on a little stool by the side of the piano. That was all I ever knew of them at that time, and even after he died I did not come to know much more, except for one fact."

She pulled Lucille's arms around her neck. "I tell you this because music teachers have a way of lingering in one's mind. It is a special kind of friendship, having almost nothing to do with anything else in life. All we had together was the music and the hour, and the beat of the metronome and the snow outside. She was the only teacher in town who gave music lessons, and she gave lessons to all the young children because at that time parents had a strange hope about their children learning to play the piano; but I was the only one to whom she gave more than I needed.

"I went there for twelve years, three times a week. The years rolled by, carrying me through Chopin and Beethoven and Mozart against my will. And yet." My mother looked about the room, straining at a thought. Then her face lit with a pleasurable concession, and her fingers played on the air with a soundless passion. They bent with tension as if the piano board were right beneath her fingertips. "And yet surely with all my will," she said, "because I never refused to go there. Chopin and Beethoven and Mozart were in my fingers, whether I wanted them there or not." She smiled at Bobby, "But suddenly one grows up and asks: where is all the rest of the life?" Her smile lapsed and she looked away from my brother. "I asked and I was answered. The morning after he died I heard my mother talking to a friend on the telephone. 'Died, has he?' she said. 'Well, I don't know whether to say it's a shame or a blessing. Too late to be a blessing, I suppose.'

"I asked my mother why she said such an awful thing. She hung the telephone back in place and looked at me with some doubts as to what she should say or how she should go about it. She took my hands and looked at them in a way that she would sometimes look at my face, absorbed with a vision. 'Tain't nothing,' she said, 'except that she had such promise. But everbody has promise sometime or other.'

"But I had caught hold of a tale and I would not let go. I pursued my mother with questions. My mother dropped my hands and turned sternly back to her baking. 'Tain't nothing else but that,' she said.

"My teacher did not stop giving lessons and the next week when I went to her my heart was beating very fast. I did not know how she would look now that he had died. I imagined that people changed fearfully when something like that happened. I did not know what I could say to her. The snow was banked on either side of me as high as my hips and I ran down the narrow path wanting not to go there, wanting not to face a house where someone had died, not knowing what I could say to her. I felt a terrible sorrow for her in spite of her sharp, loveless impatience with me, and the steady, larger patience that hovered behind her and me like a threat.

This day she did not put out her hand to feel for the snow. Her step was slower. She drifted towards the piano. The wheelchair was empty. I carefully did not notice it. But my heart was beating fast. Yet it was not the death in the house I was afraid of."

My mother stretched out her hands again. Bobby's eyes remained steadfast, faithful to the story. "I did not know then what it was I was afraid of and I did not think about it very carefully."

"Was it the she-witch?" Lucille asked.

My mother nodded her head with gratitude for the clue. "Yes, that was it. Strange how I did not know it all these years. But that's what it must have been," she shook her head gravely, "because as I began to play, a very unnatural thing happened. I sat down at the piano and did my lesson. In spite of the death and my beating heart there was nothing else to do. The hour ticked by with the metronome. I did not watch the snow shapes on the pine tree because I was too old for that. The second hour ticked its way up and the shadows began to fall. Suddenly, sitting on her stool in the crook of the piano, the witch began to disappear. First her eyes grew smaller. They became as small as yours or mine. Then her nose shrunk and became soft. Her eyes clouded over and took to dreaming; and her hands, that had always lain studiously still in her lap, began to move in the air with rhythm as if she were playing the piece with me. I finished the second hour with determination to end it right there. She looked at me with surprise, disapproval, and disappointment.

" 'You must go on,' she said.

" 'I can't,' I said, 'not today.'

"She looked at me for the first time with a granule of sad and apparent patience. 'Oh, but you mustn't mind death, or life,' she said.

"But I had grown up and discovered my will. I turned to her and said the only sympathetic words I could think of. 'I would like to hear you play.'

"She looked at me for a long time, for a very long time. I do believe it was a look fetched from all the untiring patience she had had with me for twelve years, all the unloved, wasted patience."

My mother stopped there as if the story was finished, but the children knew better. She looked at Bobby and saw him waiting.

She felt Lucille's nudging arms. She looked at me and I moved restlessly in my chair.

"And did she play?" Bobby asked.

My mother rolled him off her lap and laid him down in his bed. She stood up and straightened her dress. "Now, Lucille," she said, "you lie down too."

"But did she play?" Lucille asked, getting under her covers.

My mother turned distractedly at the door. Her hand fluttered to the doorknob, grasping it with determination. "Oh, yes," she said, "she played too well." She signaled to me to come out and let the children go to sleep. I put out the light and went unwillingly because I did not wish to meet her resigned expression in the dark hallway.

Making Jews

Nancy Datan

"WHY ARE YOU going to fast when you're an atheist?"
"Why do we go to synagogue for Kol Nidre?"
"I asked you first."

"I answered you," says my firstborn daughter, and a private chill takes me, the same chill which comes to the pit of my stomach at Pesach when my son asks, each year the curiosity greater, "Why is this night different from all other nights?" *I started this* says the voice of the private chill, and indeed I am convinced that this voice speaks to every parent of a Jew, for they are made, not born.

Choice is more obvious with my own, who came into the world with fair hair, snub noses, an Anglo-Saxon family name, and a paternal lineage which traces back to the Mayflower by

Nancy Datan says that "Making Jews" is a fair indication of her personal history. A resident of Israel for ten years, she is a married mother of three children and is Associate Professor of Psychology at West Virginia University. Her most recent works include *Transitions of Aging* and *Forbidden Fruits and Sorrow*, a collection of papers on myth, folklore, and fairy tales. "Making Jews" appeared in *Moment* magazine and is reprinted by permission of Nancy Datan and Raines & Raines. Copyright © 1976 by Continuity, Inc.

way of the Daughters of the American Revolution. Against these
odds I have only the stiff neck of the Jews and the relative
ignorance of my upbringing, including decisive acts of dropping out from—if my daughters will pardon the expression—
Sunday School. I brought to my impermanent intermarriage
the memories of festivals, wine and white tablecloths, an uncle
who would never miss Yom Kippur services and conducted
quiet games of gin rummy at the back of what I later learned was
not really a temple, but only called a temple by ignorant Jews.
"We're all ignorant Jews," a friend told me once, but: *"L'hav-
dil,"* said someone else years later, a friend who gave himself
to history on Yom Kippur in 1973 and left me the memory of
his commandment to differentiate between the sacred and the
profane. My own ignorance extended to embrace both, but:

"There is scattered about in this land a peculiar people,
whose ways are not the king's ways, and therefore it does not
profit the king to suffer them," echoes the voice of Haman over
the centuries; at that potent convergence of forces which marks
a first pregnancy I discover that my father-in-law registered as
a pacifist in 1941, perhaps the very year in which my father's
cousins were registered for death, and whatever else this pregnancy will yield, it is going to be a stiff-necked Jew, and so it was.

Now, more than a dozen years later, Merav Datan—the first
of those names chosen and given in Chicago, in anticipation of
the forthcoming trip to Israel, and the second, the heretic's
name, taken by me a decade later and taken by my children to
my surprise—remarks one day: "I'd have more friends if I were
Christian."

"Why?"

"That's just the way kids are here," in a small city in West
Virginia.

"Okay, baby, it's the easiest thing in the world to fix, we'll just
march you down to the local church and give them your pedi-
gree and register you for the D.A.R.," which met often, according to the paper, and to the amusement of the children, when
they noticed it.

"Well, obviously I don't want those kinds of friends." It is not
altogether obvious, but the pact with history is sealed within

some months at her bat mitzvah, and both of us are shocked for different reasons by the fact that I had none myself.

Of course I had *mishpoche,* and she did not. Indeed, the seasons of the life cycle are marked at the festivals: the early years, when the seder takes forever until the aunts bring out the food; the middle years, when suddenly the service seems too brief; and then adulthood, the aunts are far away and the uncles are dead and I am making seder myself.

"*You* make seder?" asks a colleague who knows of me only that my daughters cook for the family: that, among other things, is what makes this night different from all other nights. My secondborn daughter is near to her bat mitzvah, but I consider my son, eight, who calls *matzot* "Joosh bread," still ignorant of the answers to the four questions. At least I am going to teach him how to ask.

"Do we believe in God?" he asks.

"It's not a corporate decision"—and therefore different from all other decisions made in this family, ranging from country of residence to the color of the new toilet seat: "Don't forget that Gidon never lifts it," I am told. "Pick something dark."

"Do *you* believe in God?" persists my son.

"No."

"Then I don't too."

"That isn't the way to decide. It's a very personal issue, and you have to give it years of thought before you can even come to the beginning of a conclusion."

"Well, I'm *eight.*"

"Well, try to give it another four or five years at least," and the chill touches me once more: his older sister, whose countdown without food or water has already begun, asked me irritably when she was just his age:

"Why do we have to go to synagogue for Kol Nidre?"

"Because we're Jews."

"We never went to synagogue in Israel." That is certainly true: I would never set foot under a roof which featured a walled gallery for women, and it was years before I learned that a reform movement, with a synagogue, existed in Jerusalem; but prayer of any sort made me uneasy. In Jerusalem it made no difference: I had my own variety of religious experience, one not catalogued by William James, when I read the account by the Roman historian Tacitus of the fall of Jerusalem in 70 A.D.: "As I am about to relate the last days of a famous city, it seems appropriate to throw some light upon its origin," sitting in my own front yard, the bright Jerusalem sun shining on the ersatz constructions of the Jewish Agency, built to accommodate the ingathered Jews of the twentieth century.

The record of the battle was terrible and brief: ". . . (Titus) pitched his camp . . . before the walls of Jerusalem, and displayed his legions in order of battle. The Jews formed their line close under their walls . . . I have heard that the total number of the besieged, of every age and both sexes, amounted to six hundred thousand. All who were able to bore arms, and a number, more than proportionate to the population, had the courage to do so. Men and women showed equal resolution, and life seemed more terrible than death, if they were to be forced to leave their country. Such was this city and nation; and Titus Caesar, seeing the position . . . determined to proceed by earthworks and covered approaches . . . There was a cessation from fighting, till all the inventions, used in ancient warfare or devised by modern ingenuity for the reduction of cities, were constructed." Thus Tacitus concluded, and turned his attention to the Roman campaigns in Germany.

I closed the book as a neighbor paused, on her way home, and I said, "You know what? If you read about the battles of Jerusalem in 70 C.E. and in 1948, it really does sound as if the Jews are one people."

She is Orthodox, and smiles: "I don't need a Roman to tell me that."

The apperceptive mass of middle age hangs heavier on the Jew at the High Holidays: that cumulative lens of personal experience through which the world is seen, upon which the years' memories are inscribed, clouds over, distorts. My earliest Yom Kippur, a Yom Kippur of innocence when parents brought me and decisions were years away, is a happy recollection of a recitation of sins which seemed to whet my appetite, for somewhere through the rabbi's talk (the discovery that this might as well be called a sermon, and that the Orthodox did not have such things, lay ahead of me) I turned to the carnation pinned to my shoulder, and consumed it inconspicuously, petal by petal. "I ate my Yom Kippur corsage"—a memory worthy of Alexander Portnoy: but for me there was no aftertaste of guilt, indeed, I learnt to eat carnations, and couldn't be trusted around floral arrangements for years.

No doubt I would do the same today, but in every other respect Yom Kippur has been transformed. The small community of Jews in West Virginia has had to serve for *mishpoche,* and though it serves us well, I am a stranger and a sojourner here, an expatriate on two continents now, destined to be homesick no matter what my home address. My own years are scattered all over the world, while in Morgantown other children's grandparents pinch my children's cheeks. Two years ago on Kol Nidre night the rabbi spoke of the sirens which sounded and would sound forever on Yom Kippur, and my secondborn daughter sobbed in my arms with a grief she would never have known if I had not set with such ferocity on making a Jew of her: *I started this,* and, *what have I done?*

But it's done now. Yes, my son, who must be just the age I was when I discovered carnations, asks with my firstborn daughter's voice, Do I have to go to synagogue on Yom Kippur? Yes, I tell him. Will there be food afterward? asks this child, flesh of my flesh, appetites like mine. Yes, after sunset there will be food. I tell him, and the pact is sealed: women wiser than myself have prepared the way to a child's heart and soul.

And so much for the internal power politics of the High Holidays. On this campus one is as likely as not to see the Homecoming football game scheduled for Yom Kippur, and I am the only Jew in my department who never comes in to the office over the holidays. Born among the most ignorant of all the ignorant Jews, and still quite passably ignorant, the abundance of my Jewish heritage is in that stiff neck. My course calendars were ready for the start of the first academic year and so was I when, early in September, I was invited to speak on a panel which dealt with religion and the social sciences.

"Sure." I had just returned from the meetings of the International Society for the Study of Behavioral Development: it seemed unnatural to speak without a microphone in front of me, colleagues beside me, and a sea of faces before me.

"Don't you want the date?" for I was about to conclude the conversation.

"Oh. Yes."

"September 27."

"Wait a minute. That's Rosh Hashanah. I've canceled classes, and I don't think I can speak on a panel, even when I think a Jew should be there."

"Well, I do understand that, of course, but I hope you will think it over before you refuse. If it will make any difference at all to you, there is going to be another Jew on the panel"— whom I met shortly afterward, who told me with surprise, "But I'm a Unitarian!" and I replied, "Haven't you learned that in small towns there are no Jewish Unitarians?"

"I'm in a peculiar position," I told the organizer—"We're *all* in peculiar positions," my friend might have said— "because I don't go to synagogue but I don't hold classes: I can see the contribution I might make, but I don't feel right about participating."

"Perhaps you could think it over for a day."

In the interval, I inquired of the director of developmental psychology whether the department had any vested interest in representing itself on the panel; he assured me that the decision was entirely mine.

"I don't teach classes on Rosh Hashanah ..."

"Well, Rosh Hashanah is a designated Day of Special Concern. You aren't supposed to give tests or lectures which can't be made up by reading, but you aren't supposed to cancel class ..."

"*I* don't teach on Rosh Hashanah!"

"Well, if it's against your religion, of course ..."

"It's not my *religion*, it's my fucking *holiday!*" and I had my answer at last, and called the organizer: "I can't participate on the panel, and furthermore, I don't think a lecture restricted by default to *goyim* and nonobservant Jews can be considered the Distinguished Religious Lecture of the Year," a belligerent assertion which generated an enduring friendship on this contradictory campus in this contradictory city, where the fires of the crosses of the Ku Klux Klan could be seen burning on the hills just forty years ago; where a gentile shoemaker sent in a donation to Israel in the dark days of the Yom Kippur War which lay just ahead; where from time time bomb calls threaten synagogue services; where, for the eight days of Pesach, I let the crumbs of my peanut butter and matzot sandwich work an inverse baptism as they sprinkle over the faculty dining room, in violation of the injunction to bring no food into a place where food is served. But if it comes to a question of who is to violate whom, my answer is quick. Years ago I told a friend, who had learned with me to worship Socrates in his adolescence and whose interdisciplinary program now looked threatened, "If the hemlock comes, fling it at the bearer. It's better to do an evil than to suffer one." Not more than a year ago I discovered myself to be obeying another of the six hundred thirteen commandments: "If a man comes to kill you, strike first."

So, slowly, over the years, do we all discover ourselves to be keepers of the commandments, I suspect. "In Judaism we each have to discover our own road," the rabbi told me when I sought his counsel on the question of the panel convened on Rosh Hashanah. No! said the voice of the preceding decade, *Halachah* tells us. But it doesn't tell *me:* indeed, I am among those who argue that Jews make the law, law does not make us Jews.

If so—and it is so for many of us—I am recalled once more to my peculiar position, our peculiar position, that of this peculiar people. "How can you possibly rule your children's lives?" a nonJewish colleague asked me recently, and I told him, "God made man in His own image, didn't He?" My colleague, no more religious than I am, is taken aback: but it isn't blasphemy which shakes me but rather the foreknowledge of alternating currents of heresy and devotion, as it is said, for all our generations.

The Four Leaf
Clover Story

Beverly Schneider

WE WERE STILL four blocks from the cemetery, waiting for
the left turn arrow onto North and South Road, when Aunt
Bertha began apprising us of the local IT victims: Mr. Gumpfer,
from the dry cleaners, had IT; Label's son was taking radiation
treatments (you know what that means); and a TV soap opera
star had IT (I don't know whether she had IT in real life or only
on stage; Aunt Bertha was unclear). Three years earlier, my
mother had died from cancer and it was since then that Aunt
Bertha had refused to let the dreaded word fall from her lips,
as though the name itself evoked the disease's destruction. Pro-
tected in this manner, she was free to talk about IT as frequently
as possible. My other aunts were not quite ready to play the IT
game. They were reading the laundry label of Aunt Lottie's
half-priced raincoat. I was confident that Aunt Bertha would be
but momentarily thwarted. Having sheltered my own vul-
nerabilities within a cynical, condescending anticipation of an-

Beverly Schneider is coordinator of Kol Nashim, the Orthodox women's davening
group of New York's Upper West Side. A former teacher and social worker, she
lived in Israel for three years; she now works as a financial assistant on Wall
Street.

other Kaplan sisters' play of fools, I listened, half-humored, to
Aunt Bertha's horror stories as I drove the car down North and
South Road, past the house in which I had lived with my family,
and pulled into the B'nai Amoona cemetery where my mother
was buried.

This visit had started as inauspiciously as the other five visits
we had made together these past three years. Exactly one week
earlier, Aunt Bertha's daily phone calls had begun. "Becky, I'm
going with you. With Aunt Sissy and Aunt Lottie." She was
always afraid of being excluded. "We'll go to Ida's grave, I mean
Mama's, I mean your mother's grave, first. Then, you'll drive us
to the other cemetery, Cheser Shamos, uh, no, Chaim, no. You
know where it is. To see Grandma and Grandpa. You remember
them." It was futile to again remind her that her parents had
died long before I was born.

I always called my father at the nursing home before I left on
these visits. By tacit agreement, we never spoke of my mother's
death, which had coincided with his first stroke, but I liked to
hear his voice anyway. The phone was busy all morning so I
called my sister in Chicago instead. She was bored by these
visits, but I felt obliged to tell her in spite of her condescension.
"Why don't you just drop off the three Fates at the cemetery and
wait in the car while they have a good cry?" she snickered. We
chatted briefly about the baby and her new kitchen wallpaper,
but she was in a hurry to go bowling. "You don't have anything
in particular you want, do you? I've got to be running. I'm late
as it is." I hung up, hoping that somewhere between Aunt Bertha's fixations and my sister's denial, there was some room for
me.

Nothing seemed to alter these visits. They unfolded like some
inexorable ritual upon which I exercised no control. So, the
production continued as we parked the car a short distance
from my mother's gravesite. "Did you bring enough Kleenex,
Becky, should we roll up the windows, it'll get hot, it may rain,
are you bringing a purse, Bertha, we won't have to roll up the
windows." Eventually, they removed themselves clumsily from
the car, with three purses, two umbrellas, and Kleenex for an
army.

Aunt Bertha jabbered incessantly.

"Look, isn't it nice how they keep this cemetery," she said, remarking on the black man mowing the grass in the distance. "Not like that awful place where Mama is. Wait till we get to Ida's grave. I'll bet it's clean and neat."

"Quiet, Bertha. You shouldn't say that about Mama's grave. There weren't any weeds on it last year." Aunt Sissy could not tolerate ugliness. It was not respectful and threatened her vanity.

So, this year's theme is Cemetery Upkeep. I sneered silently and began to muse about my grandparents' cemetery with its trees spreading shade and leaves over crowded tombstones and its shabby old men with beards who hovered about with charity boxes, insinuating eyes, and mumbled Yiddish prayers. There, death was really Death and any form of life, even weeds, was counted as victory. I didn't want some hired hand mowing my produce when I died. Manicured cemeteries. Humpf. My poor aunts were certainly of the Depression generation.

"Oh, it was horrible! What do you mean you don't remember? Would you want to lie in a place like that? Forever?" Aunt Bertha baited her.

"When I die, I want to be buried here. Near Ida," Aunt Sissy responded.

"Do you hear that, Lottie? She doesn't want to be buried near Mama and Papa."

"Bertha!" Aunt Sissy was angry but felt obliged to offer an explanation; "I knew Ida longer."

"Oh," Aunt Bertha was stopped by the logic. So was I.

Aunt Bertha had difficulty keeping up with us. Her legs were shorter and she had to read the complete inscription on almost every gravestone. "*Jennie Greenspan,*" she whimpered. "Remember her? *Died 1952.* Lottie, what was her boyfriend's name? You know, the one with the limp ... *Sadie Schwartz.* Wasn't that a shame! She's buried near Izzy Yawitz, from the South Broadway dairy. How they used to fight!"

Curiosity overcame Aunt Sissy, who dropped back to join her older sister. They continued their banter, arguing now over biographic details. Aunt Lottie, as usual, walked close behind me. I tried to believe that she identified my silence with quiet dignity, but more often I feared she was simply guarding over

me, watching, worrying about my secrecy. I was relieved when
she too would stop to glance at the names and dates on the
tombstones. Periodically, when she would release a quiet sigh,
I would peer at her from out of the corners of my eyes.

This year, the completion of another row of graves and the
healthy thickness of ivy that now covered my mother's gravesite
gave the illusion of change. It was the same grave, the double
tombstone, as yet half-inscribed: *IDA SCHREIBER*, no middle
name, *1908-1963*. The four of us formed an automatic semicir-
cle around it. My aunts quietened abruptly and appeared to lose
themselves in thought. This was the very moment I dreaded. I
never knew what to do, never was in the right frame of mind,
never had the right feelings. I resorted to an old exercise,
closed my eyes, imagined the white bones, the lost flesh that was
now my mother, trying to remember, to feel something, anything. I pictured her skeleton deep beneath the green ivy. "This
was my mother. This was my mother," I repeated silently over
and over again. But without conviction. I could not bridge the
gap between my mother and those bones. I grew irritated with
my aunts whose shadows seemed to have returned to haunt me.
They took my feelings, they felt more, loved more, missed
more. They cried. I didn't. They cried in descending order.
Aunt Bertha with a red nose and real tears. Aunt Sissy with pink
eyes and sniffling. Aunt Lottie teary-eyed. They always cried in
that order. Maybe, if they weren't here, maybe I would dare
explode, dare cry. But they were here, watching me, waiting.
Thank God my sister wasn't here too. She would mock everything. Even me. Once again I tried to imagine my mother, but
even the white bones had been snatched away by these images
of my aunts' tears and my sister's sarcasm.

Irritated and dry-eyed, I ended the silence with a signal that
I was about to read the *Kaddish,* the traditional Jewish prayer of
mourning. I never told them that this recitation with four
women was not proper. They would have condemned the religion, would have insisted that the rightful way for a Jewish
woman to mourn is to recite the *Kaddish* from her Jewish heart
at the cemetery. I did not want to persuade them otherwise for
I too liked to hear the incantation of that prayer. Relieved to
have a prepared script before me, I read in a rolling, rumbling

monotone the practised syllables of generations, until the last cadence was maintained and the silence held for them, a sufficient time to allow for respect. They all stared, motionless, a bit teary. Three sisters, with slightly stooped shoulders, scarves carefully covering their heads, arms forming a "V" at their pocketbooks. I always repented of my anger when I saw them like this.

After a moment or two I bent down, tore up some grass, and solemnly spread it over the ivy-covered grave according to the custom in my family. Moving slowly, significantly, my aunts followed suit. I loved this form, although I never learned its source. It was sweet and simple. Final. Another visit was completed. Thank God, I made it without . . .

"A four leaf clover!" Aunt Sissy exclaimed, startling our solemnity. We stared in bewilderment as she separated a four leaf clover from the tuft of grass she had uprooted and displayed it to us.

"What're you going to do with that?" Aunt Bertha demanded.

Aunt Sissy spread the grass over my mother's grave with care and delicacy—she loved ceremony; and then, with as noble a gesture as she could manage, she bestowed the single clover upon me.

"Here, Becky. This is yours. From your mother. Now you can have everything you ever wanted."

"Thank you, Aunt Sissy. Thank you." I started to put the four leaf clover into my prayerbook with borrowed pomp while Aunt Bertha, so touched by this gesture, began hunting for a clover of her own discovery, "so I can give good luck to Becky, too."

Trying to understand, I stared blankly at her fragile gift. Is this all it takes to stop the writhing and suffering: this delicate, green clover I cradled in my palm? It seemed so easy, and yet such a betrayal. I did not know why my mother died, only that I needed something more to explain her death than this petite symmetry, mute to eternity.

Aunt Lottie stood by me with a puzzled look as though she were trying to understand a naughty game her sisters played. When I turned to her, she urged Aunt Bertha to get up and reminded Aunt Sissy that we still had to stop at Rabbi Halpern's grave before we could leave the cemetery.

I guided them to his grave at the very front of the cemetery. We always stopped there. Nothing spoiled our routine, although Aunt Bertha availed herself of various clover patches surrounding his large, simple tombstone and interrupted our meditation more than once with premature victory cries of discoveries. Aunt Sissy and Aunt Lottie remained solemn, until one of them finally sighed, "Remember how Ida used to say, 'If only Rabbi Halpern were alive now?' " Yes, my mother believed in miracles, too—not in four leaf clover miracles, she was too practical for such flimsy promises—but in Rabbi Halpern. If only he had been alive, her cancer would have gone away.

After corralling Aunt Bertha, we returned to the car and began the short trip to my grandparents' cemetery, a trip which was always a relief to me. Somewhere between the two cemeteries, Aunt Bertha, as usual, started calling her sisters by the Yiddish diminutives used when they were children. The names were soft and enchanting, "Liba" and "Lehya." From the moment I turned left from Olive Street Road into the Chesed Shel Emeth Cemetery, the sisters would argue regarding the location of the grave. It was lane no. 113b or no. 117b, across path no. 7 or no. 3. The argument continued even as we walked. I never minded. Here were the noble dead of a generation I never knew. I imagined myself immersed in that immigrant culture. Many of the graves had faded oval pictures of the dead permanently attached to the tombstones. I was intrigued by the faces. Aunt Bertha's cemetery geography fascinated me. And even though we walked for awhile, we were never lost. She seemed to know everyone on the block.

I forget which aunt was right—they probably each claimed to be—but we finally found the gravesite. "Oh, I knew it all the time. Right across from Minnie Klein. They used to walk to Soulard Market together."

Once again I waited for an appropriate length of time for silent meditation. I looked at my aunts. They did not seem so old. I tried to make them even younger, tried to imagine their bereavement when their mother died. Did they remember her kiss, her face, her voice after all these years? What she wore when she died? Did they try to communicate with her now? "Mama, I've been good, Mama. Honest, Mama. I still learn things the hard way, Mama; I'm learning only now what you meant to me. I never really knew you, Mama." Did they think that she understood her children better now that she was dead? My mother used to make these visits with them. I could not imagine her having had these thoughts and then coming home to us as she did to iron and fry liver. The thought almost made me cry.

Aunt Sissy signaled me to begin the performance of the *Kaddish*. Slow, mournful, illegitimate, I tried to read as correctly as possible, substituting the European pronunciation familiar to them for the modern Israeli one I commonly used. I felt the moment transformed. The sun withdrew respectfully behind a dark cloud, erasing all shadows. An orchestra of birds and spring breezes played an accompaniment in the trees above. My voice chronicled the death of generations.

I was sure I heard my aunts whimpering and slowed my reading to prolong the soulful mood. It seemed the birds honored the changed tempo. The leaves lay still. Only my breathing, somehow, was not completely right; the short gasps incorrectly punctuated the rhythm.

"Oh, I see one. Over there." Aunt Bertha stood next to me with her head bent downwards, eyes studying the weeds. I pretended to ignore her but raised my voice and read in a deliberate style, hoping this gentle reprimand would silence her. It did. Soon after, though, I noticed Aunt Sissy, on my left side, buckling slightly. I cast a reproving glance at her during an awkward breath stop and she straightened guiltily, but momentarily. Soon my peripheral vision became a seesaw. Right side up respectfully; left side down irresistibly until the two sisters succumbed completely.

I continued to read falteringly. The birds and breezes seemed to have deserted me. Only Aunt Lottie stood by me, a faithful attendant to my *Kaddish*. Eventually, when her knees began to bend and then straighten alternately, I knew that in a moment I would remain alone. I read on, compulsively, to silence my fears. Aunt Lottie, don't leave me. Don't leave me without my shams. Don't leave me unprotected from that wild wind that weaves through these stones, from the vultures that eye my flesh.

"Lehya, look. Here's one. Just look." Her eldest sister bid her join the search. Aunt Lottie smiled at me. Her myopic eyes beseeched forgiveness from me. They begged permission for her indulgence. And then she giggled and stooped to join her sisters.

I managed still to read. Quietly. For spite. I fulfilled the family obligation, alone, deserted by my mother's sisters, self-righteous before the crowds that mingled through the cemetery. And while I read, I thought of the story I could tell of the Kaplan sisters' play of fools. I planned to thank them for providing this grande finale after I finished the *Kaddish,* but I was haunted by Aunt Lottie's smile and could not take my mockery seriously.

So, I read to the last amen and then having finished I turned to look at them.

They did not realize I had completed the *Kaddish* or that it was time to tear up some grass and, in a gesture, end this visit. They were somewhere else. Three women in their fifties crawling over the unkempt grass, as oblivious as they were forty years ago when they made clover rings in Carondelet Park, innocent of the story I would tell. Happily, happily, they understood nothing and trusted everything.

With some coaxing, I gathered them up and brought them safely home. When I said goodbye to Aunt Bertha at her apartment, she promised she would find me a four leaf clover; and, if not, well, she would try to find something else that would be just as good. "So, call me. Don't keep away. I've got a telephone, too, you know. Instead of calling Aunt Sissy next time, you can call me."

That was the last time we visited the cemeteries together. Shortly thereafter my father died and I moved to Boston. My trips to St. Louis did not coincide with Mother's Day or fall in the month before Rosh Hashanah when my family customarily made these visits. I kept the four leaf clover that Aunt Sissy had given me in my wallet, grey and rigid, until six years later when I laid it solemnly on a solitary plot, several rows behind my parents' gravesite. It was a freshly sodded, manicured grave. Everything was just as she would have wanted it. Aunt Bertha and Aunt Lottie must have brought the pot of plastic flowers that rested at the head of her grave. They never put flowers on my mother's grave, but I didn't mind; Aunt Sissy was the lady, beautiful and refined, and she loved pretty things. I remembered Aunt Lottie's letters to me describing Aunt Sissy's long battle with cancer and I tried to imagine the angelic expression she was said to have worn when she died.

When I left, instead of tearing some grass, I placed the flattened clover ceremonially on the center of her grave because the irony comforted me and because Aunt Sissy would have appreciated the sentiment. Otherwise, I did not know what else to do.

Anniversary

Elaine Marcus Starkman

WE'VE GROWN so alike standing before our bedroom mirror this morning. Today, our fifteenth wedding anniversary. Even our reflections look alike. Two full faces, steady hazel eyes hidden beneath silver-rimmed glasses, sensitive lips, he, balding, I with the color of my hair gone drab.

Wordless he shaves, black stubble from his electric razor falling into our double-bowl vanity, onto our white carpet. Hum of his razor and my toothbrush droning under harsh fluorescent light.

He pulls out the plug, stuffs razor into our toothpaste-smudged drawer, that drawer like all our dresser drawers. Cluttered with indispensable litter that ties us together. Inside: notes, change, mismatched socks, graying underwear. Outside: surgical journals, poems, math tests, tennis shoes.

Elaine Marcus Starkman is the author of *Coming Together,* a collection of poems. She teaches Jewish literature and journal writing at the College of Marin, J.F.K. University, and St. Mary's. Her works have appeared in *Hadassah, Present Tense, Jewish Frontier, Contemporary California Poets, Tunnel Road, Studies in American Jewish Literature, Blue Unicorn,* and other publications. She lives in Walnut Creek, California, with her husband and four children.

He throws his pajamas into the old straw laundry basket and dresses, clothes unstylish and conservative as the day we met. Dark suit, narrow lapels. Reluctantly pulls on blue-flowered shirt I gave him for his birthday.

Banging of bathroom door, burnt toast, bitter coffee, frantic search for jackets and lunch money fade into morning routine. House silent. Only whirring of washer and dryer. When did I start them?

An ordinary morning. Hair unclipped, terrycloth robe stained. Yet different. Fifteenth anniversary, and I find his face among towels. How he rushed in late last night, high beneficent forehead pink with chill, glasses steamy.

"Sorry, got stuck again. Just a standard procedure. Nothing interesting. Maybe we could go to a movie tomorrow. The one by that woman film director is playing in Berkeley."

"*Swept Away?* I thought you said it was too violent."

"It's the old taming of the shrew updated, isn't it?"

"Yes. You won't like it."

"Probably not, but you said it was important to see. Ingmar Bergman's got a new film out. Maybe I'll come home early. We can go to either one."

What sudden extravagance, when has he ever cared about films? Has he remembered our anniversary this year? The year of my migraines, his weight gain, our son's running away, our daughter's school failure? The summer we fought on the Santa Cruz beach in front of a crowd of strangers, I screaming, "Doctor, doctor, doctor," he slapping me across the cheek, voice seething, "Shut up; I'm sick of you. From now on I'll do what *I* want." We drove home from his day off, the children shocked into silence. Those endless hot months, no classes, no poems to sustain me, only family responsibility, I hated what I'd once loved. Maury, a doctor before he was born. He *had* to be. And I his wife.

Throw wet towels into the dryer. What would I do in my spare time without laundry. Golf, shop, drive to the city, join the hospital auxiliary?

Brush my hair and dress. Our wedding portrait. How voguish I look. Blonde teased pageboy. Squinting through my contact lenses. A tiny pearl crown on my head. My mother sighing with

relief: *A doctor she's marrying, thank God; she's nearly twenty-three.*
Except for his baldness, he hasn't changed a bit. Same soft eyes,
same earnest smile, same uncompromising values, same rabbinical look. In those days I'd look away modestly and say, "I
love you." Even when he cut short our three-day honeymoon to
return to his residency. How understanding I was.

How quickly we fell into routine. The long weekends of his
final year, endless hours in the emergency room, his exhaustion, my posing with a huge belly in the St. Louis snow. After
lovemaking he'd stand awkwardly in the hall in his white gown
almost afraid to say those words: "I have to go now, Nina. I'll
be back tomorrow night."

"All right," I lied.

"Maybe you should phone your mother so you won't be lonely."

"No, no, everything's fine. I'd rather be alone."

"Then why are you crying? You knew it would be this way."

"It's okay. Go on." Listen to footsteps resound in the dark
hallway of our apartment building.

Five years and we never quarreled. *Nina, my friend needs a loan.
But Maury, we haven't gone anywhere for so long. I've got to lend him
some money. All right, Maury. Time to visit my family. Can't we skip this
Friday night? You don't have to say anything. Just sit with them. Listen,
let's invite them here next week. Maury, you know I can't cook anything
your mother does. Make something simple; it doesn't matter.*

How grateful I was. His family called me lucky. What could I
do to please such a giving man? Only conceive and that I
managed despite our obstetrician-friend's prognosis: *her pelvis
is small.* But they came anyway, three births in five years, the
miracle of our children's lives escaping us, distracting us from
our own goals. They ran through the town house shrieking,
crying, tumbling down the stairs, biting each other, demanding
love and attention. He loved them; they bewildered him. "Why
are they so wild?" he scratched his head.

"Because they're spoiled. Didn't your mother spoil you?"

"She didn't have time. She always worked in the grocery to
save money for our schooling."

"Why don't you humor them? Why are you so strict?"

"Because I love them, because I want them to know right from wrong."

How problematic they were—Joey repeating first grade, Amy moody and withdrawn, Rachel with her temper tantrums. Every year we were unprepared for their growing pains. And our own as well. Every year he said, *the medical profession's got to change. No, Maury, you've got to adapt to it. What you want is impossible.* Six times we moved chasing impossibilities. All the time our parents hovering in the background: *Tell him medicine is a business; his income depends on that.*

Our final move to the west coast nearly destroyed us. Here away from friends and family among capricious San Francisco temperaments, Rachel crawls out of diapers and into kindergarten. "I'm sick of your ideals. Sick of being called 'doctor's wife,' I'm going after mine now," I rant.

"What are you going to do?"

"I don't know, but I'll find out."

"Do what you want. Have I ever stopped you from doing what you want?"

"Your very presence stops me. Your—"

"That's your fault, not mine. I could never please you anyway. Just don't ask *me* to change; just leave me alone."

I don't ask. I sit in the kitchen of our new California-style house late at night writing poems. For the first time in years. Those poems, that passion, born of my guts, my joy alone, not his, *mine.* Published in an obscure feminist university journal. I'm a feminist, liberated. Suburban mother of three, I howl with delight. Dance with the children, drive to the top of Mt. Diablo, shout from its peaks: *Mamma's gone mad.*

With that madness 1970 breaks, and I'm transformed. Nina the Iconoclast. Chipping away at his pedestal. He's rigid, unathletic, boring, *too moral.* I'll leave. Go to live in a women's commune in Berkeley, fly to Israel and build the desert, make up for lost time. Drown myself in Bergman, look for the young Chicano I met in the poetry stacks. But I watch him say *Kaddish* for the death of his patient, listen to the sound of his Danish rocker and favorite Oistrakh, look into his deep hazel eyes that refuse to see the senselessness of our lives, and bound off to the laundry room like a hurt puppy. There in that familiar maze of underwear, old texts and paperbacks, I announce, "I'm starting school again."

"Good idea, but don't become too compulsive about it."

How well he knows my compulsiveness. School's not so easy now. My forehead tingles, my stomach cramps. Rachel asks why I'm not room-mother. "Because I have to study," I snap, a dragon at dinner hour. Course after course. Women and Madness, La Raza Studies, Seminar in Faulkner, Tai Chi, the Yiddish Novel.

The children's diapers are replaced by braces, lessons, tutors, car pools, conferences, puberty. They alone grow. We merely age, I studying at night toward some unknown pursuit, Maury reading journals and Middle East news reports.

"Ten o'clock. I'm on call. I've got to get some rest."

"Go ahead. I'm studying."

"Why do you play this game every night?"

"What game?"

"All right, study. Study until you beg me to touch you. I'm fed up. You and your games."

"I'm not playing games. I just have no desire."

"Then why don't you leave? It's fashionable for women to leave men these days. I'll give you anything you want. Just go so I can have some peace."

"Don't be ridiculous; you think I'd leave you and the children?"

"Why not? You probably have a lover anyway."

"Are you mad? Are you *absolutely* mad?"

"Then why do you act like this?"

"Like what?"

"Your lack of desire, your inability to manage the kids. Why don't you go for help?"

"Because I'm trying to change? Because I'm trying to do something for myself? You're the one who should go. You've lost touch with reality."

"Go in the kitchen and study. You don't respect anything I believe in. You want something I can't give you. I'm just a small man."

The yellow wallpaper rages in silence. All these years—wasted. He with his kindness has made me afraid of the world, he with his selflessness has made me nothing, and I've let it happen. What am I next to him?

The phone rings. He dresses and leaves. I close my text and creep into our bedroom, lie by the telephone on his side of the bed. Browse in a new novel. What reckless heroines, what cads the men are. Why can't we be like that?

He's gone an hour now. The rage dissolves into a whimper. The wind bangs at the patio windows, dogs bark, children moan, the faucet drips. What if Maury dies? Would I mourn him for years? Would I ever take a lover?

Phone again. A woman I met at school.

"One partner in fourteen years? This is the Age of Aquarius."

"For him it isn't."

"And for you?"

"Me? I don't know."

"You're still hung up because he's a doctor."

"It's not that. It's the kind of person he is."

"You mean *you are*. You'll change, you'll see. By the end of the year you'll change."

"Not in *that* way. You know I still have some traditional values."

"You and he are just alike, killing yourselves with an outmoded moral code. You have to move with the times."

"I know, I know."

"No you don't. Otherwise you'd forget your fantasies or admit you still care for him."

"I can't."

At 2:00 A.M. he comes in, face sallow, tired, blood on his undershorts. "A terrible case, Nina, a young man. Motorcycle accident. He'll be dead by morning. Let me hold you. I can't do my work without you."

A winter moon floods our bedroom. Succumb but don't surrender. Don't share his act of love. Separate mind, nourish it with illusions of young men in my classes. He falls asleep immediately, not waking to wash. Listen to his snoring. Anesthetic on his fingers, spittle on his lip. How could I ever leave? He'd work himself to death. I'm the small one, not he. If only

I'd let go of my anger, if only I'd stop blaming him for my failures. Sleep, morning obligation, make lunch, the children—

We wake, shut off from one another, two strangers. Wordless, he shaves, runs off to the hospital. Phones me at ten. A sudden joy in his voice. "Nina, he's going to *live*. There *must* be a God, do you hear? When I told that to the men, they laughed. Nina, say something."

I can't. He waits for my silence to end. "Listen, I know this has been a hard month. One of the men told me about a place in Mexico. Maybe we could drive down with the kids when they're on spring vacation."

"I don't think they'll want to go. Last time we took them with us it was a disaster. You hollered at Joey the whole time, and Amy's complaints drove me crazy."

"We could leave them with Mrs. Larsen."

"Rachel hates Mrs. Larsen."

"How about Mrs. Bertoli?"

"Too expensive."

"Well, I just wanted to check before I take extra call this month. This malpractice insurance will either kill me or make me retire."

"Take the call, Maury; we'll stay at home."

"You're sure?"

"I'm sure; you're not ready to retire. Maury—I'm glad about your patient."

"Don't be glad for me, be glad for him."

He didn't even mention our anniversary; he didn't remember. Every year he forgets. Yes, we'll stay home this time as we have all the other times. And yet there's something different this year as I sort the towels. His key in the door, breakfast dishes unwashed. He's home so soon flipping on the news.

"It's too early for lunch."

"I know." Hands me a single rose, kisses my neck. "Happy Anniversary." Looks so helpless I want to reach out but don't. My eyes wet. "Come on, I'll make you lunch. What time do you have to be back?"

"I don't; the anesthesiologist is on strike. No work."

He changes into his gardening pants. When did he let his sideburns grow? They're nearly gray. How he loves watering the garden. Always has been more nurturing than I. Awkward eating without the children. What to say to each other—just two of us alone. A new phase we're entering this fifteenth year.

"The salad's great. You know, we should become vegetarians," he suddenly laughs.

"Can you see Joey existing without his sloppy joes and hot dogs?"

"Give him five more years, he will. He get off okay this morning? He was mumbling about some science project."

"Fine, he's even turning into a decent kid. Decent but different from us."

"He's growing up in such different times; it's hard on him. Good to be home. After seeing that patient this morning I promised myself not to worry about anything. Are you angry at me?"

"Why do you ask?"

"You seemed upset this morning."

"I was angry at myself."

"What for?"

"Because I've let myself become too much like you."

"Why do you say that? We have our separate friends, interests—"

"Even Bob Stoller said we're getting to look alike."

He grins. "Only our noses. Did you know that Stoller and his wife broke up last week?"

"Nothing surprises me these days. How come you didn't tell me?"

"What's the use of telling bad news? Nina, let's sell the house; let's go live in the country. I'm sick and tired of everything. I'm going to look at a place this weekend."

"Are you kidding?"

"I'm not. Let's finish lunch and talk about it in bed."

"But Rachel comes home at two, and I've got to finish a poem."

"Forget the poem. If you work too hard, you'll become a poet. Then what would I do?"

"Maury, you're a chauvinist!"

"No, I'm not, just jealous."

"*You're* jealous of *me*?"

"You've more time to think, to be yourself."

"I suppose I do."

"More time to do what you want."

"Oh, come on now."

"Well, I can't do what I want either. People like us have too many responsibilities. We live limited lives."

He stands there in his underwear, his pale skin covered with black down. The veins in his neck pulsate like the days in our old St. Louis apartment when we were first married. March twenty-first, 1960. First day of spring. *I still care, I still care.* I didn't know that I did, but I do.

My Mother Was a Light Housekeeper

Thyme S. Seagull

HELLO, BERKELEY, YOUR acid sparkled streets glistening
through the smog, heartland in the production of rhetoric,
land of free boxes, neighborhood warning systems, block
dances, food conspiracies, and my relatives. Aunt Riba and
Uncle Roy's bright one-story stucco, catty-corner to a decaying
mansion—where some of their children live communally.

Rosh Hashonah. I wonder why Jewish New Year begins in the
Fall instead of the Spring. The Spring would feel more natural.
I reach their doorbell just as mom and dad drive up in their
camper. Everyone on time for the holiday dinner. Me, mom,
and dad have never been here before because Aunt, Uncle, and
Sarah, the Old Mother, have just moved to Berkeley to be near
their children. Everyone very keyed up. Riba, Roy, and Sarah all
answer the door. Excited talking, sharing information about

Thyme S. Seagull lives in Eugene, Oregon, where she does lesbian feminist radio
programming. She is the author of "Rima Comes to Emerald City" and "Get
It Right the First Time," unpublished sequels to "My Mother Was a Light
Housekeeper." "My Mother Was a Light Housekeeper," copyright © 1978 by
Thyme S. Seagull, was first published in *Sinister Wisdom* 6 (Summer 1978).

missing members of the clan. Showing family photos. I drift to the rear and notice Sarah, the Old Mother, standing at the doorway to the back porch.

"We had a nice house in D.C.," Sarah says to me in familiar yet surprising Yiddish accents, a sound I have not heard for years. She is very short and stooped, wrinkled, not older but ancient. "It had a lot of room, big backyard, lots of flowers and trees." I can see into the backyard here: tiny.

"Yes, but they left that house and moved here?"

"They wanted to be near the children."

"Your great-grandchildren."

"Yes, them especially, Lillakah and Lil'Umbillakah."

I look wonderingly at the Old Mother, a fantastic survivor. A Ukrainian. She is so short it is easy to overlook her wrinkled face. But I look at her carefully. I had overlooked my own grandmother.

"You knew my Bubie?" (I ask after my grandmother.)

"Yes," Sarah whispers. "A very progressive woman, very progressive. I knew her in Elsinore, when I lived in Los Angeles." The rest of the family is floating towards us. I see mom's attention about to catch onto our conversation. I tighten up and respond quickly, "Yes! I was there too."

"Elsinore is a Yiddishe shtetl," Sarah comments.

"Yes, I know," I whisper quickly, as mom interjects. "Yiddishe shtetl! She doesn't know what you mean, grandma, these kids don't know what it means—" Ha ha ha ha, they laugh about how these kids don't understand.

"*I know what it means,*" I say, but she and Sarah are talking away in Yiddish. (Oy Gottenyu, she's auf tsurus, A Shaynim Donk in Pupik.) It is true I don't understand much.

"It means Jewish ghetto," mom stops long enough to tell me.

"I *know.*"

"Well, that's better than the rest of these kids."

"You only spoke Yiddish to each other, not to us." You and dad spoke in your thick private flavors. We were outside of it; we spoke English in harsh unhappy tones, coping with public school in rural America . . . "But I *was* in Elsinore and I'm *not* a total idiot."

Mom blue-eyes me, smiling. Is it ok to come out with it like that? Did I hurt her? A record in Hebrew I never heard before is playing on the stereo. "Anachnu Ve'Atem" is the refrain, a powerful chant from Israel.

"What's that, mom?"

"A song about Us and Them."

I don't know how to ask mom if I have hurt her. It is very beautiful music so it catches us for awhile, then she wanders off to join a conversation with my aunt, who is setting the table. I turn back to the Old Mother. "I know Elsinore is the West Coast shtetl. I could easily see that. The only ones in the streets and the stores are elderly Jews."

"Yes, and they have a community center," says Sarah.

"Yes, I know. Bubie and I went there. To a concert. A woman was singing in an evening gown. Bubie started singing too."

"Yes, she loved to sing. Such a good voice too."

"The people who were running the show didn't think she should sing because it wasn't her concert. A man came over and told her to stop singing. She got really pissed off. We had to leave. She was mad and didn't want to stay anymore. As we walked out, she muttered resentful curses at the people who ran the community center, all the way out, real loud, everyone heard and turned around as we left."

"She was an individual, very stubborn, very progressive."

The dinner table is covered with white paper, centered with candelabra and dotted with red wine bottles. For a moment I recall the ancient ceremonies, chanting in Hebrew for three hours around the table before we could eat, the ancient ceremonies during which I stared at the matzoh crumbs and the red wine stains on the white paper. While the grandfather chanted in a language I didn't learn, and all the relatives jabbered away in yet another language I did not learn. What does anything mean? I long ago tired of asking, or maybe I never did ask. I am a foreigner in the ancient culture, the languages, the traditions. I am light years away. Or has it only been a generation? In me, the tradition of five thousand years dies. I am the daughter who cannot carry on the family name, practice the ceremonies. I am the daughter who searches for a new tribe. Who searches for primitive solidarity in a new culture of women. What was coherent for them has never been coherent for me.

"Maybe you'd want to write a book review for *Freiheit*?" asks Uncle Roy. (*Freiheit* is a socialist journal which he edits, modeled after the old *Freiheit*.)

"No," I say, flatly and glumly. "I've done that already. Book reviews are fine, but first I want a different space."

"She doesn't want to do journalism anymore, Roy." Aunt Riba. I look at her in surprised gratitude.

"What do you want to write? For whom? To be published in a book? Magazine, where?" Uncle Roy demands.

"A book maybe."

"What, a novel, fiction, what?"

"Something which emanates from the dream consciousness. *Freedom begins in the realm of dreams,*" I quote.

"Freedom is only in the realm of dreams," says Sarah, in Yiddish. Mom translates to the rest of us, the younger generation.

A silence follows. Then Uncle Roy continues dominating the dinner conversation with social, political issues. Mom, dad, and Aunt Riba follow along avidly while the rest of us red-diaper babies, in various stages of dress and stress, delicately slurp and gobble the split pea soup, chicken, and mushrooms.

"Do you think the working class is becoming more progressive?" asks Uncle Roy of my father.

Dad clears his throat. "Well, I can tell you, from traveling around the country a lot and living in trailer parks these last several years, I can tell you they are still very reactionary," says dad, in his slow laryngitic voice.

"Or maybe it's the union leaders who are," adds mom.

Why is it that I am always surrounded by people speculating on the working class—is it capable of transforming itself in the U.S.? can there be a revolution? I am still in the heartland of theory, with my relatives. I haven't seen mom and dad in a year; we've all been traveling around. I want to talk about experiences.

"Who have you met lately? Who travels in these trailers?"

"We met some travelers in Montana who used to live down the road from us," says mom.

"Really, who?"

"Oh, we never knew them when we lived there. They were on their way to moving to Grants Pass, Oregon. . . . *We* could never move to Grants Pass," mom ends sharply.

"Why not?" I ask, still not getting it.

"Because we're Jews." (Get it, get it?)

"I can't just move anywhere I want either," I say. "I mean lesbians can't." Mom looks at me, somewhat pained.

"Isn't that where you spent the summer, Cheike, around there? At a festival?" Dad.

"What kind of festival?" asks Uncle Roy, perking up.

"A women's spiritual gathering."

"What's that?" he persists.

"Ummm, uh, uhmmm," I look around the table. Everyone is staring down at their chicken, listening intently. What to say? "It was women getting together on land, like a campout, to center ourselves as a group. We're developing our own culture." Unfortunately, I get into it and go on. "But we didn't own the land, and the man who owned the land insisted on being there."

"You've gone too far," says dad. "Why do you have to have all-women gatherings and always say, 'Too bad there was a man there'? It's like colored people when they got money at first they went out and bought Cadillacs but now some of 'em drive VW's."

I can't follow the logic of dad's remark so I turn to my aunt and mom, who are sitting together, seeming to agree with dad. "You have to experience working with all women and being with all women. You've been married for decades and decades, how would you know?"

"Oh, I have experience," answers mom, with a touch of hauteur.

"The women at B'nai B'rith used to get together every week," adds Aunt Riba.

"It's not the same thing. You went home to husbands afterwards. Living with men and visiting or going to meetings is different than living with all women . . ."

At this point my uncle gets up, grandiosely announcing that he will wash the dishes.

"I'm going to help him," says mom, with laughing emphasis.

"How long can a group of women stay together?" asks dad. "It's not like you have kids to keep you together."

I move my mouth to protest. Some lesbians have kids. Why do you need kids to stay together? What does stay-together mean? How important is it? But how can I ask them? *They* don't know.

"Women living just with women, ay meshugge," continues dad. "It's absurd." Almost everyone laughs, thinking of the absurdity of it. Not maliciously, though, it is just ludicrous to them. Nothing I say can make it real; I don't have the answers, the experiences, five thousand years of ritual at my fingertips, five thousand years of red wine at my lips, to make them speak the words from beyond the heartland of rhetoric. I try to imagine my tribe, we who will shout *KinsWoman!* to each other in a tribal tongue. I imagine us in a dance to the light, our own festival of light, into ourselves and into each other, dancing around candles on the Solstice. I imagine saying to the children, "We have danced this dance and chanted this chant for five thousand years. It celebrates the eternal return of the light."

These are the words, but I do not have them.

Walking along the streets of the colonial town where I went to high school, I am with a very open being. A being who has just come into the country from Nepal or Ceylon. But I sense she is the same one from high school, the mysterious Sing, who appeared those years to us in stately silence, elegant, impeccable. Sing, forever the profile of the kiss not taken. I am showing her Main Street.

Then the scene shifts to the farm: Nuovev Jasmine. She has a room under our roof, like a nest in the eaves. We go up to my little bedroom overlooking the pond, right under her nest. As we lie in bed together, we can see the sun rising over the trees around the pond. We are touching, I am touching her face, so tender and clear. She is open to me.

I ask her questions. I take off the last of my clothes and then she does too, smiling, watching me. The softness of her caress across my breast is like silky seaweed on underwater skin. Everywhere I am opened, sensual.

Suddenly, the sense of another. Vashti is sitting hidden in the blankets at the foot of the bed, staring at the sunrise. My younger sister. I feel around the blankets. "So there you are. Why don't you open the downstairs drapes?" (Same view.)

"That's OK, I'm going outside," she says, and goes. I lie back. We're

spending the whole day in bed together, timelessly. "I don't know what time it is because I don't have any clocks around," I explain, although it is not necessary. Then the dream changes, turns round. I'm waking up.

Cheike! Cheike! "Are you ready to face reality?" asks my mother, with her own brand of gentle sarcasm. The fragile film of the dream is dissolving. Oh, what was it? The feeling of spending the whole day in bed with a woman, a very large woman who holds me, with long, thick red-gold hair. And cascading matzoh boxes at the very end.

Daylight streams into the trailer. Mom turns on the nine o'clock news. Patty Hearst capture news. Reality. I am not lying with my lover. I have no lover. I am with mom and dad in their trailer. California sunshine is bouncing off all the cement and metal in this trailer court.

"Can I turn off the radio?" I leap up, turning off the radio.

"Don't you want to hear what's really happening in the world?"

"I can't do anything to help Patty Hearst. I want to write in my journal."

Mom is washing the dishes, standing firmly in sneakers and anklets. She glances over at the marbled cardboard notebook I open, like the ones from grade school. Back on the farm, it hadn't occurred to me to write in front of anyone, and I had never seen anyone else write. It was a deep dark secret, like what happened behind closed doors in bathrooms and bedrooms.

"Do you ever read it, or do you just write in it?" mom asks.

"No read, just write, ha ha ha." No, I don't show my writing. What if I opened my books to mom and dad, showed my whole self, dark green and silent childhood? But my flippant manner has closed the subject.

"Yes, I reread it sometimes. I learn from it." Whoever wrote in a journal on the farm? All I ever saw was a locked wooden box of mom and dad's love letters. And my older sister's locked diary, in which she vowed never to tell a future husband she had lost her chastity. Nuovcv Jasmine, a paradisiacal Jewish chicken farm in the forties and fifties, when adventuring into the interior was called "too subjective." Politics and economics were going to save the era. And politics was what got you in trouble and made people hate you. The childhood faces of the Rosenberg boys haunted my childhood from the back cover of *Death-House Letters*. Which sat on their dresser for years, like a permanent fixture. I recall that bedroom, which looked out over the pond. The double bed I had to cover so precisely—but never lie on. The night table next to it on mom's side, upon which sat *The Well of Loneliness* (in paper) and a lamp, also for years.

"Why don't we ever share what it felt like to live at Nuovev Jasmine?"

Mom looks at me warily. I used to be so critical of her. She finishes drying her hands on a dish towel. "What do you want to talk about?"

I feel shaky, on thin ice, but ready to skate—"I hear you calling my name. Like a shattering reverberation over fifty acres of corn stubbles, rattling through the woods. 'Cheikk-kkeeeeeeee. . . .'

"It is winter, the corn stubbles are frozen, my feet crunch in the snow. I want to explore how the eastern woods look in the snow, the density, the designs, the feeling of the snow transforming an already secret place. It was not a place where anyone accompanied me. I could see dad driving the pick-up on a far western cornfield, heading toward the garbage pit. You were calling from the porch, you wanted me to help with the laundry . . ." Mom's tan face is frowning.

Is it ok to talk like this? Dad is outside the trailer, I can see him setting up a vise-grip on the back of the camper, his new workroom. A condensation of the garage and feedroom at Nuovev Jasmine. I can see his white hair curling up the back of his neck as he bends forward in concentration. He is making earrings out of nickels. Mom gets up to sweep the floor, commenting that what she does and what dad does is what is most comfortable for each. There is no problem. As she moves around, the trailer shakes, the floor shakes, and the ceiling shakes. Reminding me of dawn. (At dawn the rocking trailer woke mom up. "What's going on?" she asked in a startled urgent voice. From my berth I stopped wiggling and didn't tell her what was going on. Just laughed that I had had a farm dream again.)

"So what? I was doing the laundry . . . dad was dumping the garbage, you were—"

"What? What was I?"

Mom's eyes light up to answer, "I didn't want you to do the laundry, Cheike. Actually, I wanted you to do the eggs!"

"Ah yes, you wanted me to do the eggs. Remember when the bouncing trailer woke us this morning? I was having a dream of packing eggs!" (I still won't say I was masturbating.) "I was bouncing in my dream." At this point dad comes in and leans against the door frame, listening to us. "Only I'm not packing eggs for Nuovev Jasmine, I'm packing eggs for *Amazonia*. It's clearly printed in blue on the side of each thirty-dozen box. The eggs are all packed strangely, all different sizes—jumbos and peewees together, checked and cracked, flats and fillers not filled to the proper amounts . . ."

We all laugh. Yea, the egg room, grading and packing all those years, a fragile egg myself, thin and unexposed, not like those hardy egos developing in the outside world. Eggs falling off the machine and smashing on the cement—eaten by wild chicken coop cats, darting in at the sound—eggs crunched together on the way from the washer to the grader, squeezed and falling, eggs outside crunched by tractor tires, eggshells in the mud. Huge white eggs and little inverts, soft-shelled eggs, malleable in fingers, floppy, lacking—calcium? Lacking the right support . . . The Large go in the large, the Mediums go in the medium, the Pullets go in the pullet . . . Experiences rolling down the blue runways of the grader table, and you pack them away fast, so they don't pile up, and ship them in caseloads to the Cities . . .

But the soft ones, maybe they didn't smash as hard and fast as the firm ones. Eggshells in Amazonia, which exists in our northwoods minds like an Atlantis on land. Like the new continent of Mu. The trick is to reach Amazonia without these old, almost fatal wounds. Might this trailer understand Amazonia— understand it as the total space, separate culture, the earth and sky. And eggs, mom and dad understood: eggs, seeds, and ponds.

"I want to ask you something, Cheike." Mom, in a serious tone. Oh, no! What is it? "Why did you change your name?"

Reflex: defense. "Because these Anglos can't pronounce Cheike properly."

"It doesn't make sense to me. People will mispronounce your new name too."

"It's a tribal name. I belong to a different tribe now. But I have many names. To you I am still Cheike."

"To me, you are still Baby." She laughs. I don't mind her laugh, but I bring her up to date. "I'm not a baby anymore though, you know, I'm a lesbian woman . . ."

"Why do you always have to bring up being a lesbian?"

"I hardly ever do—that you hear."

"Like last night."

"Because it fit in. You always think you're different and can't fit in anywhere in small town America, and that's true, but there are lots of reasons why people don't fit in and can't move anywhere they like. It goes double for me. There are very few places I can live. You wonder why I don't settle down, and that's why. I have to find a women's community I can live in . . ." I look up at dad, who is shaking his head. "What, no?"

"Tell me, Cheike," his old hoarse voice, "do you have to be a lesbian to be a feminist?"

Oh no, that question again. I can pretend I don't know. "I don't know. I did—have to become a lesbian before I could be anything but a feminist literary critic. But that was because my ideas were years ahead of my behavior. Some of my ideas."

"Don't you think women can oppress other women?" pursues dad. "I know some very domineering women."

"Yea, sure. The difference is in a group awareness. Now we try to avoid the roles that reinforce oppression."

"That's you and your friends. There are domineering women."

"I'm talking about what lesbians all over the country are trying to do these days . . . Let's go to the beach!" I say in sudden inspiration, my fingers almost burning against the hot silver metal outside the open door.

It is our last day together. Mom and dad are heading for Arizona in their trailer and I to Oregon in my VW bug. Everyone agrees to the trip to the beach. We do not rush.

"Tell me, what are you going to do from here? Are you going to settle down?" mom continues.

"You sound like Bubie."

"We're worried about you."

"I see my life as a story: at first I was very threatened. I escaped by running into the pond and going underwater. I held out for a long time, long enough, although once when I did pop up I got shot at. I went under again—long enough to be in a later age, a different time and place. I come up. It feels quiet now, safe now. I go to a house where I feel attracted; a woman is there I want to see. To leave, we have to climb out the second story window down an escape, because of her husband, who wants to continue to possess her. But I want to leave, and she follows me. We go out on a road, which is a ledge, a narrow ledge of ourselves. To the right is an enormous drop; to our left, a sheer cliff wall. We are following the path to Amazonia."

"Where's Amazonia?"

"It's an erotic hillside in Brazil. It's a scenario."

"A scenery? A Brazil scenery?"

"Huh. It's women, all kinds of women, egg women, crying young egg girls growing up in so many shapes and sizes, checked and cracked, who grew up in so many conditions but together at last. Not sorted out into hierarchies, you might say . . . or I might say, anyway . . . anarchy and variety are our beginning characteristics."

Silence. Then, "Your generation has had a much better opportunity to associate with each other from different social, religious, and economic backgrounds." Wow! She understands. "Then there's psychological backgrounds and astrological backgrounds . . . !" I have to add.

"Let's go."

On the way we stop to pick up Daro, a young woman who wants a ride with me to Oregon. May as well start early. Although I don't know Daro at this point, I know that with her along I won't be outnumbered. I associate her as one on my path.

Daro smiles calmly and swings in the front seat of my bug. Mom and dad are in back. Her vibrant brown eyes beam familiarity.

"Why do women wear beards these days?" asks dad. Oh no, he has noticed Daro's strong stray chin hairs. Daro looks at me suddenly and then turns around to the back seat. "Why don't you?"

Mom comes in here, rendering a textbook lecture on hor-

monal balances in each sex. She remembers a dark-haired girl-
friend from high school who had had chin hair. I glance over
at Daro's shoulder, covered with glistening reddish-dark hair.
"Was that the one who didn't want you to get married, mom?"
I pipe up. "Yes, that was the one."

"It's defiance," says dad. Dad still believes in some of the
hierarchies of family and society.

"Defiance! It takes courage to be ourselves in a society with
its overpowering demands for a certain look!"

Mom agrees. Dad goes on, "You'd be safer on the streets if
your appearance conformed. That's why the Jews got away from
wearing payess [side curls], yarmulkahs, and black robes. Why
do you think? I see some women walking around in ripped, dirty
jeans. People aren't tolerant. They'll attack you if you look different."

I can tell dad is recalling his boyhood in eastern Poland. He
knows what it is like to be hated because of how you look. He
is trying to warn us compassionately, but I am pretty sure he is
offending Daro, who stares down at her velvet jeans patches.

"How you look is not reason for men to attack women," says
mom.

"Yes, but it makes you stand out, that's when people attack
you, when they think you hate them."

"We're into love, not hate, dad."

"The world isn't ready for love."

I stare out along the gorgeous coastline. What is the world
ready for, then?

"Let's pull over," I say, and I pick a beach, a pull-in near an
artichoke field. Beyond that, there is a promontory with a lighthouse on the end.

"Can you pick any beach?" "Yes," I assure them, "that is what
I always do." They have not been to a Pacific beach before. Daro
bounds out over the dunes as soon as we stop. Mom and dad
settle faces down on a blanket. Dad goes to sleep, and mom
reads a *Country Women* magazine I gave her. She unzips the back
of her sundress. Only the skin around her neck is freckled and
tan. Dad's whole back is dark-red bronze, like their faces. The
contrast with their white hair strikes me. Mom's blue eyes sparkle out to me. Together with them at last on a Pacific beach, we

are a flock of water-sharers. No one else is on the beach, just us refugees from the East—and Daro. Here the ocean is not blocked into swimming areas like the Middle Atlantic, no boardwalks, no saltwater taffy stands, no screaming rides. Just dunes, wildflowers, cliff walls, spun sponge rocks, phosphorescent caves. A freshwater stream—flowing through a crater of sand nearby. Around us—trails of seagull feathers and transparent sacs of jelly.

Daro reappears, examining the purple sac inside one, a glob of jelly fish, watching the bubbles blow within it. She hands me a feather and sinks down on the blanket, resting her hand on my knee. Mom on my other side reaches her hand around me to touch Daro. Her hand doesn't quite reach so she wiggles around and moves up an inch so she can reach. Daro's self-absorption is like soft tissue wrapped around a sharp object. Mom wants to make up for the car conversation. Dad decides to tell a joke. "Once there was a kid who dared her father to eat half a worm: 'I'll eat half if you eat half.' The father takes up the dare and eats half the worm. He gives the other half to the kid, but the kid says, 'You ate the wrong half!' " Daro likes this story and laughs, bowing her head over my lap, laughing.

"I didn't mean anything before about how you look, honey, I was just talking." Dad's laryngitic kindly voice. He has a cold. Daro looks at him and relaxes. He is a grandfather, and tired, smiling inside his thinning curly mop of white hair, his red skin criss-crossed with lines.

"Mom and dad used to be farmers, Daro, now they are gypsies, like us." I want her to know them, to feel safe and accepted with them, as I do, because I feel how suspicious she is of parents. Later, I discover she is more like them than I will ever be. Those three are of the earth, and I am of the air. For years I resisted mom and dad, not just their parental intonations, but as representatives of the material plane itself. The maintenance of a real farm. They had long ago freely admitted to not being philosopher-poets—my one requirement for the people I live with—but bread-and-butter folks, the people who keep the home front repaired. I was a little Rimbaud monster hatched from the cosmic egg, seeking visions. Later, I learned that air needs the protection of earth, and the earth needs the air to breathe. We unite in the sight of the water and the fire. It would be neat to stay and have a camp fire on the beach.

"I wish I hadn't felt so separated from you two for so long. We could have shared a lot more."

"You wouldn't unlock your door," says mom.

"You didn't ask the right questions."

"We didn't realize you felt separated. Parents assume they can tell what's going on, they don't ask questions," says dad.

"Your father didn't converse with you, draw you out, did he, dad?" Dad exhales sharply, like *Are you kidding?* His father was a rabbi from the Old Country, not attentive to the psychology of childhood.

"You know," says mom, "my mother always asked a lot of questions and I resented it. I kept my distance from you. I didn't want to intrude like that."

"Oh, I'm a bird, I love like a bird," I say. What is the use of going over the past, the years I spent behind a closed door, a little alcove where I wrote things I never admitted to and gazed at the pond from my attic window. "I was a bird, trapped in an attic." I laugh. And then lapse into broody silence. Daro smiles brightly sparkling brown eyes at me and reaches around, tentatively touching my shoulder. I reach around mom and knead her shoulders. Smooth the little knots. Imagine she is doing the same to me. Dad goes back to sleep. I concentrate on breathing in and out. Mom looks over the *Country Women* magazine I gave her, an issue on "older women." After awhile she says, "What about older men? I don't want to leave my boyfriend." And puts her arm around dad's sleeping form. I don't know; I don't know. My eyes feel tired, either from the sun or from uncried tears. *When* am I going to be with whomever I should be with? And *when* am I going to be wherever I should be? And they, who have each other only, where can they settle down, their new Jerusalem? Not in the same direction as Amazonia. We are cultural refugees together for only a few weeks each year, on our separate roads. Nuovev Jasmine is gone, the pond a swamp again. I haven't been back, but I saw that in a dream. Never again can we skinny dip, boat, or skate on it. The pond is shrunk and dirty, receded from the pier, ukky. The man who bought it turned it into a sewage disposal for his trailer park.

I jump up, facing the vast expanse before us. I want to swim; I rip off my clothes and run down into the tide. Raising my arms high and jumping, a tremendous wave crests beneath me. There is only the Adventure left, only the quest for a new native land. Look at them on the shore, here for only one moment do we inhabit the same reality, here at land's end, mom, dad, Daro and me in the same shot, the same frame. Click!

Over the dunes a man in street dress appears. He says, "This isn't a public beach, it's my beach." So we have to leave here. Dad wants to go anyway, he's not feeling that well. I slip into my soft gym pants, but the waist drawstring is lost down its slot. I feel tired, I want to flop down, not leave. I feel like a baby, wanting to cry in frustration because I can't get the string to come through the slot. To scream and cry like a baby.

"Mom . . .?"

"You do it with a safety pin. Here." She stands in front of me, patiently threading the knot through the opening. I stand silently watching, like a pacified toddler. I can see the lighthouse behind her, at the edge of the promontory. Victorious, finished, she stands straight and smiles. Sardonically, she says, "Your mother is a light housekeeper . . ."

Virgo woman, steadiness and continuation in seas of change, *I salute you.*

IV
NEW
DIRECTIONS

X: A Fabulous Child's Story

Lois Gould

ONCE UPON A time, a baby named X was born. This baby was
named X so that nobody could tell whether it was a boy or
a girl. Its parents could tell, of course, but they couldn't tell
anybody else. They couldn't even tell Baby X, at first.

You see, it was all part of a very important Secret Scientific
Xperiment, known officially as Project Baby X. The smartest
scientists had set up this Xperiment at a cost of Xactly 23 billion
dollars and 72 cents, which might seem like a lot for just one
baby, even a very important Xperimental baby. But when you
remember the prices of things like strained carrots and stuffed
bunnies, and popcorn for the movies and booster shots for
camp, let alone 28 shiny quarters from the tooth fairy, you
begin to see how it adds up.

Also, long before Baby X was born, all those scientists had to

Lois Gould is a former police reporter who served as editor of the *Long Island
Star Journal* and as executive editor of the *Ladies' Home Journal.* Her four published novels are *Such Good Friends, Necessary Objects, Final Analysis,* and *A Sea
Change;* a collection of her essays, *Not Responsible for Personal Articles,* appeared
in 1978. "X: A Fabulous Child's Story," copyright © 1978 by Lois Gould, is
reprinted by permission of Daughters Publishing Co., Inc.

be paid to work out the details of the Xperiment, and to write the *Official Instruction Manual* for Baby X's parents and, most important of all, to find the right set of parents to bring up Baby X. These parents had to be selected very carefully. Thousands of volunteers had to take thousands of tests and answer thousands of tricky questions. Almost everybody failed because, it turned out, almost everybody really wanted either a baby boy or a baby girl, and not Baby X at all. Also, almost everybody was afraid that a Baby X would be a lot more trouble than a boy or a girl. (They were probably right, the scientists admitted, but Baby X needed parents who wouldn't *mind* the Xtra trouble.)

There were families with grandparents named Milton and Agatha, who didn't see why the baby couldn't be named Milton or Agatha instead of X, even if it *was* an X. There were families with aunts who insisted on knitting tiny dresses and uncles who insisted on sending tiny baseball mitts. Worst of all, there were families that already had other children who couldn't be trusted to keep the secret. Certainly not if they knew the secret was worth 23 billion dollars and 72 cents—and all you had to do was take one little peek at Baby X in the bathtub to know if it was a boy or a girl.

But, finally, the scientists found the Joneses, who really wanted to raise an X more than any other kind of baby—no matter how much trouble it would be. Ms. and Mr. Jones had to promise they would take equal turns caring for X, and feeding it, and singing it lullabies. And they had to promise never to hire any baby-sitters. The government scientists knew perfectly well that a baby-sitter would probably peek at X in the bathtub, too.

The day the Joneses brought their baby home, lots of friends and relatives came over to see it. None of them knew about the secret Xperiment, though. So the first thing they asked was what kind of baby X was. When the Joneses smiled and said, "It's an X!" nobody knew what to say. They couldn't say, "Look at her cute little dimples!" And they couldn't say, "Look at his husky little biceps!" And they couldn't even say just plain "kitchy-coo." In fact, they all thought the Joneses were playing some kind of rude joke.

But, of course, the Joneses were not joking. "It's an X" was absolutely all they would say. And that made the friends and relatives very angry. The relatives all felt embarrassed about having an X in the family. "People will think there's something wrong with it!" some of them whispered. "There *is* something wrong with it!" others whispered back.

"Nonsense!" the Joneses told them all cheerfully. "What could possibly be wrong with this perfectly adorable X?"

Nobody could answer that, except Baby X, who had just finished its bottle. Baby X's answer was a loud, satisfied burp.

Clearly, nothing at all was wrong. Nevertheless, none of the relatives felt comfortable about buying a present for a Baby X. The cousins who sent the baby a tiny football helmet would not come and visit any more. And the neighbors who sent a pink-flowered romper suit pulled their shades down when the Joneses passed their house.

The *Official Instruction Manual* had warned the new parents that this would happen, so they didn't fret about it. Besides, they were too busy with Baby X and the hundreds of different Xercises for treating it properly.

Ms. and Mr. Jones had to be Xtra careful about how they played with little X. They knew that if they kept bouncing it up in the air and saying how *strong* and *active* it was, they'd be treating it more like a boy than an X. But if all they did was cuddle it and kiss it and tell it how *sweet* and *dainty* it was, they'd be treating it more like a girl than an X.

On page 1,654 of the *Official Instruction Manual*, the scientists prescribed: "plenty of bouncing and plenty of cuddling, *both*. X ought to be strong and sweet and active. Forget about *dainty* altogether."

Meanwhile, the Joneses were worrying about other problems. Toys, for instance. And clothes. On his first shopping trip, Mr. Jones told the store clerk, "I need some clothes and toys for my new baby." The clerk smiled and said, "Well, now, is it a boy or a girl?" "It's an X," Mr. Jones said, smiling back. But the clerk got all red in the face and said huffily, "In *that* case, I'm afraid I can't help you, sir." So Mr. Jones wandered helplessly up and down the aisles trying to find what X needed. But everything in the store was piled up in sections marked "Boys" or "Girls." There were "Boys' Pajamas" and "Girls' Underwear" and "Boys' Fire Engines" and "Girls' Housekeeping Sets." Mr.

Jones went home without buying anything for X. That night he
and Ms. Jones consulted page 2,326 of the *Official Instruction
Manual.* "Buy plenty of everything!" it said firmly.

So they bought plenty of sturdy blue pajamas in the Boys'
Department and cheerful flowered underwear in the Girls' Department. And they bought all kinds of toys. A boy doll that
made pee-pee and cried, "Pa-pa." And a girl doll that talked in
three languages and said, "I am the Pres-i-dent of Gen-er-al
Mo-tors." They also bought a storybook about a brave princess
who rescued a handsome prince from his ivory tower, and another one about a sister and brother who grew up to be a
baseball star and a ballet star, and you had to guess which was
which.

The head scientists of Project Baby X checked all their pur-
chases and told them to keep up the good work. They also
reminded the Joneses to see page 4,629 of the *Manual,* where
it said, "Never make Baby X feel *embarrassed* or *ashamed* about
what it wants to play with. And if X gets dirty climbing rocks,
never say 'Nice little Xes don't get dirty climbing rocks.'"

Likewise, it said, "If X falls down and cries, never say 'Brave
little Xes don't cry.' Because, of course, nice little Xes *do* get
dirty, and brave little Xes *do* cry. No matter how dirty X gets,
or how hard it cries, don't worry. It's all part of the Xperiment."

Whenever the Joneses pushed Baby X's stroller in the park,
smiling strangers would come over and coo: "Is that a boy or
a girl?" The Joneses would smile back and say, "It's an X." The
strangers would stop smiling then, and often snarl something
nasty—as if the Joneses had snarled at *them.*

By the time X grew big enough to play with other children,
the Joneses' troubles had grown bigger, too. Once a little girl
grabbed X's shovel in the sandbox, and zonked X on the head
with it. "Now, now, Tracy," the little girl's mother began to
scold, "little girls mustn't hit little—" and she turned to ask X,
"Are you a little boy or a little girl, dear?"

Mr. Jones, who was sitting near the sandbox, held his breath
and crossed his fingers.

X smiled politely at the lady, even though X's head had never
been zonked so hard in its life. "I'm a little X," X replied.

"You're a *what?*" the lady exclaimed angrily. "You're a little b-r-a-t, you mean!"

"But little girls mustn't hit little Xes, either!" said X, retrieving the shovel with another polite smile. "What good does hitting do, anyway?"

X's father, who was still holding his breath, finally let it out, uncrossed his fingers, and grinned back at X.

And at their next secret Project Baby X meeting, the scientists grinned, too. Baby X was doing fine.

But then it was time for X to start school. The Joneses were really worried about this, because school was even more full of rules for boys and girls, and there were no rules for Xes. The teacher would tell boys to form one line, and girls to form another line. There would be boys' games and girls' games, and boys' secrets and girls' secrets. The school library would have a list of recommended books for girls, and a different list of recommended books for boys. There would even be a bathroom marked BOYS and another one marked GIRLS. Pretty soon boys and girls would hardly talk to each other. What would happen to poor little X?

The Joneses spent weeks consulting their *Instruction Manual* (there were 249½ pages of advice under "First Day of School"), and attending urgent special conferences with the smart scientists of Project Baby X.

The scientists had to make sure that X's mother had taught X how to throw and catch a ball properly, and that X's father had been sure to teach X what to serve at a doll's tea party. X had to know how to shoot marbles and how to jump rope and, most of all, what to say when the Other Children asked whether X was a Boy or a Girl.

Finally, X was ready. The Joneses helped X button on a nice new pair of red-and-white checked overalls, and sharpened six pencils for X's nice new pencilbox, and marked X's name clearly on all the books in its nice new bookbag. X brushed its teeth and combed its hair, which just about covered its ears, and remembered to put a napkin in its lunchbox.

The Joneses had asked X's teacher if the class could line up alphabetically, instead of forming separate lines for boys and girls. And they had asked if X could use the principal's bathroom, because it wasn't marked anything except BATHROOM. X's teacher promised to take care of all those problems. But nobody could help X with the biggest problem of all—Other Children.

Nobody in X's class had ever known an X before. What would they think? How would X make friends?

You couldn't tell what X was by studying its clothes—overalls don't even button right-to-left, like girls' clothes, or left-to-right, like boys' clothes. And you couldn't guess whether X had a girl's short haircut or a boy's long haircut. And it was very hard to tell by the games X liked to play. Either X played ball very well for a girl, or else X played house very well for a boy.

Some of the children tried to find out by asking X tricky questions, like "Who's your favorite sports star?" That was easy. X had two favorite sports stars: a girl jockey named Robyn Smith and a boy archery champion named Robin Hood. Then they asked, "What's your favorite TV program?" And that was even easier. X's favorite TV program was "Lassie," which stars a girl dog played by a boy dog.

When X said that its favorite toy was a doll, everyone decided that X must be a girl. But then X said that the doll was really a robot, and that X had computerized it, and that it was programmed to bake fudge brownies and then clean up the kitchen. After X told them that, the other children gave up guessing what X was. All they knew was they'd sure like to see X's doll.

After school, X wanted to play with the Other Children. "How about shooting some baskets in the gym?" X asked the girls. But all they did was make faces and giggle behind X's back.

"How about weaving some baskets in the arts and crafts room?" X asked the boys. But they all made faces and giggled behind X's back, too.

That night, Ms. and Mr. Jones asked X how things had gone at school. X told them sadly that the lessons were okay, but otherwise school was a terrible place for an X. It seemed as if Other Children would never want an X for a friend.

Once more, the Joneses reached for the *Instruction Manual*. Under "Other Children," they found the following message: "What did you Xpect? *Other Children* have to obey all the silly

boy-girl rules, because their parents taught them to. Lucky X—
you don't have to stick to the rules at all! All you have to do is
be yourself. P.S. We're not saying it'll be easy."

X liked being itself. But X cried a lot that night, partly because
it felt afraid. So X's father held X tight, and cuddled it, and
couldn't help crying a little, too. And X's mother cheered them
both up by reading an Xciting story about an enchanted prince
called Sleeping Handsome, who woke up when Princess Charm-
ing kissed him.

The next morning, they all felt much better, and little X went
back to school with a brave smile and a clean pair of red-and-
white checked overalls.

There was a seven-letter-word spelling bee in class that day.
And a seven-lap boys' relay race in the gym. And a seven-layer-
cake baking contest in the girls' kitchen corner. X won the
spelling bee. X also won the relay race. And X almost won the
baking contest, except it forgot to light the oven. Which only
proves that nobody's perfect.

One of the Other Children noticed something else, too. He
said: "Winning or losing doesn't seem to count to X. X seems
to have fun being good at boys' skills *and* girls' skills."

"Come to think of it," said another one of the Other Children, "maybe X is having twice as much fun as we are!"

So after school that day, the girl who beat X at the baking
contest gave X a big slice of her prizewinning cake. And the boy
X beat in the relay race asked X to race him home.

From then on, some really funny things began to happen.
Susie, who sat next to X in class, suddenly refused to wear pink
dresses to school any more. She insisted on wearing red-and-
white checked overalls—just like X's. Overalls, she told her
parents, were much better for climbing monkey bars.

Then Jim, the class football nut, started wheeling his little
sister's doll carriage around the football field. He'd put on his
entire football uniform, except for the helmet. Then he'd put
the helmet *in* the carriage, lovingly tucked under an old set of
shoulderpads. Then he'd start jogging around the field, pushing the carriage and singing "Rockabye Baby" to his football
helmet. He told his family that X did the same thing, so it must
be okay. After all, X was now the team's star quarterback.

Susie's parents were horrified by her behavior, and Jim's parents were worried sick about his. But the worst came when the twins, Joe and Peggy, decided to share everything with each other. Peggy used Joe's hockey skates, and his microscope, and took half his newspaper route. Joe used Peggy's needlepoint kit, and her cookbooks, and took two of her three baby-sitting jobs. Peggy started running the lawn mower, and Joe started running the vacuum cleaner.

Their parents weren't one bit pleased with Peggy's wonderful biology experiments, or with Joe's terrific needlepoint pillows. They didn't care that Peggy mowed the lawn better, and that Joe vacuumed the carpet better. In fact, they were furious. It's all that little X's fault, they agreed. Just because X doesn't know what it is, or what it's supposed to be, it wants to get everybody *else* mixed up, too!

Peggy and Joe were forbidden to play with X any more. So was Susie, and then Jim, and then *all* the Other Children. But it was too late; the Other Children stayed mixed up and happy and free, and refused to go back to the way they'd been before X.

Finally, Joe and Peggy's parents decided to call an emergency meeting of the school's Parent's Association, to discuss "The X Problem." They sent a report to the principal stating that X was a "disruptive influence." They demanded immediate action. The Joneses, they said, should be *forced* to tell whether X was a boy or a girl. And then X should be *forced* to behave like whichever it was. If the Joneses refused to tell, the Parents' Association said, then X must take an Xamination. The school psychiatrist must Xamine it physically and mentally, and issue a full report. If X's test showed it was a boy, it would have to obey all the boys' rules. If it proved to be a girl, X would have to obey all the girls' rules.

And if X turned out to be some kind of mixed-up misfit, then X should be Xpelled from the school. Immediately!

The principal was very upset. Disruptive influence? Mixed-up misfit? But X was an Xcellent student. All the teachers said it was a delight to have X in their classes. X was president of the student council. X had won first prize in the talent show, and second prize in the art show, and honorable mention in the science fair, and six athletic events on field day, including the potato race.

Nevertheless, insisted the Parents' Associaton, X is a Problem Child. X is the Biggest Problem Child we have ever seen!

So the principal reluctantly notified X's parents that numerous complaints about X's behavior had come to the school's attention. And that after the psychiatrist's Xamination, the school would decide what to do about X.

The Joneses reported this at once to the scientists, who referred them to page 85,759 of the *Instruction Manual.* "Sooner or later," it said, "X will have to be Xamined by a psychiatrist. This may be the only way any of us will know for sure whether X is mixed up—or whether everyone else is."

The night before X was to be Xamined, the Joneses tried not to let X see how worried they were. "What if—?" Mr. Jones would say. And Ms. Jones would reply, "No use worrying." Then a few minutes later, Ms. Jones would say, "What if—?" and Mr. Jones would reply, "No use worrying."

X just smiled at them both, and hugged them hard and didn't say much of anything. X was thinking, What if—? And then X thought: No use worrying.

At Xactly 9 o'clock the next day, X reported to the school psychiatrist's office. The principal, along with a committee from the Parents' Associaton, X's teacher, X's classmates, and Ms. and Mr. Jones, waited in the hall outside. Nobody knew the details of the tests X was to be given, but everybody knew they'd be *very* hard, and that they'd reveal Xactly what everyone wanted to know about X, but were afraid to ask.

It was terribly quiet in the hall. Almost spooky. Once in a while, they would hear a strange noise inside the room. There were buzzes. And a beep or two. And several bells. An occasional light would flash under the door. The Joneses thought it was a white light, but the principal thought it was blue. Two or three children swore it was either yellow or green. And the Parents' Committee missed it completely.

Through it all, you could hear the psychiatrist's low voice, asking hundreds of questions, and X's higher voice, answering hundreds of answers.

The whole thing took so long that everyone knew it must be

the most complete Xamination anyone had ever had to take. Poor X, the Joneses thought. Serves X right, the Parents' Committee thought. I wouldn't like to be in X's overalls right now, the children thought.

At last, the door opened. Everyone crowded around to hear the results. X didn't look any different; in fact, X was smiling. But the psychiatrist looked terrible. He looked as if he was crying! "What happened?" everyone began shouting. Had X done something disgraceful? "I wouldn't be a bit surprised!" muttered Peggy and Joe's parents. "Did X flunk the *whole* test?" cried Susie's parents. "Or just the most important part?" yelled Jim's parents.

"Oh, dear," sighed Mr. Jones.

"Oh, dear," sighed Ms. Jones.

"*Sssh,*" ssshed the principal. "The psychiatrist is trying to speak."

Wiping his eyes and clearing his throat, the psychiatrist began, in a hoarse whisper. "In my opinion," he whispered—you could tell he must be very upset—"in my opinion, young X here—"

"Yes? Yes?" shouted a parent impatiently.

"*Sssh!*" ssshed the principal.

"Young *Sssh* here, I mean young X," said the doctor, frowning, "is just about—"

"Just about *what*? Let's have it!" shouted another parent.

". . . just about the *least* mixed-up child I've ever Xamined!" said the psychiatrist.

"Yay for X!" yelled one of the children. And then the others began yelling, too. Clapping and cheering and jumping up and down.

"SSSH!" SSShed the principal, but nobody did.

The Parents' Committee was angry and bewildered. How *could* X have passed the whole Xamination? Didn't X have an *identity* problem? Wasn't X mixed up at *all*? Wasn't X *any* kind of a misfit? How could it *not* be, when it didn't even *know* what it was? And why was the psychiatrist crying?

Actually, he had stopped crying and was smiling politely through his tears. "Don't you see?" he said. "I'm crying because it's wonderful! X has absolutely no identity problem! X isn't one bit mixed up! As for being a misfit—ridiculous! X knows perfectly well what it is! Don't you, X?" The doctor winked. X winked back.

"But what *is* X?" shrieked Peggy and Joe's parents. "*We* still want to know what it is!"

"Ah, yes," said the doctor, winking again. "Well, don't worry. You'll all know one of these days. And you won't need me to tell you."

"What? What does he mean?" some of the parents grumbled suspiciously.

Susie and Peggy and Joe all answered at once. "He means that by the time X's sex matters, it won't be a secret any more!"

With that, the doctor began to push through the crowd toward X's parents. "How do you do," he said, somewhat stiffly, And then he reached out to hug them both. "If I ever have an X of my own," he whispered, "I sure hope you'll lend me your instruction manual."

Needless to say, the Joneses were very happy. The Project Baby X scientists were rather pleased, too. So were Susie, Jim, Peggy, Joe, and all the Other Children. The Parents' Association wasn't, but they had promised to accept the psychiatrist's report, and not make any more trouble. They even invited Ms. and Mr. Jones to become honorary members, which they did.

Later that day, all X's friends put on their red-and-white checked overalls and went over to see X. They found X in the back yard, playing with a very tiny baby that none of them had ever seen before. The baby was wearing very tiny red-and-white checked overalls.

"How do you like our new baby?" X asked the Other Children proudly.

"It's got cute dimples," said Jim.

"It's got husky biceps, too," said Susie.

"What kind of baby is it?" asked Joe and Peggy.

X frowned at them. "Can't you tell?" Then X broke into a big, mischievous grin. "*It's a Y!*"

from A Weave of Women

E. M. Broner

THE BIRTH

THEY EMBRACE AND face Jordan. They are turned golden in the evening light, like the stone. There are several of them. The weeping one will not turn to salt. In fact, she drinks her tears. She is a full-bellied sabra and her fruit is sucking away inside.

The women breathe with Simha. Heavy labor has not started yet. They sit in the doorway of their stone house in the Old City. They move inside and breathe with Simha into the stones.

Simha groans. They echo. Simha loses her water. The Dead Sea. The River Jordan. The Nile. They wait for the baby to float on a basket from Simha's reeds.

They have notified two midwives. It is a mistake. The doctors have refused home delivery. A nurse warned them against it.

E. M. Broner commutes regularly to a loft in New York from Detroit, where she is Associate Professor and Writer-in-Residence at Wayne State University. Co-editor of *A Lost Tradition: A History of Mothers and Daughters in Literature,* she is at work on her fifth novel. This excerpt from *A Weave of Women* by E. M. Broner, copyright © 1978 by E. M. Broner, is reprinted by permission of Holt, Rinehart and Winston, Publishers.

Deedee leans against the stones and tells of a friend who bore a son on Christmas Eve under the Christmas tree.

"Was it planned?"

"No. It was an accident."

"Which?"

"Both the pregnancy and the birth."

"What happened to the baby?"

"He was put into the Dirty Baby Ward at the hospital because he was covered with pine needles."

The midwives arrive. One is a Jews for Jesus girl, dressed modestly in kerchief, long skirt, covered arms. She knows her Old and New Testaments but not her Biology. The other is a Swede who is into health. She worked as a volunteer at a border kibbutz and volunteered herself to a kibbutz member. She arrives nursing her new baby. The Swede is intent on smearing ointment onto her sore nipples. The other midwife is reading Leviticus in variant texts.

Simha exclaims. She is in pain. The women are joyous. Pain quickens the moment to birth. Pain quickens the excitation.

They see the cervix. It is purple, a reddish purple.

The midwives look disturbed.

"Hot water?" asks the social worker.

They don't think so.

Simha is sitting on a stool. The women put a soft blanket between Simha's knees.

One midwife tries to hear the baby's heartbeat. She cannot. The Swede listens and hears the regular beat. The midwives do not know how many fingers Simha is dilated. Simha shouts at them from her stool. They leave.

The social worker goes to a house with a phone and, from there, she telephones accomplished women. She phones Martin Buber's granddaughter, Golda Meir's cousin, Ben Gurion's niece. She phones women in the parliament, the law courts, at the university.

Gradually the experts gather. They surround Simha, crouched on her stool. They have books of instructions in several languages.

Antoinette is in the room, a Shakespearean from London. Joan is there, a playwright, a Britisher, but from Manchester. A scientist arrives, originally from Germany. Dahlia is there, a singer from Beer Sheva. Tova has been there all along, the curly-haired actress from New York. Hepzibah jitneys down from Haifa wearing her padded scarf against the wrath of the Father-Lord. Mickey arrives in the midst of her divorce. Gloria, the redhead, has been there for the fun. She came over from California for the fun. Another social worker arrives from Tel Aviv, serious Polish Vered.

Simha has left her stool for the mattress on the floor. Her labor has stopped and she dozes. Why is the baby so bad? It will do nothing on time or within reason. It will cry and the mother will never know why. Simha, matted hair, parched lips, is having nightmares.

The scientist says this is not her field of expertise but nothing seems wrong, the head down, labor proceeding.

Hepzibah barely refrains from covering Simha's full, long hair with a kerchief. Simha is not married and, therefore, does not need a head covering, but perhaps the rules are different when it comes to unwed mothers.

Deedee is both intense and amused. The Jews are something else! She is Irish and prefers her own, and then the Greeks and then the Jews. But Israel is warm and she has women friends here who will neither let her starve nor weep.

They are up all night on this night of vigil. The women brew tea. The redhead, Gloria, knows a special way to make Turkish coffee that she learned from an Arab cab driver. He added cardamom seed. She talks on about the cab ride. All of her tales wander, often with cab drivers, jitney drivers, young students from the university who cannot resist her and follow her across the wadi near campus.

The women drink the thick coffee. They are not sleepy. It becomes chilly and they put naphtha into the heater. They open the door a moment. The bad odor escapes, the blue flames light and the early morning air is warmed.

The Shakespearean has a crisp accent and a bustling manner.

"Did someone call the father?" she asks.

Gloria from California did.

At dawn the father runs into the little stone house. He has hitchhiked from his kibbutz. Gloria's message was delivered to the dining room and shouted from table to table. Ah! He is on his shift in the cow shed. His brother takes over and his mother gives him a basket of freshly baked bread from the kibbutz oven, also her own jam and a plant from her garden.

The kibbutz, accepting paternity, sends wishes of easy birth and warm blankets to receive the son.

A daughter is born.

By the time of the birth the father does not care what comes from Simha's cave, what small, furtive animal that is gnawing at her and making her scream. When the animal slides out, it has soft hair on its head and soft fur on its body. It is a daughter-puppy.

The women prepare the mother.

Mickey, in the midst of her divorce and of her hatred, combs Simha's hair. She braids it. She brushes it out again and puts it up. She lets it hang down Simha's back.

Antoinette gathers flowers from the valley of the Old City.

"There's rosemary, that's for remembrance. . . . And there is pansies, that's for thought. There's fennel for you, and columbines . . . daisy . . . violets . . ."

"That's morbid," says Joan. "Ophelia of all things!"

Antoinette does not deign to reply. What does a Manchester person know of repartee, of the deft thrust? She wraps herself in London imperial dignity.

Gloria stares at the father of the child. He fell asleep wearily. He interests her, the natural man who eats hungrily without good or bad manners, sleeps easily, loves shyly. Gloria looks at his kibbutz stomach stretching the buttons of his cotton shirt. His hand is curled. She touches it and it jerks.

Hepzibah takes out her Daily Prayer Book. Terry, the social worker, readies a manifesto. Gerda, the scientist born in Germany, looks at this new marvel of science.

Dahlia from Beer Sheva goes out to exercise her face and chest. The total person sings, not just the vocal cords. She returns red-cheeked and lively-eyed. She sings to Simha of happiness, of bodies, of seas of the moon, of inner caverns that hold tropical fish, of waters that flood and the fish swims clear. The fish has no gills and now must sing instead of gulping.

Tova, the actress, strokes and smoothes the baby daughter.

No one will spank her, croons Tova. Life is not a slap on the behind.

The women stroke the animal, pet it behind its ears, pet its scaly legs, its stretching turtle neck, its lumpy head.

Tova brings the stage property—an Indian bedspread with monkeys and fruit-bearing trees. Simha is sat up on the chattering monkey and the lush tree. A garland is twined for her hair.

Gloria tries again to awaken the kibbutznik. He opens his eyes, looks into Gloria's goyishe pale blue and smiles. He has forgotten Simha, who was his happiness. He has forgotten the new daughter. He looks at Gloria's incandescent hair, her straight nose, her American long legs.

The women watch him silently. The kibbutznik feels a crick in his neck. He is a father. He must speak up at kibbutz meetings, in public, and ask for her maintenance. He is the lover of Simha, and she is a head taller than he. She has wide hips, pendulous breasts, large brown eyes, thick hair. He sighs. Never will he feel that canopy of red above him, those blue eyes sunlit upon his arrival. He belongs to furry animals and hairy, big women.

They surround the mattress and chant:

"Welcome to the new mother. Welcome to the new daughter."

Simha is happy but sloppy. She grabs at her breasts, which are beginning to fill and hurt. She cannot close her legs. The womb is sore. But she looks young again. That old woman who went into childbirth is rejuvenated.

Their home is a busy one and across the narrow street is a busier one. That is the Home for Wayward Girls, actually the Home for Jewish Wayward Girls. They are wayward because they ran away. Or because they stand along the roadside near the universities, secular or religious, crying out in the holy tongue, "Come and fuck me!"

Committees have met on these girls. Terry has sat on such a committee as Director of the Home. It is the committee decision that the girls are prostitutes because they are psychologically disturbed.

"No," says Terry, "economically disturbed."

She brings out charts on inflation, lack of education, illiteracy.

"What is left for these girls to do?" asks Terry.

"No one tells them to," says the committee.

But they, the girls, know it's what they have to do. And, afterward, their mothers scratch at their eyes. Their fathers whip them. The daughters have failed the religion and the socialist state.

The girls leave both religion and socialism. They wear pointy bras, beehive hairdos or they straighten and blow-dry Arabic-Jewish-African hair. They wear high-heeled chunky shoes and miniskirts when no one is mini anymore, not the Israeli policewomen or the women in the army, who have lengthened skirts to mid-knee.

Rina arrives for the ceremony, Rina from development town, court and prison. Rina wears a long skirt. She wears eyeliner around her almond eyes. She covers her pointy breasts with a shawl. Her parents threw her out because she was lazy in the house. Her lovers threw her out because she was fearful in bed.

Shula is invited, Shula the Westerner, the Pole. She is blonde and buxom. She spits on her parents. She does not honor their days in the land. She spits on her teachers. She does not follow the command to honor the teacher above all. She spits on the police. She spits on all uniforms: traffic, civil guard, nurses, beauty parlor.

"Who taught you to spit, Shula?"

"My grandmother. She spat on me when she saw me and said, 'An ugliness. May the Evil Eye leave her on this earth. May she only be seen as ugly and undesirable so that we never lose her.' And so I am—ugly and undesirable."

The ceremony begins.

Simha wears a wraparound skirt to cover either taut or flabby belly. The kibbutznik is present, bearing another basket from his kibbutz, sensible girls' clothing of strong kibbutz material.

He stares at both of the women, his daughter and his love. And he feels jealous. His daughter fits on the mother's hip, on her breast. There is no need for a father as there was no need for a husband, and he has traveled by bus a winding route for four hours to arrive in Jerusalem.

"Find a girl in the kibbutz," advises the kibbutz psychologist. "Forget her. She takes advantage of you."

Ah, she did! She did! His first love. She took advantage of him and deflowered him.

Gloria is there wearing a low-cut dress. She has found sun during this chilly weather, and her freckles reach into her cleavage.

The kibbutznik stares into the basket he is carrying.

Tova from New York is there. She has an Arab lover. He is too shy to attend, but he sends a song.

Mother, I would leap from the mountain for you.
Mother, I will never forget you.

Shh. It is Simha's prayer.

"I come into your house, O Mother God. You inclined your ear toward me, and I will whisper into it all the days of my life.

"The cords of life and death encompassed me. From the hollow of the grave, from the cave of the mouth of birth I called. I knew happiness and anguish. You delivered my soul from death into birth, my eyes from tears, my feet from falling. I shall walk before You in the land of the living."

The baby is poking at her own eyes. She grimaces. A thin cry.

Hepzibah says, "Let her become a comfort to Simha in her old age."

Hepzibah puts down her prayer book and kisses Simha.

"She may need it," murmurs Hepzibah.

Terry says, "Let there be peace. Grant this daughter of her people peace."

Ah, they do not know what will befall or that there will be no room for the daughter or for her people.

The kibbutznik says: "May she serve however she wishes, in the chicken house, the barn, the rose garden, the cotton field, the kitchen, the guesthouse. May she be a member of the community of people."

Simha knows why she chose him to be the father.

CEREMONIES ON
THE THRONE OF MIRIAM

It is during the second orange harvest that Simha's baby has her hymenotomy. The air smells of orange blossoms. The clementines are sweet, the grapefruits not tart. Cucumbers are light green and long. Radishes are large and mild. Nothing growing in this season is bitter.

Simha has not taken her baby from her breast these eight days. If she does for an hour or two, she worries about what else she should be doing.

The wayward girls, Rina and Shula, wander in, washing their faces, arms and hands carefully before they sponge Simha or handle the baby.

Mickey attends them between appointments at the rabbinical house. She burps the baby and says, *Momzera,* little illegitimate girl.

Vered, the Polish social worker from Tel Aviv, comes with warnings. She tells Terry about the statistics dealing with bastards. There is no longer the old, benign kibbutz attitude about marriage or the lack of it. This is a conservative time. The baby will suffer.

Vered's clients these days are the Russians, the dwindling number of them who still want to settle in The Land. Vered wants the Israelis to provide a good example. Simha, lying indolently, her robe always open, her breasts leaking, does not provide such an example.

Nor later will Vered.

The women gather for the ceremony.

They giggle nervously.

"What should it be called?"

"Hymenectomy."

"No. That sounds like an appendectomy."

"It sounds like you're getting rid of your Uncle Hymen."

They wait for Gerda. They enclose the house, covering the windows with cloth, placing lace on the chosen chair. Tova has brought lace that she uses in the theater, old, torn, delicate lace she found in the suk in Old Jaffa. Tova drapes it. Simha sits in lace, the baby on her lap. Deedee, the oldest of many sisters and brothers, has made a christening dress for this baby.

"Christening?"

Deedee sighs. Jews and etymology. Jews and sensitivity. Here in the land of her God, also, they are still fighting any mention of His name. "B.C." they call "Before the Common Era." "Christendom" they don't mention at all. December 25 falls into whatever Jewish month it falls into—Tevet or Shevet the twenty-fifth. No one is named Christine or Christopher. No one buys Christian Brothers wine. They tease her about New Year's Eve. It's either Christ's circumcision or they call it Sylvester, and no one gives a party but a few lonesome Americans. The flora is not called Christmas fern, Christmas rose, Christmas berry. There is no Christ's thorn that she can find. Christmas trees they call a German invention. . . .

"It's such a beautiful dress," says Simha. "We're proud in it."

Deedee relaxes and Gloria tenses. Too much attention on Deedee.

Gerda enters.

"Name the baby."

They tell her the name of the baby.

"Hava, mother of everything living."

Hava translates into Eve, they explain to Gloria, a recent convert. Gloria tells them about her conversion and about the young Reform rabbi laying her on the floor of his study.

"Is this part of the conversion?" she asked him.

The girls don't want to hear Gloria.

"Name the mother," says Gerda.

Simha is the mother.

Simha says, "Here am I acting upon the command that is not yet written that the daughter of eight days shall be pierced."

Simha rises and hands the baby to the godmother, her roommate Terry. Simha walks with difficulty to her bed. Terry sits in the draped chair.

"This is the Throne of Miriam the Prophetess," says Gerda. "May she be remembered for greatness."

Gerda lifts Hava from Terry's arms.

"This is a daughter of Eve."

"What do you mean?"

"We trace our descent from Eve."

Rina and Shula are whispering. They object to the baby being called "a daughter of Eve."

"They use that name for us," says Shula. "It is another name for whore."

"But the son of Adam means human being," says Tova.

"So it is," say the girls.

Terry says her part.

"This baby is descended from Eve. This baby is descended from Sara. Sara's name is princess, the origin of 'Israel.' From her will come tribes and ceremonies."

Tova lifts Hava.

"This child Hava, may she one day be great."

Hepzibah cannot bring herself to say unfamiliar prayers. They are difficult, as well, for Antoinette, a traditionalist.

The women of the room bless the fruit of the vine. They bless the fruit from Simha's womb.

Simha begins to cry from her bed. Terry's arms are shaking. The wayward girls dry Simha's tears and avert their eyes from the ceremony.

Gerda hesitates.

"Do you want it?"

"Yes," says Simha sobbing.

"Yes," says Terry trembling.

"No, no," say Rina and Shula. "She should be a virgin at her wedding."

"I stop here," says Gerda and refuses to continue.

"Explain it to us, Gerda," says Dahlia from Beer Sheva. "No one ever explains to us so how can we choose?"

Gerda lectures easily at the university, over the phone, at the homes of friends.

She diagrams. Two views. A lovely mouth. It is surrounded by lips, the labia majora and the labia minora.

"*Menorah?*" ask the wayward girls. "Lamp?"

It is like an opening, parted lips, with a kind of jagged tooth, with the jagged bits of membrane.

Gerda makes another diagram. The tiny hymen.

"Just a poke with a pick, with something sharp," says Gerda, "that will pierce it. The hymen is so tiny in a baby."

A third diagram. The entrance, the tissue that blocks it, the vaginal wall, the cervix.

"It is usually broken," says Gerda, "by the time young girls see doctors, either by accident or through intent."

"Do it, Gerda," says Simha.

"I did not invent this ceremony," says Gerda. "You did. I'm the scientist. You're the mystic. I will not proceed alone without agreement."

"What is it called, Gerda?"

"It has no name. It has not been done before."

"Name it."

"Hymenotomy."

"Sounds like lobotomy," says Gloria.

"Why hymenotomy?"

"*Tomy,*" says Gerda, "a cutting of a tissue."

Antoinette becomes alert.

"Actually," says Antoinette in her crisp London accent, "it is from the root *tem,* to cut."

"What are you using?" ask the women of Gerda.

"Any sharp cutting instrument will do," says Gerda. "I have one here."

"Will it bleed?"

"Not really."

"Will it hurt?"

"Scarcely at all."

"And," says Antoinette to Hepzibah, who is also trying not to participate, "*tome* is a cutting from a larger roll of paper, one book in a work of several volumes."

Gerda says, "There is the thin membrane that separates the outside from the inside of the vagina. It is a vestigial structure."

"Cut it," says Terry, against all vestigial structures, social, physical.

Antoinette's voice rises. "*Dichotomy, anatomy.*"

Gerda is swift. The hymeneal membrane is pierced. She has poked easily through the hymeneal ring.

Hava is startled and wails. Simha gives Hava her nipple, first dabbing wine on it.

There is a loud sigh from the group.

Tova says, "Now you are one of us."

Terry, the godmother, says, "May all orifices be opened."

Dahlia says, "May she not be delivered intact to her bridegroom or judged by her hymen but by the energies of her life."

The baby drinks and lets go of the nipple to cry. Hepzibah

frowns. The wayward girls are shocked. There is so much to shock wayward girls, much they encounter that others do not—physical violence, rape, but this devirginizing of an eight-day-old is the most shocking of all.

"Who will love her?" they whisper to each other, "once they find out?"

Deedee awakens. She fills a large silver cup with sacramental wine.

"May she never suffer again from piercing," says Deedee, "of the body or of the heart."

The lace at the window stirs. It is old Shlomo Sassoon. They shoo him away.

There is a knock at the door. It is the father. He is too early. Would he mind waiting? Gloria brings him a cup of her Turkish coffee. The bitter brew will cool him, will rest him from his hard journey.

"Did you ask his permission?" asks Vered from Tel Aviv.

Simha says, "I told him I wanted to do it, but I did not ask his permission."

"Did he want to do it?" asks Vered.

"No," says Simha.

"Then you did it without his permission."

"I do not have to ask his permission."

"It's being done to his baby," says Vered.

"It's being done to a girl child," says Simha, "and he knows nothing of that."

"Of what?" ask the wayward girls.

"Of the ways that women must open themselves."

Shula sulks. She opens herself. She is a wishbone, sometimes bending her legs around small, bony men, sometimes around large, fat men. One day she will crack in half with no wishes ever granted her.

Dahlia sings in her throaty voice: "I will open my lips with song and my bones declare, Blessed is she that cometh in the name of the Shehena, the womanly God."

They seat themselves on chairs, pillows, an Arab rug and around Simha's bed.

Dahlia sings of women's chairs: the birthing stool, the throne of Miriam, the chair of the longing woman at the window, of the cooking woman at the table, of chariots of war and chariots of angels ascending.

The song ends shrilly. The women worry. Does little Hava so soon have to think of war?

"We are always at war," says Dahlia, "in our land and in our lives."

Deedee is bored. These Jewish friends never cease from whining and dining. The Irish talk, lovely, lively chatter, but this endless talmudic tract, spiritual gossip, this daily poop of prayer. Who is she, Deedee, to such commentary and ceremony?

Tova says, "It is not only Simha's baby who has been pierced. We should each tell of the piercing."

You first, Tova.

"I was pierced," says Tova, "by the angry glance of my enemy."

"Arab lover!" says Mickey. "But what's the difference? Your friends become your enemies too. I stayed a virgin and I will always regret it—that I was pierced by the bastard, my husband. I saved it for the man who threw it away."

"Threw what away?" asks Rina.

"Threw me away, stupid," says Mickey. "What are *they* doing here?" she asks about the girls from across the way. "Isn't it their bedtime?"

The girls huddle together.

"He had me," Mickey says, "and told me, 'What do I need you for? You're not a virgin anymore, you're common and any man can have you.'"

"He was not a son of Adam," says Hepzibah, reaching for Mickey's shaking hands. "He wasn't human."

Deedee relaxes with her friends. They take a long time getting there but, eventually, they do.

"My boss pierced me," says Deedee. "Small, fat boss. I, his secretary, towered over him. Only when I was at my desk and he standing next to me each morning was he taller than I. On my nineteenth birthday he took me for drinks to the bar in our building. Sitting next to him in the booth I could see down on the top of his head where his pink scalp shone through the thinning hair. He bought me a cocktail, one, two, a few. He helped me to his car to take me home. We ended up at the park. Not dark yet. Dusk. People walking around us. What did he care? He parked near the fountain. The water was turned off because it was getting cold and the pipes would freeze. Not his. He had his heater on. I was dozing. 'Want to see who's bigger,' he said, 'you or me?' I bled on his car seat, which he didn't appreciate. He took me home. 'It's my period, ma,' I said and ran upstairs. My ma followed me. When she saw me sobbing, she knew it wasn't and slapped me down into the bed. 'You're of no use to anybody, including yourself,' said my ma. In those days I, only nineteen, was supporting my ma and all the kids, for my dad had left us years before."

Deedee's head is on Tova's shoulder. Terry holds Deedee's hand.

"Hava," says Deedee, "let your piercing be among friends Let it be ceremonious and correct. Let it be supervised. Let it be done openly, not in anger, not in cars. Ah, Hava," weeps Deedee, "how I envy you."

Gloria says, "The guy who pierced my ears pierced my hymen. On his jewelry shop window was a sign, FREE. EARS PIERCED FREE. I went in. 'I've pierced women all over the world,' said the jeweler. 'Is it free?' I asked. 'You doubt it?' said the jeweler. 'I could be arrested for false advertising.' I said, 'I'm afraid. I'm afraid of pain.' He said, 'I'll be gentle. You won't feel a thing. Only choose an earring and I'll pierce you with it.' 'What are those numbers on the earrings?' 'Nothing. My bookkeeping,' he says. I chose pearls with the number forty. He smiled, seated me in the Piercing Chair and pierced me with the pearls. 'That's forty dollars,' he said, 'for the earrings.' Of course I didn't have it. 'Ask your mother.' 'I don't have one.' 'Ask your father.' 'He'd beat you first and me afterward.' He said, 'Only one way I'll get my money's worth.' "

Gerda, the scientist, says, "I pierced myself. 'Why make a fuss?' I asked myself. 'If I ever marry do I need blood on a sheet? Do the neighbors have to be called in? I went through my Ph.D. to be judged this way?' I had no boyfriend, no one really interested in me, but I could not wait. One must control one's destiny. I am my own bridegroom."

Antoinette has not married. She is shy about not marrying

and about having a hymen and about the stories the women have told.

"It is there," says Antoinette softly, "like tonsils or appendix. It never really gave me any trouble. It's there, a part of me, like a scab or a scar, a lock or protection. Let it be there. I like politeness, someone knocking, announcing. All doors and windows need not be open."

Antoinette sits self-consciously. She double-crosses her legs.

Hepzibah does not speak. She refastens her scarf more securely. Hepzibah always smiles. She refers to her husband and to her male sons as her "soldiers," and to her daughter as "one day the mother of soldiers." Yet she is with these women and full of love for them. But she cannot speak of what is under the scarf, the blouse, the skirt, the stockings, between the legs.

Vered says, "I was lucky. A fifty-two-year-old man did it, skillfully, carefully. No young man could have been so kind to me."

They listen.

"And even now," says Vered, who is twenty-nine, "I can be with no man younger than fifty."

Some have not spoken yet—the wayward girls, Dahlia, Joan from Manchester, Terry or Simha.

It is getting dark.

"Ach! Where's my daughter's father?" asks Simha.

Gloria opens the door. The kibbutznik has gone. The Turkish coffee cup is on its side. There is a thick residue of the coffee on the step.

"I'm such a shit!" says Simha.

Abruptly she smiles. "I always was. I lived in an isolated part of town—Jerusalem—where no houses had been built. We lived together, Jews and Arabs. I played with everything in The Land, stones in the wadi, the insides of caves, snakes, insects. I played with the Arab shepherds and their goats. I lay with them in the grass and we had each other, watching the goats."

Hepzibah sighs. Why does she come here after all? This is irrelevant to her. She rises and leaves silently. The women do not always notice when she goes but long for her afterward. Her hand in theirs is dry and steady.

"And you, Dahlia?" asks Simha.

"I pierced myself with a high note," says Dahlia.

That is good enough. The women applaud.

Terry said, "I lived in New York. I worked there but hated it. I had a scholarship offer to one of the schools in the state system to work on my M.S.W. and I accepted. But to leave the city a virgin, to be pierced in Schenectady or Binghamton. What would the choices be? A midget or someone with stumps or a Paul Bunyan who would cripple me? The week before the school semester began I quit my job and spent the day looking for my piercer. I found him easily, a fellow from the lunch counter where I ate, the fastest waiter, smooth, everything in one motion, athletic, younger than I. I waited until his shift was over and asked him to accompany me home. I said I was afraid to walk alone in the dark. But he was street smart. He never held my hand or looked at me, he just accompanied me up the stairs to my room and closed the door himself. I was right—everything in one motion, elegant, smooth. I never regretted it and did not eat at the counter again."

Joan, the playwright, said, "I was pierced on the Mediterranean. I was starting a new life and had to start with a new body. He was a tourist from some northern country, one of those that invaded England. I let him invade me on deck, under the bright moon."

The wayward girls are shocked. They would not dream of speaking about such a private matter.

The women cut cheese, eat it with fresh white bread and slices of mild radish. They cut sweet cucumbers, tomatoes and green peppers into small pieces for a kibbutz salad. They drink wine and say the blessing afterward.

"As it shall be written, may the mother be gladdened with the fruit of her body and the father rejoice in his offspring. May they live to rear her, may her friends learn to help her, may the law accept her and wisdom guide her."

Gerda says, "Terry, all the guests present and the mother Simha have observed this hymenotomy. Let us rejoice that we have performed this deed of piety."

The women make a tent around the baby.

Terry says, "Let us send forth the tidings that a daughter of the blood has joined us."

Simha is weary. She and the baby have both bled into the chair, Simha through her stitches, the baby through its tiny wound. Tova's lace is stained, torn, lying awry. The ceremony has ended.

Rina and Shula decide not to tell the girls of Wayward what they have witnessed. It might get Terry into more trouble. The young girls return to their house wondering and silently crying.

No one welcomed them at birth. Rina's mother said:

"I had hoped for a daughter that looked like an angel, and you, dark one, came along. I had hoped for a son, and a daughter was sent. I had hoped for a good baby, a crier lay. I had hoped for an eater, a fusser was in my arms. Why did God punish me? I had hoped for a circumcision, instead there was blood on her diaper. I screamed for the nurse. She laughed. 'Well, you have a girl for sure,' she said."

The women are dozing. Gloria stays over another night. She has some data for Deedee.

"In Japan," says Gloria, "you can have an operation and have a hymen sewed in. They stick in goatskin for one hundred thirty-seven dollars and no one ever knows. When it tears, you bleed."

"Gross," says Deedee.

They sleep and dream.

They are all virgins again.